Evidence-Based Management

How to use evidence to make better organizational decisions

Eric Barends and Denise M Rousseau

KoganPage

First published in Great Britain and the United States in 2018 by Kogan Page Limited

2nd Floor, 45 Gee Street
London
EC1V 3RS
United Kingdom
www.koganpage.com

c/o Martin P Hill Consulting
122 W 27th Street
New York, NY 10001
USA

4737/23 Ansari Road
Daryaganj
New Delhi 110002
India

© Center for Evidence Based Management, 2018

ISBN   978 0 7494 8374 6
E-ISBN   978 0 7494 8375 3

British Library Cataloguing-in-Publication Data

A CIP record for this book is available from the British Library.

Library of Congress Cataloging-in-Publication Data

Names: Barends, Eric, author. | Rousseau, Denise M., author.
Title: Evidence-based management : how to use evidence to make better
    organizational decisions / Eric Barends and Denise M. Rousseau.
Description: 1 Edition. | New York : Kogan Page Ltd, [2018] | Includes
    bibliographical references and index.
Identifiers: LCCN 2018029623 (print) | LCCN 2018030628 (ebook) | ISBN
    9780749483753 (ebook) | ISBN 9780749483746 (pbk.)
Subjects: LCSH: Industrial management. | Decision making.
Classification: LCC HD31.2 (ebook) | LCC HD31.2 .B357 2018 (print) | DDC
    658.4/03–dc23

Typeset by Integra Software Services Pvt Ltd, Pondicherry
Print production managed by Jellyfish
Printed and bound by 4edge Limited, UK

To the lifelong learners who are evidence-based managers

CONTENTS

Downloadable resources are available at **www.koganpage.com/EBM**

ABOUT THE AUTHORS

Eric Barends is the Managing Director of the Center for Evidence-Based Management. He has 20 years of management experience, 15 years at the senior management level, including 5 years as an executive. He advises management teams and boards of directors of large and medium-sized companies and non-profit organizations on evidence-based management and the development of managers. He serves as visiting faculty at Australian National University and New York University. He received the first doctorate in Evidence-Based Management, from the Vrije Universiteit Amsterdam.

Denise M Rousseau is the H J Heinz II University Professor at Carnegie Mellon University's Heinz College and Tepper School of Business. Formerly president of Academy of Management and editor-in-chief of *Journal of Organizational Behavior*, Rousseau founded a network of scholars, consultants and managers promoting evidence-informed organizational decisions, operating today as the Center for Evidence-Based Management – of which she is Academic Board President. She is a winner of the Academy of Management's Lifetime Achievement Award for Scholarly Contribution and twice winner of its Terry Award for best book in Management. She received her doctorate in Psychology from the University of California at Berkeley.

CONTRIBUTORS

Rob Briner is Professor of Organizational Psychology in the School of Business and Management at Queen Mary University of London. He is also very active in developing evidence-based practice in management, HR and organizational psychology. He was a founding member, Vice-Chair and now Scientific Director of the Center for Evidence-Based Management, which through its teaching, training and dissemination activities aims to help managers make better decisions by adopting the principles of evidence-based practice. Rob's work in this area has led to him being named in 2016 the Most Influential HR Thinker by *HR Magazine*.

Barbara Janssen is Director of projects and teaching at the Center for Evidence-Based Management and an independent consultant and project manager. She has 15 years of consultancy experience, advising organizations on implementing organizational change. To support organizational decision-making processes, she frequently coordinates and conducts rapid evidence assessments on various topics. In addition, she advises management of large and medium-sized companies and non-profit organizations on implementing the principles of evidence-based practice.

Martin Walker is Director for Banking and Finance at the Center for Evidence-Based Management. He has extensive experience in investment banking IT and operations. His roles included Global Head of Securities Finance IT at Dresdner Kleinwort and Global Head of Prime Brokerage Technology at RBS Markets. He also held roles at Merrill Lynch and HSBC Global Markets, where he was the Blockchain lead in Markets Operation, and produced research for financial consultancy Finadium.

Alessandra Capezio is a senior lecturer in organizational behaviour in the Research School of Management at the Australian National University. She is core member of the Work Effectiveness and Leadership Lab (WELL), which conducts high-quality research on workplace behaviours. Alessandra is passionate about promoting and teaching evidence-based practice in management and is a Fellow of the Center for Evidence-Based Management.

FOREWORD

The need for evidence-based management is stronger than ever. Although evidence-based practice and discussions of evidence-based management have increased over the last decade or more, and there are now organizations devoted to building evidence-based management activities in business management and the policy sciences, much remains to be done to make evidence-based management more ubiquitous in managerial decision-making. This book marks an important step forward by providing scholars, teachers, policymakers and organizational leaders both the knowledge and the practical tools necessary to teach evidence-based management in classrooms so as to produce more evidence-based practitioners, and to apply evidence-based management in workplaces to produce more scientifically sound decisions and policies.

The case for evidence-based management rests on several truths. First, knowledgeable observers have noted that progress in management scholarship and concomitant advances in theoretical understanding of social processes, and also the translation of that knowledge into action, are mostly notable by their absence.[1] Accumulating important and relevant evidence is essential for making scientific progress, as medicine nicely illustrates. A new journal, *Academy of Management Discoveries*, was launched in part because its founding editorial board correctly believed that most journals overemphasized 'new' theory, and that there was insufficient attention to explicating interesting phenomena and data for their own sake. It is too soon to tell to what extent *AMD* will change the emphasis journals place on sound evidence as contrasted with the newness or cuteness of ideas. But many scholars believe that the journal will help move management research away from an excessive preoccupation with theory[2] and with novelty for its own sake, both practices that have retarded the development of replicable knowledge.[3]

There are other hopeful signs consistent with an emphasis on evidence-based management. One is the founding of organizations consistent with bringing evidence-based management more to the fore. For instance, consider the Responsible Research in Business and Management initiative. That effort is 'dedicated to inspiring, encouraging and supporting credible and useful research in the business and management disciplines.'[4] This virtual organization seeks to increase research on socially significant topics and to encourage replication and the development of knowledge that stands up to scrutiny – research that is both useful for formulating organizational and social policy and also credible.

What editors of many academic journals seem to have missed is that in the quest for novelty and 'new' theory, social science has mostly built a knowledge base on quicksand. We have lots of new ideas and findings that don't stand up to scrutiny and can't be replicated – precisely the opposite of what one would want to build an evidence-based science and practice upon. In that regard, recently the National Academies of Sciences, Engineering and Medicine empanelled an ad hoc committee to 'assess research and data reproducibility and replicability issues'.[5] The problem is enormous. In social psychology, a working group published results that showed that only about a third of social psychology results published in major, refereed journals were replicated, with effect sizes about half of those originally reported.[6] This result represents a sobering wake-up call for scholars and highlights the need for better, more rigorous evidence.

Other recently founded or expanded organizations are also helping build an evidence-based management agenda. Most directly, there is the Center for Evidence-Based Management, an independent non-profit providing resources to people interested in learning more about evidence-based management.[7] The two authors of this book, Rousseau and Barends, are prominent in the Center, with Barends its director. The Center has built a network of practitioners, educators and researchers and is an important repository for teaching materials, articles, columns, blogs and research about evidence-based management.

The Behavioral Science and Policy Association (BSPA), which publishes a journal, *Behavioral Science and Policy* and also holds an annual conference, was founded to bring social science research – evidence and theory – into the realm of policy-making. 'We believe a clear understanding of the power of behavioural science research and interventions can provide innovative solutions for addressing challenges faced by policymakers and other practitioners.'[8] Clearly, some people and organizations are lining up with the EBM agenda, but much more remains to be done.

Another argument for the importance of evidence-based management is that in many domains, extensively documented in the subject area of human resource management[9] but in numerous other topics, too, managers don't use the best – or maybe any – evidence in implementing policies and practices. By ignoring evidence, managers damage organizational performance and the people who depend on those organizations. For instance, mergers continue apace, notwithstanding evidence on their ineffectiveness in creating value.[10] Downsizing persists, even though evidence suggests it mostly harms people while not benefiting companies.[11] Work hours grow longer even as research shows that long hours adversely affect both people's health and productivity.[12] The list of topics where evidence seems notable by its absence in organizational policies and practices is truly frightening. We would not tolerate such casual, non-fact based decision-making in fields such as medicine or engineering, and we should stop excusing it in management, as well.

Third, fad-chasing and casual benchmarking remain all too common, particularly in management training and development where the use of 'happy-sheets' that measure how much people enjoyed some session or material places an inevitable premium on entertainment and, worse than that, foments the goal of seeking to make people feel comfortable and not challenged so they will 'like' the presenter. Thus, in the important topic of leadership, evidence gives way to 'inspiration' and crowd-pleasing rhetoric. At a dinner in Australia, a senior human resources executive defended a speaker at a recent conference, notwithstanding this individual's lack of substantive knowledge and the fact that the person behaves quite opposite to what he advocates for others. Her defence: noting the standing ovation this presenter received. Entertainment is not evidence, and if we are to choose our educators and sources of information based on whether or not they can get people on their feet, the Rolling Stones or Bruce Springsteen would put even the best leadership 'guru' to shame. The fact that an enormous leadership industry rolls along, notwithstanding truly miserable levels of employee engagement, low levels of trust in leaders and numerous measures of abysmal leadership development performance, speaks to the ongoing need to confront myths and edutainment with evidence.[13]

Yet another reason the need for evidence-based management remains singularly crucial is the importance of the decisions made in and by organizations. Organizations have profound effects on their employees' psychological and physical well-being, and thus indirectly on mortality, morbidity and healthcare costs.[14] Organizations have reached vast scale. Product markets are increasingly concentrated, potentially harming consumers.[15] Monopsonistic power in labour markets affects employee wages, wage growth and income inequality.[16] Organizational size and scale has enabled these entities to affect political outcomes, in turn permitting the organizations to become ever more profitable through their control of the political economy. Simply put, organizations are increasingly powerful, and it would be nice if that power was deployed more frequently using good evidence rather than ideology or managerial capriciousness. The case for evidence-based management remains a strong one for numerous reasons.

Evidence comes in many ways, in many forms, and from many sources. One of the strengths of this book is that it considers evidence from academic research, from practitioners, from the organization itself and from stakeholders surrounding the organization. For each of these sources of evidence, the book addresses how to acquire evidence and appraise its relevance and usefulness, as well as practical insights as to how to turn evidence into action. This work is truly the definitive text on how to develop and use an evidence-based approach to management, and an important step forward from an earlier *Handbook* that, while obviously useful, was neither as integrated nor as focused on implementation as this volume.[17]

In the end, actually implementing evidence-based management requires three things. First, it requires a reasonably comprehensive evidentiary base. While much progress has occurred through the ongoing publication of important research in the social sciences, journals could do much to accelerate this evidence-development process by changing the criteria for publication to emphasize evidence and to change a review process that invariably requires multiple rounds of submissions that often bring astonishingly little gain for all the time and effort expended.

Second, it requires the tools and techniques that make implementing evidence-based management accessible to a wider audience. This book and the efforts of the BSPA, CEBMa, RRBM and other organizations offers substantial and substantive guidance and examples.

Third, and possibly most importantly, making evidence-based management more widespread and routine requires the motivation to apply knowledge and logical thought to organizational and public policy decision-making. As I write these words, the United States has no national science advisor, many of the cabinet departments lack scientific advisory commissions or senior scientific positions, and science seems to be on the defensive, elsewhere in the world as well. Evidence-based medicine increased in prominence not just from growing scientific knowledge. To get evidence-based medicine implemented, it took health systems and insurance companies requiring compliance with scientifically determined standards of care and financial reimbursement coming to increasingly depend on the application of best practices. Unless and until similar pressures come to bear on businesses and governments, evidence-based management will remain, as it mostly is today, a discretionary activity and optional method of managing. These facts suggest that evidence-based management, beyond knowledge and skill, requires a social movement and social pressure to truly deliver its potential for improving decision-making and, as a consequence, people's lives and organizational performance.

One can only hope that the factors that would make evidence-based management more widespread arrive sooner rather than later. The work of Denise Rousseau and Eric Barends, as represented in this book and in so many other places, represents important steps on a long road to making evidence-based management routine and its benefits universal.

Jeffrey Pfeffer, June 2018

Notes and references

1 Davis, GF (2010) Do theories of organizations progress? *Organizational Research Methods,* **13** (4), pp 690–709

2 Hambrick, DC (2007) The field of management's devotion to theory: Too much of a good thing? *Academy of Management Journal,* **50** (6), pp 1346–52

3 Mone, MA and McKinley, W (1993) The uniqueness value and its consequences for organization studies, *Journal of Management Inquiry,* **2** (3), pp 284–96

4 https://www.rrbm.network/

5 http://www8.nationalacademies.org/cp/projectview.aspx?key=49906

6 Open Sciences Collaboration (2015) Estimating the reproducibility of psychological science, *Science,* **349** (6251), http://dx.doi.org/10.1126/science.aac4716

7 https://www.cebma.org/

8 https://behavioralpolicy.org/about/

9 See, for instance, Rynes, SL, Colbert, AE and Brown, KG (2002) HR professionals' beliefs about effective human resource practices: Correspondence between research and practice, *Human Resource Management,* **41** (2), pp 149–74; and Rousseau, DM and Barends, EGR (2011) Becoming an evidence-based HR practitioner, *Human Resource Management Journal,* **21** (3), pp 221–35

10 Lubatkin, M (1988) Value-creating mergers: Fact or folklore? *Academy of Management Executive,* **2** (4), pp 295–302

11 Cascio, WF (1993) Downsizing: What do we know? What have we learned? *Academy of Management Perspectives,* **7** (1), pp 95–104

12 Pfeffer, J (2018) *Dying for a Paycheck,* HarperBusiness, New York

13 Pfeffer, J (2015) *Leadership BS,* HarperBusiness, New York

14 Pfeffer, *Dying for a Paycheck,* op cit

15 See, for instance, Galston, WA and Hendrickson, C (2018) A policy at peace with itself: Antitrust remedies for our concentrated, uncompetitive economy [Online] https://www.brookings.edu/research/a-policy-at-peace-with-itself-remedies-for-our-concentrated-uncompetitive-economy/

16 Naidu, S, Posner, EA and Weyl, EG (2018) Antitrust remedies for labor market power, *Harvard Law Review,* forthcoming

17 Rousseau, DM (ed) (2012) *The Oxford Handbook of Evidence-Based Management,* Oxford University Press, New York

PREFACE

We wrote this book for decision makers in organizations and for the faculty, coaches and management professionals who help them develop. It lays out essential concepts in evidence-based practice and guides the reader in taking an evidence-based approach to decisions related to management and organizations. In doing so, we also hope to challenge and inform management professionals and scholars regarding an alternative, more effective approach to making decisions in an increasingly complex, dynamic environment. Albert Einstein said, 'We cannot solve problems by the same kind of thinking we used when we created them'.[1] Evidence-based management changes our thinking about decisions in organizations, and how we teach and coach others to deepen their professional competencies.

Evidence-based management is a career-long pursuit – not just a tool or a course. It challenges conventional wisdom, authority and tradition regarding the way decisions are made. It raises a seldom-discussed issue in contemporary organizations – the quality of the evidence we use. All evidence-based practice, from its initiation in medicine to its contemporary uptake in policy and management, has as a key focus the critical appraisal of evidence quality. In our age of alt-facts and 'news and views' and at least one government's initiative to ban the term 'evidence-based'(!),[2] attention to the trustworthiness of our information and judgement is needed more than ever.

Our journey into evidence-based management

Learning is essential to evidence-based management. This is also true for us as authors. Both of us have been on our own journey into evidence-based management, starting from two very different places.

Eric Barends is an artist-turned-manager-turned-educator, who first learned of evidence-based practice working with physicians. 'People often ask what brought me to evidence-based management. Of course, my higher motive is "making the world a better place", but 10 years ago the big reason was frustration. As a senior manager, I was frustrated with the way decisions are made. Regardless whether it's a local hospital or a global banking firm, too many decisions are based on a single source, typically the

HIPPO – the highest paid person's opinion. A pivotal moment in my career was when I oversaw a large organizational change programme and asked three senior directors how they thought the change should be managed. To my big surprise, they all recommended a different approach. But what worried me more was I could tell their recommendations were influenced by where they were trained and which management books they had read. When I discussed this with a group of physicians they advised me to take an evidence-based approach: People can make any recommendation they like, but have them rate on a scale the quality of evidence backing it. If a recommendation is based on evidence from multiple, high-quality sources, such as a systematic review and controlled organizational data, it should be rated as high-quality evidence. If the evidence is a single case study or based only on their personal experience, the recommendation should still be entertained, but it should be rated as lower-quality evidence. Recommendations receive a weight consistent with their evidence quality. As you will see in this book, a true evidence-based approach is a bit more complicated, but at the time I thought that this approach was brilliant! This discussion in 2007 was a defining moment and marked my journey into evidence-based management. Fortunately, at that time, several other people were already promoting it, including Denise Rousseau, Jeffrey Pfeffer and Rob Briner. The problem was, however, that these people were all academics. They were promoting the *idea* of evidence-based management, but they did not explain how evidence-based management can be *applied* in daily practice. And to be honest, even though I was one of the few management practitioners in the movement, neither did I.

'It took us several years to figure out how the evidence-based practice skills developed in medicine – such as systematically acquiring evidence, appraising its quality, and calculating a probability estimate – apply to the domain of management. This book takes a big step forward to the practice of evidence-based management. I wish I had this book 10 years ago, when I was struggling with well-meant but often misguided advice from colleagues, consultants and famous management thinkers. It would have made me a better manager.'

Denise Rousseau is a professor, an academic researcher concerned with worker well-being and positive organizational practices, and a professional educator teaching MBAs and other graduate students and executives, many of whom hope to be better managers than those they themselves have had. 'I became interested in evidence-based management about 20 years ago as I came to believe in what could be called a research-practice gap. This meant that what I believed to be scientific findings of practical value were seldom used by managers or other practitioners. Naively, I thought it was a motivation issue, managers not being interested in research findings.

'Over time I have come to understand the research-practice "gap" quite differently. First, I have learned that thoughtful practitioners tend to be interested in all sorts of information, including scientific evidence.[3] (In all honesty, the best theorists I have met in my career have been highly successful, thoughtful senior executives, whose high need for cognition and understanding rivals professional academics.) However, scientific evidence is hard for managers to find, and often they don't know where or how to look for it. Second, educators in professional schools of business and management are very inconsistent regarding whether they base their teaching on the scientific evidence related to their subject. Professional schools do very little to prepare their graduates for seeking new evidence from science or other sources once out of school, and fail to prepare them for updating their knowledge as new evidence becomes available. Third, scholars in general do very little to make their research accessible to practitioners. For the most part, scholars create few if any evidence summaries that practitioners might find useful, instead writing vague Implications for Practitioner sections to their articles in order to get published – but not necessarily to put their findings to use. Last but not least, evidence is not answers. Regardless of the array and quality of evidence available to a working manager, that person still needs to interpret and apply the evidence in hand, an application that can require considerable judgement, consultation and learning by doing. Educators pay little attention to helping managers figure out how best to apply evidence in real life. It became clear that a family of approaches is needed to build a better bridge over the research-practice gap.'

What we have learned

Together we have 20 years of experience teaching evidence-based management. In truth, we began teaching it while we were still learning what it was or could be. We have needed to understand better what evidence-based management meant in daily practice. We came to appreciate the special skills and knowledge involved in interpreting science for practical use, the several kinds of evidence critical to organizational decisions (for example, organizational data, professional experience and stakeholder perspectives), and the different evidence-gathering processes needed for different kinds of decisions. We also came to realize the need to develop frameworks for critically appraising different kinds of evidence.

We also offer some observations:

- Asking good questions is a central skill in evidence-based practice, particularly the question 'What do I need to know to make this decision?'

- Obtaining evidence is a very different skill than merely searching the web. Because we can google doesn't mean we know how to find the best available evidence.

- Practitioners will sometimes gather new evidence and other times just apply the evidence they have in hand. They need to learn how to do both. This can mean priming the pump with preparatory reading and networking with researchers and other professionals in order to have easy access to evidence – when a decision arises.

- The biggest worry students express is not whether they have enough time or can get good evidence, it's whether their boss will be open-minded enough to listen to the evidence.

- And last, but not least, the perfect is the enemy of the good. The goal is better decisions, not perfect decisions. Effective evidence-based practitioners are lifelong learners prepared to deal with uncertainty in making decisions and solving problems.

Happy reading,
Eric Barends and Denise Rousseau
Leiden, NL and Pittsburgh, USA

Notes and references

1 Einstein, there is some dispute regarding the origins of this quote. https://en.wikiquote.org/wiki/Talk:Albert_Einstein, 11 February 2018

2 Kaplan, S and McNeil, DG (2017) Uproar over purported ban of words like 'fetus', *New York Times*, 17 December

3 Barends, EG *et al* (2017) Managerial attitudes and perceived barriers regarding evidence-based practice: An international survey, *PloS One*, 2017, **12** (10), e0184594

HOW TO READ
(AND USE) THIS BOOK

Our advice could be simple: sit down in a comfortable chair, and start reading from cover to cover. But we understand that you want something more elaborate. Here are some tips.

What background knowledge do I need?

Anyone who wants to know more about evidence-based management can read this book. Our target audience includes students, management professionals, consultants and teachers across a wide range of management disciplines (including but not limited to HR, strategy and change, healthcare management, public management, policy making, marketing and entrepreneurship) who want to learn how to make better decisions in organizations. No degree or technical knowledge is required. However, *some* experience with organizations, either as an employee or a manager, is helpful.

What is the structure of the book?

The chapters in this book follow the six steps of evidence-based management: *Ask*, *Acquire*, *Appraise*, *Aggregate*, *Apply* and *Assess*. In addition, the chapters follow the four sources of evidence: *Practitioners*, *Scientific literature*, *Organizations* and *Stakeholders*. Together the chapters represent the evidence-based management skills framework that forms the structure of this book (see Table 0.1).

Must I read the book from cover to cover or can I read separate chapters?

If you want to practise evidence-based management, you should be able to apply all six steps and make use of all four sources. Thus, it makes sense to consecutively read all chapters. However, although the steps, skills and

Table 0.1 Evidence-based management skills framework

	Practitioners (professional expertise)	Research literature (empirical studies)	Organization (internal data)	Stakeholders (values and concerns)
Ask Translating a practical issue into an answerable question		Chapter 2		
Acquire Systematically searching for and retrieving the evidence	Chapter 3	Chapter 6	Chapter 8	Chapter 10
Appraise Critically judging the trustworthiness of the evidence	Chapter 4	Chapter 7	Chapter 9	Chapter 11
Aggregate Weighing and pulling together the evidence		Chapter 12		
Apply Incorporating the evidence into the decision-making process		Chapter 13		
Assess Evaluating the outcome of the decision taken		Chapter 14		

sources are the same for all types of decisions, some may be more relevant than others – depending on the issue and organizational context at hand. In addition, your knowledge of some of the steps and sources may be more advanced whereas your understanding of others may be limited. For this reason, the chapters in this book can also be read separately – cherry picking is allowed. To ensure a thorough understanding when reading separate chapters, we have provided some overlap. Important core concepts such as PICOC, bias, confounders and methodological features are discussed in several chapters. In addition, a glossary is provided to help you when encountering unfamiliar terms or concepts.

Three chapters are not about the six steps or four sources, what is their purpose?

In addition to the 12 chapters that represent the evidence-based management skills framework, we have provided three more chapters. Chapter 1 provides a succinct and readable overview of the basic principles of evidence-based management: what is it, why do we need it, and common misconceptions. This chapter is a good introduction for those who are unfamiliar with evidence-based management. You might want to share it with your colleagues (a free downloadable copy can be retrieved from www.CEBMa.org). Chapter 5 provides a short introduction to science. It discusses basic scientific principles such as the scientific method, peer review and replication, and explains important concepts such as statistical **significance**, bias, confounders and moderators and mediators. In Chapter 15 we discuss how you can build the capacity for evidence-based management – not only in yourself, but also among your peers, bosses and the organization at large.

Why are there so many examples in this book?

Evidence-based management is not a philosophy or an abstract idea, it is something people do (or don't do) to make better decisions in organizations. It is about following the six steps, applying the six corresponding skills and using the four sources of evidence day-to-day. To illustrate how this works we have used many practical examples.

So, is this a textbook or a management book?

Both. The book can be used as a 'textbook' for universities, business schools and other educational institutions, as well as a 'management book' for managers, leaders, policymakers and consultants. But first and foremost, this is a '*How to*' book. It is meant to be used not just to read. For this reason, we have incorporated checklists and flowcharts useful in daily practice. We hope this book gets a privileged spot on your desk or bookshelf to be consulted whenever an important decision is made.

What is on the companion website?

Two websites are available to help supplement this book and help continue your development as an evidence-based practitioner:

- Carnegie Mellon's Open Learning Initiative offers a set of training modules so you can learn about different aspects of evidence-based management and test your understanding of them: http://oli.cmu.edu/. Once you get to the opening page, sign up and then search for Evidence-Based Management (open + free courses).

- The Center for Evidence-Based Management (CEBMa) offers a variety of supports for practitioners, teachers and scholars, including articles, presentations and access to a network of EBMgt practitioners: https://www.cebma.org/

ACKNOWLEDGEMENTS

The inspiration for this book came from *Evidence-Based Medicine: How to practice and teach EBM*, the landmark publication by David L Sackett, Sharon E Straus, W Scott Richardson, William Rosenberg and R Brian Haynes. We owe these pioneers a great debt for their wisdom and insight into evidence-based practice, and hope our book will take its place alongside theirs for any professional seeking to make better decisions.

This book is really a community effort. We thank the members of the Center for Evidence-Based Management (CEBMa) for their insights into EBMgt teaching and practice and their critical contributions to the book itself. Truth to be told, this book is as much theirs as ours.

We give a special shout out to our 'proofreaders', who gave us critical feedback on previous drafts. In particular, we want to thank David Creelman, John Zanardelli, Sandy Mchalko, Mrs Walker, Wendy Hirsh, Courtney Bigony, Jageshwar (Jag) Sungkur, Arjan Haring, Laura Fennimore, Vincent Cassar, Luca Bugelli, Christian Criado-Perez, Joe Moore, Peter West, Gergely Németh, Marijn Van Cauwenberghe, Darryl Howes, Sue Gerrard, Judith Zielstra, Ian Moorhouse, Sergio Ribeiro, Blake Jelley and especially Pietro Marenco. We hope they can see the difference they made in the final product.

A sincere thanks to Clare Peel for clever editing and Rosemarie Lang for savvy preparation of our manuscript.

We have tried to be scrupulous about the origins of the ideas, insights and examples used in this book, but some individuals have had a greater impact than their number of citations might suggest. We gratefully stand on the shoulders of giants including Gordon Guyatt, Daniel Kahneman, David Sackett, Nate Silver, Herb Simon and Neil deGrasse Tyson.

Denise Rousseau greatly benefited from a Bellagio residency supported by the Rockefeller Foundation and the collegiality and time to write it provided. She also deeply appreciates the years of support for EBMgt teaching provided by Carnegie Mellon deans Ramayya Krishnan (Heinz College) and Bob Dammon (Tepper School of Business), as well as the ongoing support of an HJ Heinz II Professorship.

Finally, this book wouldn't be written without Quint Studer and Tony Kovner. Thanks to the generous financial support from the Studer Foundation and NYU's Kovner Visitor-in-Residence Fund we were able to invest the time and effort needed to write this book. Thanks for supporting this opportunity to make a difference.

Evidence-based management: the basic principles

> The fact that an opinion has been widely held is no evidence whatever that it is not utterly absurd.
>
> BERTRAND RUSSELL

Consider this hypothetical situation. You pay a visit to a dietician after gaining a bit of weight over the holiday season. The dietician advises you to try diet X. It's very expensive and demands a radical change in lifestyle, but the prospect of having a slim and healthy body motivates you to stick to the diet. After a few weeks, however, you have gained five pounds and suffer serious side effects that require medical treatment. After searching the internet, you learn that most scientific studies find diet X to be ineffective and fraught with such side effects. When you confront the dietician with these findings, he replies, 'Why should I pay attention to scientific studies? I have 20 years of experience. Besides, the diet was developed by a famous American nutritionist, whose book sold more than a million copies.'[1]

Does that sound like malpractice? It probably does. Unfortunately, in management, disregarding sound **evidence** and relying on personal experience or the popular ideas of management gurus is daily practice. Yet managerial decisions affect the working lives and well-being of people around the world. As Henry Mintzberg said: 'No job is more vital to our society than that of a manager. It is the manager who determines whether our social institutions serve us well or whether they squander our talents and resources.'[2]

In this book we will explain what evidence-based management is and how it can help you and your organization make better decisions. Whether we work in a bank, hospital, large consulting firm or small startup, as practitioners affecting the lives of so many, we have a moral obligation to use the best available evidence when making a decision. We can do this by learning how to distinguish **science** from folklore, **data** from assertions, and evidence from beliefs, anecdotes or personal opinions.

1.1 What is evidence-based management?

The basic idea of evidence-based management is that good-quality decisions require both critical thinking and use of the best available evidence. Of course, all practitioners use some kind of evidence in their decisions. But few pay attention to the quality of the evidence. The result is decisions that rely on unfounded beliefs, fads and fashions, and the unsupported though popular ideas of management gurus. The bottom line is bad decisions, poor outcomes and little understanding of why things go wrong. Evidence-based management seeks to improve the way decisions are made. It is an approach to decision-making and day-to-day work practice that helps practitioners to critically evaluate the extent to which they can trust the evidence they have at hand. It also helps practitioners identify, find and evaluate additional evidence relevant to their decisions.

In this book, we use the following definition of evidence-based management.[3] This definition not only provides a clear statement of what evidence-based management means, but also describes the main skills required to manage in an evidence-based way:

Evidence-based management is about making decisions through the conscientious, explicit and judicious use of the best available evidence from multiple sources by:

1 **Asking**: translating a practical issue or problem into an answerable question.

2 **Acquiring**: systematically searching for and retrieving the evidence.

3 **Appraising**: critically judging the trustworthiness and relevance of the evidence.

4 **Aggregating**: weighing and pulling together the evidence.

5 **Applying**: incorporating the evidence into the decision-making process.

6 **Assessing**: evaluating the outcome of the decision taken

to increase the likelihood of a favourable outcome.

1.2 What counts as evidence?

When we say 'evidence', we mean **information,** facts or data supporting (or contradicting) a claim, **assumption** or hypothesis. Evidence may come from scientific research suggesting some relatively generalizable facts about the world, people or organizational practices. Evidence may also come from local organizational or business indicators, such as company metrics, KPIs or observations of practice conditions. Even professional experience can be an important source of evidence, as in the case where an entrepreneur learns from having launched a variety of businesses that one particular approach seems more likely to pay off. Last, stakeholders, people who affect and/or are affected by a decision, can provide important information on potential consequences and interests related to the decision.

Think of it in legal terms. In a court of law, evidence from many different sources is presented, including eyewitness testimony, forensic evidence, security camera images and witness statements. All this evidence may help a judge or a jury to decide whether a person is innocent or guilty. The same is true for management decisions. Regardless of its source, all evidence may be included if it is judged to be **trustworthy** and relevant.

1.3 Why do we need evidence-based management?

Most management decisions are not based on the best available evidence. Instead, practitioners often prefer to base decisions solely on their judgement based on personal experience. However, personal judgement alone is not a very reliable source of evidence because it is highly susceptible to systematic errors – we have cognitive and information processing limits that make us prone to biases that have negative effects on the quality of the decisions we make.[4, 5, 6, 7]

Even practitioners and industry experts with many years of experience are very bad at making forecasts or calculating risks when relying solely on their personal judgement, whether it concerns the credit rating of bonds,[8] the growth of the economy,[9] political developments[10] or medical diagnoses.[11] In Chapter 4 you will gain a better understanding of the nature of **professional expertise** and learn how to detect common cognitive biases that can negatively affect practitioner judgement.

Another heavily used source of evidence is what other organizations are doing. Through benchmarking and so-called 'best practices', practitioners sometimes copy what other organizations are doing without critically evaluating whether these practices are actually effective and, if so, whether they are also likely to work in a different context. Benchmarking can demonstrate alternative ways of doing things, but it is not necessarily a good indicator in itself of what would work elsewhere. Chapters 8 and 9 further explain how to gather and evaluate organizational evidence.

At the same time, there are many barriers to evidence-based management. Few management practitioners have been trained in the skills required to critically evaluate the trustworthiness and relevance of the information they use. In addition, important organizational information may be difficult to access and what is available can be of poor quality. Finally, practitioners are often unaware of the current scientific evidence available on key issues related to their decisions. For example, a survey of 950 US HR practitioners showed large discrepancies between what practitioners think is effective and what the current scientific research shows.[12] This study has been repeated in other countries with similar findings.[13] Such results suggest that most practitioners pay little or no attention to scientific or organizational evidence. Instead, the typical practitioner seems to place too much trust in low-quality evidence such as personal judgement and experience, best practices and the beliefs of corporate leaders. As a result, billions of dollars are spent on management practices that are ineffective or even harmful to organizations, their members and the public.

 Example

For years, the US technology company Google believed that technical expertise was the most important capability for their managers. They thought that the best managers left their people alone as much as possible, focusing instead on helping them with technical problems when people got stuck. When the company examined what employees valued most in a manager, however, technical expertise ranked last among eight qualities. More crucial were attributes like asking good questions, taking time to meet and caring about employees' careers and lives. Managers who did these things led top-performing teams and had the happiest employees and lowest turnover. These attributes of effective managers, however, also are well established in scientific studies, so Google's improvement efforts could have started years earlier.

To give evidence-based management a shot at success, we need to increase the capacity of managers and organizations to prioritize quality evidence over unfounded personal opinion – and incorporate what the body of evidence indicates into their better-informed professional judgement. In Chapter 15, we will discuss how to build the capacity for evidence-based management – not only in yourself, but also among your peers, bosses and the larger organization.

1.4 What sources of evidence should be considered?

Before making an important decision, an evidence-based practitioner starts by asking, 'What's the available evidence?' Instead of basing a decision on personal judgement alone, an evidence-based practitioner finds out what is known by looking for evidence from multiple sources. According to the principles of evidence-based management, evidence from four sources should be taken into account (Figure 1.1):

Figure 1.1

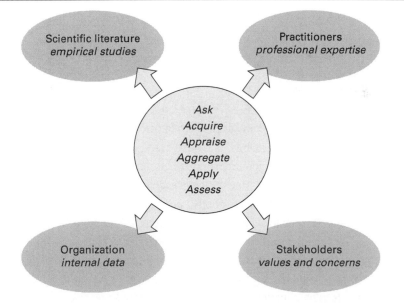

Practitioners: The professional experience and judgement of practitioners.

The scientific literature: Findings from empirical studies published in academic journals.

The organization: Data, facts and figures gathered from the organization.

Stakeholders: The values and concerns of people who may be affected by the decision.

Evidence from practitioners

The first source of evidence is the professional experience and judgement of managers, consultants, business leaders and other practitioners. Different from intuition, opinion or belief, professional experience is accumulated over time through reflection on the outcomes of similar actions taken in similar situations. This type of evidence is sometimes referred to as 'tacit' knowledge. Professional experience differs from intuition and personal opinion because it reflects the specialized knowledge acquired by repeated experience and practice of specialized activities such as playing the violin or making a cost estimate. Many practitioners take seriously the need to reflect critically on their experiences and distil the practical lessons. Their knowledge can be vital for determining whether a management issue really does require attention, if the available organizational data are trustworthy, whether research findings apply in a particular situation or how likely a proposed solution is to work in a particular context.

 Example

A Dutch university hospital has decided to implement personal development plans for all its nurses. These plans would include a statement of the nurse's aspirations and career priorities. The HR director points out that according to Maslow's hierarchy of needs, a well-known motivation theory, basic levels of needs (such as health and safety) must be met before an individual can focus on his or her higher-level needs (such as career and professional development). The nurses at the emergency department are increasingly exposed to serious safety hazards from offensive language to physical violence. The HR director therefore recommends excluding these nurses until the safety hazards are under control and significantly reduced.

How did evidence from practitioners help?

Experienced managers and nurses were asked independently about their view on the director's recommendation. Most of them failed to agree and indicated that their professional experience tells them that often the opposite is true: nurses who work in difficult circumstances tend to be strongly interested in professional development and self-improvement. In addition, a search was conducted in online scientific databases. This yielded a range of studies indicating that there is no empirical evidence available to support Maslow's theory, therefore the managers' and nurses' experience is a better quality source of evidence.

In Chapter 3 we explain how to gather evidence from practitioners in a valid and reliable way, covering aspects such as what, who, and how to ask, the sample size needed, and how to develop appropriate questionnaires.

Evidence from the scientific research literature

The second source of evidence is scientific research published in academic journals. Over the past few decades the volume of management research has escalated hugely, with topics ranging from evaluating merger success and the effects of financial incentives on performance to improving employee commitment and recruitment.

There is also much relevant research from outside the management discipline, since many of the typical problems that managers face, such as how to make better decisions, how to communicate more effectively and how to deal with conflict, are similar to those experienced in a wide range of contexts. Although many practitioners learn about research findings as students or on professional courses, new research is always being produced, which often changes our understanding. In order to include up-to-date evidence from the scientific literature in your decisions, it is essential to know how to search for studies and to be able to judge how trustworthy and relevant they are.

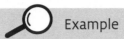

Example

The board of directors of a large Canadian law firm has plans for a merger with a smaller firm nearby. The merger's objective is to integrate the back-office of the two firms (IT, finance, facilities, etc) in order to create economies of scale. The front offices and legal practices of the two firms will remain separate. The board has been told by the partners that the organizational cultures of the two firms differ widely, so the board wants to know whether this can create problems for the merger. Partners of both firms were asked independently about their professional experience with mergers. Those who had been involved in one or more mergers stated that cultural differences matter, and can cause serious culture clashes between professionals.

How did evidence from the scientific literature help?

A search was conducted in online scientific databases, which yielded a **meta-analysis** based on 46 studies with a combined sample size of 10,710 mergers and acquisitions. The meta-analysis confirms the partner's judgement that there is a negative association between cultural differences and the effectiveness of the post-merger integration. However, the study also indicates that this is only the case when the intended level of integration is high. In mergers that require a low level of integration, cultural differences are found to be positively associated with integration benefits. In the case of the two law firms, the planned integration concerns only back office functions, making the **likelihood** of a positive outcome higher.

In Chapter 6 you will learn the skills necessary to successfully search for evidence from the scientific literature using online research databases such as ABI/INFORM Global, Business Source Premier and PsycINFO.

Evidence from the organization

A third source of evidence is the organization itself. Whether this is a business, hospital or governmental agency, organizational evidence comes in many forms. It can be financial data such as cash flow or costs, or business measures such as return on investment or market share. It can come from customers or clients in the form of customer satisfaction, repeat business or product returns statistics. It can also come from employees through information about retention rates or levels of job satisfaction. Evidence from the organization can be 'hard' numbers such as staff turnover rates, medical errors or productivity levels, but it can also include 'soft' elements such as perceptions of the organization's culture or attitudes towards senior management. Evidence from the organization is essential to identifying problems that require managers' attention. It is also essential to determining likely causes, plausible solutions and what is needed to implement these solutions.

 Example

The board of a large insurance company has plans to change its regional structure to a product-based structure. According to the board, the restructuring will secure the company's market presence and drive greater customer focus. The company's sales managers strongly disagree with this change, arguing that ditching the region-based structure will make it harder to build good relationships with customers and will therefore harm customer service.

How did evidence from the organization help?

Analysis of organizational data revealed that the company's customer satisfaction is well above the industry average. Further data analysis showed a strong negative **correlation** between the account managers' monthly travel expenses and the satisfaction of their customers, suggesting that sales managers who live close to their customers score higher on customer satisfaction.

In Chapter 8 you will develop a better understanding of evidence from the organization and learn to acquire it in a valid and reliable way.

Evidence from stakeholders

A fourth source of evidence is stakeholder values and concerns. Stakeholders are any individuals or groups who may be affected by an organization's decisions and their consequences. Internal stakeholders include employees, managers and board members. Stakeholders outside the organization such as suppliers, customers, shareholders, the government and the public at large may also be affected. Stakeholder values and concerns reflect what stakeholders believe to be important, which in turn affects how they tend to react to the possible consequences of the organization's decisions. Stakeholders may place more or less importance on, for example, short-term gain or long-term sustainability, employee well-being or employee output, organizational reputation or profitability, and participation in decision-making or top-down control. Organizations that serve or respond to different stakeholders can reach very different decisions on the basis of the same evidence (compare ExxonMobil and Greenpeace, for example). Gathering evidence from stakeholders is not just important for ethical reasons. Understanding stakeholder values and concerns also provides a frame of reference from which to analyse evidence from other sources. It provides important information about the way in which decisions will be received and whether the outcomes of those decisions are likely to be successful.

 Example

To assess employees' satisfaction with their supervisors, a British telecom organization conducted a survey among its 12,500 employees. The survey contained some demographic questions such as postcode, date of birth and job title, and five questions on employee satisfaction with their immediate supervisor. The introductory letter by the CEO stated that all answers would remain anonymous. After the survey was sent out, only 582 employees responded, a response rate of less than 5 per cent.

How did evidence from stakeholders help?

A **focus group** discussion with employees from different parts of the organization was conducted to find out why so many members did not participate in the survey. The employees in the focus group stated that they were concerned that the demographic data would make it possible to identify the person behind the answers. Given the sensitive nature of the survey's topic they therefore decided not to participate. Based on this outcome the survey was modified by dropping the postcode and replacing the date of birth with an age range. The modified survey yielded a response rate of 67 per cent.

In Chapter 10 we explain how to identify a company's most relevant stake-holders. We also discuss methods for exploring stakeholder interests and concerns, and describe how paying attention to both practical and ethical aspects in the decision process can improve the quality of your decisions. Finally, in Chapter 12 we demonstrate how you can weigh and combine evidence from all four sources of evidence.

1.5 Why do we have to critically appraise evidence?

Evidence is never perfect and sometimes can be misleading. Evidence can be overstated such that a seemingly strong claim turns out to be based on a single and not particularly reliable piece of information. A colleague's confident opinion regarding the effectiveness of a practice might turn out to be based on little more than an anecdote. An organization's long-standing way of doing things may actually never have been evaluated to see whether it really works. All evidence should be critically appraised by carefully and systematically assessing its trustworthiness and relevance.

How a piece of evidence is evaluated can differ slightly depending on its source; however, **critical appraisal** always involves asking the same basic questions. Where and how is the evidence gathered? Is it the best available evidence? Is there enough evidence to reach a conclusion? Are there reasons why the evidence could be biased in a particular direction? So, for example, if we are critically appraising a colleague's experiences with a particular problem, we may wonder how many times he or she has experienced that issue and whether the situations were comparable. For example, if a colleague proposes a solution to high levels of staff absenteeism, but his or her experience relates to only one previous instance, and that was among migrant workers picking fruit, then it would not have much to teach you about dealing with absenteeism of orthopaedic surgeons in a hospital. Similar questions need to be asked about evidence from the organization such as sales figures, error rates or cash flow. How were these figures calculated? Are they accurate? Are they reliable? In the case of evidence from the **scientific literature** we would ask questions about how the study was designed. How were the data collected? How was the outcome measured? To what extent are alternative explanations for the outcome found possible? Evidence-based management is about using the best available evidence, and critical appraisal plays an essential role in discerning and identifying such evidence.

In Chapter 4 you will learn how to detect common cognitive biases that may negatively affect practitioner (and your own) judgement. Chapter 7 will help you to critically appraise the trustworthiness of external evidence such as journal articles, business books, newspaper articles or textbooks based on scientific research. Chapter 9 will teach you the skills needed to critically appraise organizational evidence. Finally, Chapter 11 focuses on the critical appraisal of stakeholder evidence; that is, the perceptions and feelings of people who influence and/or are affected by a decision.

1.6 Why focus on the 'best available' evidence?

In almost any situation it is possible to gather different types of evidence from different sources, and sometimes in really quite large quantities. But which evidence should we pay more attention to and why? A fundamental principle of evidence-based management is that the quality of our decisions is likely to improve the more we make use of trustworthy evidence – in other words, the best available evidence. This principle is apparent in every-day decision-making, whether it is buying someone a birthday present or wondering where to go out for dinner. In most cases, we actively seek out information from multiple sources, such as our partner's opinion, the expe-riences of friends or the comments of a local food critic. Sometimes this information is so weak that it is hardly convincing at all, while at other times the information is so strong that no one doubts its correctness. It is therefore important to be able through critical appraisal to determine what evidence is the 'best' – that is, the most trustworthy – evidence. For instance, the most trustworthy evidence on which holiday destination has the least chance of rain in Ireland in early August will obviously come from statistics on the average rainfall per month, not from the personal experi-ence of a colleague who only visited the country once. Exactly the same is true for management decisions. When making a decision about whether or not to use a quality management method such as Six Sigma to reduce medical errors in a British university hospital, information based on the findings from a study of 150 European university hospitals in which medical errors were measured before and after the introduction of Six Sigma is more trustworthy than the professional experience of a colleague who works at a small private hospital in Sydney. However, such a study may never have been done. Instead, the best 'available' evidence could be case studies of just one or two hospitals. For some decisions, there may be no evidence from the scientific literature or the organization at all, thus we may have no option but to make a decision based on the professional experience of colleagues or to pilot test different approaches and see for ourselves what might work best. Given the principles of evidence-based management, even if we rely on the experience of colleagues, this limited-quality evidence can still lead to a better decision than not using it, as long as we are aware of its limitations when we act on it.

1.7 Some common misconceptions of evidence-based management

Misconceptions about evidence-based management are a major barrier to its uptake and implementation. For this reason, it is important that misconceptions are challenged and corrected. In most cases, they reflect a narrow or limited understanding of the principles of evidence-based management.

Misconception 1: Evidence-based management ignores the practitioner's professional experience

This misconception directly contradicts our definition of evidence-based management – that decisions should be made through the conscientious, explicit and judicious use of evidence from four sources, including evidence from practitioners. Evidence-based management does not mean that any one source of evidence is more valid than any other. Even the professional experience and judgement of practitioners can be an important source if it is appraised to be trustworthy and relevant. Evidence from practitioners is essential in appropriately interpreting and using evidence from other sources. If we are trying to identify effective ways of sharing information with colleagues, evidence from the organization may be informative but professional experience and judgement are needed to help to determine what practices make good sense if we are working with professionally trained colleagues or relatively low-skilled workers. Similarly, evidence from the scientific literature can help us to understand the extent to which our experience and judgement is trustworthy. Research indicates that years of experience in a technical speciality can lead to considerable expertise and tacit knowledge. On the other hand, an individual holding a series of unrelated jobs over the same number of years may have far less trustworthy and reliable expertise. Evidence-based management is hence about using evidence from multiple sources, rather than merely relying on only one.

Misconception 2: Evidence-based management is all about numbers and statistics

Evidence-based management involves seeking out and using the best available evidence from multiple sources. It is not exclusively about numbers and quantitative data, although many practice decisions involve figures of some sort. You do not need to be a statistician to undertake evidence-based management, but understanding basic statistical concepts helps you to critically evaluate some types of evidence. The principles behind such concepts as sample size, statistical versus practical significance, confidence intervals and effect sizes, can be understood without mathematics. Evidence-based management is not about statistics, but *statistical thinking* is an important element.

Misconception 3: Managers need to make decisions fast and don't have time for evidence-based management

Sometimes evidence-based management is about taking a moment to reflect on how well the evidence you have can be trusted. More often it is about preparing yourself (and your organization) in advance in order to make key decisions well. Evidence-based management involves identifying the best available evidence you need, preferably before you need it. Some management decisions do need to be taken quickly, but even split-second decisions require trustworthy evidence. Making a good, fast decision about when to evacuate a leaking nuclear power plant or how to make an emergency landing requires up-to-date knowledge of emergency procedures and reliable instruments providing trustworthy evidence about radiation levels or altitude. When important decisions need to be made quickly, an evidence-based practitioner anticipates the kinds of evidence that quality decisions require. The need to make an immediate decision is generally the exception rather than the rule. The vast majority of management decisions are made over much longer time periods – sometimes weeks or even months – and often require consideration of legal, financial, strategic, logistic or other organizational issues, which all take time. The inherent nature of organizational decisions, especially important ones, provides plenty of opportunity to collect and critically evaluate evidence about the nature of the problem and, if there is a problem, the decision most likely to produce the desired outcome. For evidence-based management, time is not normally a deal breaker.

Misconception 4: Each organization is unique, so the usefulness of evidence from the scientific literature is limited

One objection practitioners have to using evidence from the scientific literature is the belief that their organization is unique, suggesting that research findings will simply not apply. Although it is true that organizations do differ, they also tend to face very similar issues, sometimes repeatedly, and often respond to them in similar ways. Peter Drucker, a seminal management thinker, was perhaps the first to assert that most management issues are 'repetitions of familiar problems cloaked in the guise of uniqueness'.[14] The truth of the matter is that it is commonplace for organizations to have myths and stories about their own uniqueness.[15] In reality they tend to be neither exactly alike nor completely unique, but somewhere in between. Evidence-based practitioners need to be flexible enough to take such similar-yet-different qualities into account. A thoughtful practitioner, for instance, might use individual financial incentives for independent salespeople but reward knowledge workers with opportunities for development or personally interesting projects, knowing that financial incentives tend to lower performance for knowledge workers while increasing the performance of less-skilled workers.[16, 17]

Misconception 5: If you do not have high-quality evidence, you cannot do anything

Sometimes little or no quality evidence is available. This may be the case with a new management practice or the implementation of new technologies. In some areas the organizational context changes rapidly, which can limit the relevance and applicability of evidence derived from the past situations. In those cases, the evidence-based practitioner has no other option but to work with the limited evidence at hand and supplement it through learning by doing. This means pilot testing and treating any course of action as a prototype, that is, systematically assess the outcome of decisions made using a process of constant experimentation, punctuated by critical reflection about which things work and which things do not.[18, 19]

Misconception 6: Good-quality evidence gives you the answer to the problem

Evidence is not an answer. It does not speak for itself. To make sense of evidence, we need an understanding of the context and a critical mindset. You might take a test and find out you scored 10 points, but if you don't know the average or total possible score it's hard to determine whether you did well. You may also want to know what doing well on the test actually means. Does it indicate or predict anything important to you and in your context? And why? Your score in the test is meaningless without this additional information. At the same time, evidence is never conclusive. It does not prove things, which means that no piece of evidence can be viewed as a universal or timeless truth. In most cases evidence comes with a large measure of uncertainty. Evidence-based practitioners typically make decisions not based on conclusive, solid, up-to-date information, but on probabilities, indications and tentative conclusions. Evidence does not tell you what to decide, but it does help you to make a better-informed decision.

1.8 What is the evidence for evidence-based management?

Sometimes people ask whether there is evidence that an evidence-based approach is more effective than the way managers already typically make decisions. This is, of course, a very important question. To measure the effect of evidence-based management would require an evaluation of a large number of situations and contexts where evidence-based management was applied, and the measurement of a wide range of outcomes, preferably by means of a double blind, randomized controlled study. Such a study might well be too difficult to carry out. However, there is plenty of scientific research that suggests that taking an evidence-based approach to decisions is more likely to be effective. We noted earlier in this chapter that the human mind is susceptible to systematic errors – we have cognitive limits and are prone to biases that impair the quality of the decisions we make. The fundamental questions to ask include: How can we make decisions without falling prey to our biases? Are there decision practices or processes that can improve decision quality? Fortunately, there are a large number of studies that indicate the following:

- Forecasts or risk assessments based on the aggregated (averaged) professional experience of many people are more accurate than forecasts based on one person's personal experience (provided that the forecasts are made independently before being combined).[20, 21, 22, 23, 24]

- Professional judgements informed by hard data or statistical models are more accurate than judgements based solely on individual experience.[25, 26, 27]

- Knowledge derived from scientific research is more accurate than the opinions of experts.[28]

- A decision based on the combination of critically appraised evidence from multiple sources yields better outcomes than a decision based on a single source of evidence.[29, 30]

- Evaluating the outcome of a decision has been found to improve both organizational learning and performance, especially in novel and non-routine situations.[31, 32, 33]

Notes and references

1 This example is partly adapted from Pfeffer, J and Sutton, R (2011) Trust the evidence, not your instincts, *New York Times*, 3 September

2 Mintzberg, H (1990) The manager's job: folklore and fact, *Harvard Business Review*, 53 (4)

3 This definition is partly adapted from the Sicily statement of evidence-based practice: Dawes, M *et al* (2005) Sicily statement on evidence-based practice, *BMC Medical Education*, 5 (1)

4 Kahneman, D (2011) *Thinking, Fast and Slow*, Penguin Group, London

5 Clements, MP (2002) An evaluation of the survey of professional forecasters probability distribution of expected inflation and output growth, *Journal of Economic Literature*, 22 November

6 Bazerman, MH (2009) *Judgment in Managerial Decision Making*, Wiley, New York

7 Simon, HA (1997) *Models of Bounded Rationality*, Vol 3, MIT Press, London

8 Barnett-Hart, AK (2009) The Story of the CDO Market Meltdown: An empirical analysis, Harvard University, Cambridge, MA

9 Loungani, P (2000) The arcane art of predicting recessions, *Financial Times*, 18 December

10 Tetlock, PE (2006) *Expert Political Judgement*, Princeton University Press, Princeton, NJ

11 Choudhry, NK *et al* (2005) Systematic review: The relationship between clinical experience and quality of health care, *Ann Intern Med*, **142** (4)

12 Rynes, SL, Colbert, AE and Brown, KG (2002) HR Professionals' beliefs about effective human resource practices: Correspondence between research and practice, *Human Resource Management*, **41** (2), pp 149–74

13 More educated managers do, however, show somewhat greater knowledge of scientific findings, Rynes *et al*, ibid.

14 Lowenstein, R (2006) When business has questions, Drucker still has answers, *New York Times*, 22 January, Bu 7

15 Martin, J *et al* (1983) The uniqueness paradox in organizational stories, *Administrative Science Quarterly*, pp 438–53

16 Ariely, D *et al* (2009) Large stakes and big mistakes, *The Review of Economic Studies*, **76** (2), pp 451–69

17 Joseph, K and Kalwani, MU (1998) The role of bonus pay in salesforce compensation plans, *Industrial Marketing Management*, **27** (2), pp 147–59

18 Pfeffer, J and Sutton, RI (2010) Treat your organization as a prototype: The essence of evidence-based management, *Design Management Review*, **17** (3), pp 10–14

19 Weick, KE and Sutcliffe, K (2007) *Managing the Unexpected: Resilient performance in an age of uncertainty*, Wiley, New York

20 Silver, N (2012) *The Signal and the Noise: Why so many predictions fail – but some don't*, p 286 and p 690, Penguin, London

21 Bauer, A *et al* (2003) Forecast evaluation with cross sectional data: The blue chip surveys, *Economic Review*, Federal Reserve Bank of Atlanta

22 Servan-Schreiber, E *et al* (2004) Prediction markets: Does money matter? *Electronic Markets*, **1** (31)

23 Armstrong, JS (2001) Combining Forecasts in *Principles of Forecasting: A handbook for researchers and practitioners*, Kluwer Academic Publishers, New York

24 Yaniv, I and Choshen-Hillel, S (2012) Exploiting the wisdom of others to make better decisions: Suspending judgment reduces egocentrism and increases accuracy, *Journal of Behavioral Decision Making*, **25** (5), pp 427–34

25 Lewis, M (2003) *Moneyball: The art of winning an unfair game*, Barnes and Noble

26 Grove, WM (2005) Clinical versus statistical prediction, *Journal of Clinical Psychology*, **61** (10), pp 1233–43

27 Ayres, I (2007) *Super Crunchers*, Bantam Books, New York

28 Antman, EM *et al* (1992), A comparison of results of meta-analyses of randomized control trials and recommendations of clinical experts, *JAMA*, **268** (2), pp 240–48

29 McNees, SK (1990) The role of judgment in macroeconomic forecasting accuracy, *International Journal of Forecasting*, **6** (3), pp 287–299

30 Tetlock, PE (2006) *Expert Political Judgement*, Princeton University Press, Princeton, NJ

31 Anseel, F, Lievens, F and Schollaert, E (2009) Reflection as a strategy to enhance task performance after feedback, *Organizational Behavior and Human Decision Processes*, **110** (1)

32 Ellis, S and Davidi, I (2005) After-event reviews: Drawing lessons from successful and failed experience, *Journal of Applied Psychology*, **90** (5), pp 857

33 Tannenbaum, SI and Cerasoli, CP (2013) Do team and individual debriefs enhance performance? A meta-analysis, *Human Factors*, **55** (1), pp 231–45

ASK: Critical questions about assumed problems and preferred solutions

02

The important thing is to never stop questioning

ALBERT EINSTEIN

At the outset of a decision, it is critical to figure out the problem you need to solve, or the opportunity you are trying to address. A good start begins with asking questions – lots of them. Doing this kicks off the process of deliberate search for evidence and understanding – gathering intelligence to get a full grasp of the need, the opportunity or crisis. Asking questions to identify uncertainties – and thus the need for evidence – is therefore the first step of evidence-based management. In fact, asking questions and framing diagnoses and problems properly may be the most important step in the evidence-based process.

Indeed, this first step of evidence-based management is not so much about critical thinking or logical reasoning, but first and foremost about your capacity for asking the right questions – as illustrated by the US astrophysicist Neil deGrasse Tyson:

> If someone comes up to you and says, 'I have these crystals. If you rub them together, it will heal all your illnesses. I'm happy to sell them to you for 100 dollars.' What would your response be? Would it be: 'Oh, great. Wow! Here's the money.' Or would it be: 'Oh, that's rubbish. That will never work.' Each of those responses is equally scientifically lazy. In the first case, you say it's definitely true; in the second case, you say that it couldn't ever be true. But each

of those responses – the acceptance and the rejection – requires no thought. So, extreme gullibility and extreme scepticism are two equal ways of not having to think much at all. It's harder to ask good questions. For example, 'Where did you get the crystals? What are the crystals made of? What kind of diseases do you say they cure? How do you know it works? By what mechanism does it work? What evidence do you have that it would work on me? Can you demonstrate?' By the time you've finished, the person will probably have walked away.[1]

Dismissing something as nonsense or embracing something as the truth before you have fully considered the evidence – even when it is the result of critical thinking or logical reasoning – is risky. Often when we assume we are thinking critically or logically, that is, when we think we have a sound reason for our judgement, our decision-making may be tainted by cognitive biases and systematic errors. You can read more about this in Chapter 4. A better approach is to ask questions to determine whether strong evidence exists to support a claim, hypothesis or assumption regarding a problem or solution. Therefore, asking questions is the first step of evidence-based management. Is the claim a person makes based on trustworthy evidence? Evidence-based professionals always try to maintain an open mind and a healthy dose of scepticism. They always (respectfully) question the information they are given, whether it is from their superior, a consultant or a highly esteemed professor. In this chapter, you will learn how to ask questions to identify uncertainties and the need for evidence.

2.1 Identifying underlying assumptions

The main function of asking questions is to identify assumptions. An assumption is a claim, assertion or hypothesis that we believe (or accept) to be true, even though there is no evidence available (yet). In daily life and in the context of organizations we make assumptions all the time. We assume that our car will be in the same spot we parked it in yesterday. We assume that our company did not burn down during the night. We assume that we will receive our pay cheque at the end of the month. Some assumptions turn out to be based on solid evidence, while others may have no supporting evidence, and some may even be false. In daily life, this is not necessarily a problem. After all, most of the assumptions we make are rather harmless and won't have serious consequences if they turn out to be incorrect. In the realm of management and organizations, however, an assumption underlying an important business decision that turns out to be based on fiction rather than solid evidence can have a devastating impact. It may affect the company's business results and damage the working lives of employees. It is therefore important to identify assumptions underlying important managerial decisions and to check whether they are based on evidence.

A key problem with assumptions is that they are sometimes hidden. For example, consider the following assertion: *'Teenagers nowadays spend hours sitting at their computer. So, their school performance will suffer.'* On closer inspection, you will notice there are two hidden assumptions underlying this assertion. *'Teenagers nowadays spend hours sitting at their computer. They don't use the computer to do their homework, but to play games. Because they play games they don't have time left to do their homework. So, their school performance will suffer.'* The same applies to the following claim: *'Most organizations with an HR department have a low absenteeism rate, so all organizations should have an HR department.'* Here the hidden assumption is that an organization's low absenteeism rate is thanks to the HR department – excluding all other possible explanations. The question is whether these (hidden) assumptions are correct, that is whether they are supported by trustworthy evidence. For this reason, it is important not only that you identify explicit assumptions, but also to check for assumptions that are hidden.

As mentioned above, people make assumptions all the time, and the same is true for managers, policymakers and business leaders. Documents such as policy papers, project proposals, strategy documents and change plans are often rife with (both hidden and explicit) assumptions. Obviously, it would not make sense – nor would it be feasible – to check the evidence for each assumption that is made, as most assumptions are rather trivial. However, the opposite is true for 'critical' assumptions. As mentioned earlier, when a critical assumption turns out to be false, the policy plan or decision may have severe negative consequences. Thus, the purpose of asking questions in the first stage of the evidence-based process is: 1) to identify critical assumptions, and 2) to check whether there is sufficient evidence to support these assumptions.

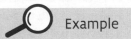 **Example**

On February 2013 Marissa Mayer, CEO of Yahoo, sent a memo to all her 12,000 employees. In this memo, she stated that it is critical that all employees are present in their offices. 'Some of the best decisions and insights come from hallway and cafeteria discussions, meeting new people, and impromptu team meetings. Speed and quality are often sacrificed when we work from home. We need to be one Yahoo, and that starts with physically being together.' She therefore cancelled all work-from-home arrangements and instructed all employees to work in the Yahoo offices. 'Being a Yahoo isn't just about your day-to-day job, it is about the interactions and experiences that are only possible in our offices.'

While you may already have a strong opinion on the wisdom of the CEO's decision to eliminate all work-from-home arrangements, the first step in the evidence-based process is to identify the most critical assumption(s) underlying this decision. In this case, there are several critical assumptions that if found to be incorrect (or overstated) may have a severe negative impact on the company. For example, in the memo it is stated that 'some of the best decisions and insights come from hallway and cafeteria discussions and meeting new people'. The same counts for the assertion that 'speed and quality are often sacrificed when we work from home'. If these two critical assumptions turn out to be incorrect, the CEO's decision may not only have a negative impact on the job satisfaction and commitment of the employees in question, but also on the creativity and performance of the company's workforce as a whole. So, after identifying these statements as being critical assumptions, the obvious next question would be 'What is the evidence for this?'

2.2 Starting point: What is the problem to solve or opportunity to address?

In evidence-based management the starting point for asking questions is the assumed problem or opportunity, rather than the preferred solution. Often we dedicate a significant amount of time to determining what exactly the problem or opportunity might be. You may ask yourself why this is important.

In medicine, there are strong indications that wrong diagnoses account for the most severe cases of patient harm – in fact, the leader of a recent study on misdiagnosis stated that 'there's a lot more harm associated with diagnostic errors than we ever imagined'.[2] You may wonder if this is also true for management. When managers or business leaders decide to take action to address an assumed problem or opportunity, how accurate and reliable is their diagnosis? After all, if the definition of the problem is incorrect, you will not be able to address it well, even if you take an evidence-based approach. We therefore sympathize with this famous quote by Albert Einstein: 'If I were given one hour to save the world, I would spend 59 minutes defining the problem and one minute solving it.' In fact, our experience is that, in some cases, there is not even a problem to be solved. For example, an organization may learn about a new, interesting solution (for example, 'Talent Management'), assume that the company somehow will benefit from this, and thus decide to implement this new solution. However, implementing a solution when there is no evident problem or real opportunity makes little sense and can be a serious waste of time and resources. In the Yahoo example, the preferred solution is clear (eliminating all work-from-home arrangements), but the assumed problem is less apparent. Is it poor performance, lack of creativity and innovation, or low product quality? And what is the evidence that these problems really exist? For this reason, an evidence-based approach always starts with the following question, 'What is the problem you are trying to solve, and what is the evidence for this problem?'

2.3 PICOC

When asking questions, it is important to make explicit the professional or organizational context that you should take into account. This is especially important when you ask questions to people outside the organization, or consult external sources such as the research literature. For example, a question such as 'Does team-building work?' may make sense in the context of your organization, but when consulting external sources the question is obviously too vague. After all, you may be interested to know whether team-building in the form of an outdoor survival game improves the performance of a team of newly hired call centre workers. Or whether team building in the form of working with a coach may improve the collaboration among a group of surgeons who have a very poor relationship with each other. To make your question more context-specific, it helps to formulate what's called a PICOC. A PICOC is a conceptual tool to help you find evidence that takes into account your professional context. The PICOC acronym stands for:

Table 2.1

Population	Who?	Type of employee, people who may be affected by the outcome
Intervention	What or how?	Management technique/method, factor, independent variable
Comparison	Compared to what?	Alternative intervention, factor, variable
Outcome	What are you trying to accomplish/improve/change?	Objective, purpose, goal, dependent variable
Context	In what kind of organization/circumstances?	Type of organization, sector, relevant contextual factors

In the Yahoo example above, we could formulate the PICOC as follows:

P = IT workers, knowledge workers

I = work-from-home arrangements

C = traditional work arrangements

O = task performance, creative performance

C = a multinational technology company

The underlying thought is that all five elements are relevant to your questions, and that each change in the P, I, C, O, or C may lead to a different answer. Thus, a general question such as 'Are work-from-home arrangements effective?' yields answers of limited practical value because only the I (work-from-home arrangements) is addressed in the question, without taking account of:

- the P: the effect may be different for blue collar workers than for knowledge workers;
- the C: the effect may be different for agile working than for traditional working;
- the O: the effect on performance is possibly different from the effect on employee satisfaction;
- the C: the effect may be different for a tech company than for an academic hospital.

In short: Your PICOC will help you to determine whether evidence from external sources (for example, the findings of a scientific study) will be generalizable and applicable to your organizational context. For this reason defining your PICOC is an important element of evidence-based management.

Note

In the next sections, we provide an overview of questions you can ask to determine whether there is evidence to support (or contradict) an assumed problem/opportunity or a preferred solution. In most organizations decisions are not made by one person, but rather by a group of people, such as a board of directors, a committee or a project team. In those situations, you would ideally take the role as 'Chief Evidence Officer', monitoring and safeguarding the quality of the decision-making process by asking the questions provided below. In the situation where you are the sole decision maker, however, it will be hard to question yourself. In that case you should ask another person to take the role of critical enquirer to identify the underlying assumptions – and thus the need for evidence – in your reasoning. As we go forward we will talk about both problems and opportunities under the label of 'problems to be solved'.

2.4 Step 1: What is the assumed problem to be solved?

As explained in the previous sections, our first question is 'What is the problem to be solved?' In most organizations, an assumed problem is often composed of several underlying assumptions. Thus, 'chunking' or breaking the problem down – decomposing it into smaller, more specific, problems – is often useful, in particular when you find the problem overwhelming or daunting. For instance, in the Yahoo example above the problem may be that the company's performance is below the average in the sector, but a smaller, more specific underlying problem is that speed and quality are sacrificed when people work from home. If the organization struggles with multiple problems at the same time, it is advisable to start with the most serious and urgent one (see question 3). When you have a satisfying answer to what the most important problem is, you can ask five follow-up questions.

How clearly defined is the problem?

Having a clear description of the assumed problem is the best first step to solving it. After all, if you do not clearly define the problem you probably cannot solve it. A good problem description entails at least four elements:

Flowchart 2.1

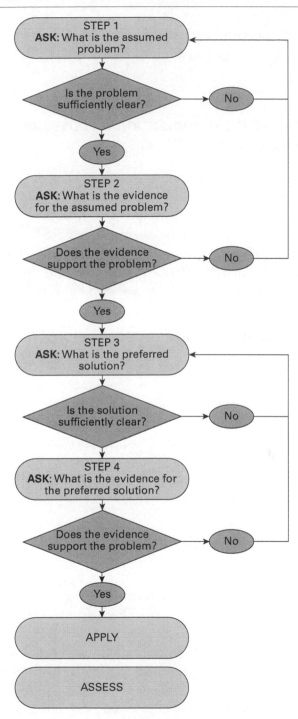

1 The problem itself, stated clearly and concisely. (What? Who? Where? When?)
2 Its (potential) organizational consequences (see question 2).
3 Its major cause (see question 4).
4 The PICOC.

Is it clear what the organizational consequences of the problem are?

A problem is only a problem when it has (potential) organizational consequences. For example, a low level of job satisfaction may only be a problem if it negatively affects a company's business objectives (for example, patient outcomes, innovation or net profit margin) or the interests of its stakeholders (for example, employee well-being, share price or demands for community services). It is therefore critical that you clearly state how the problem (potentially) affects important aims and outcomes.

Is it clear how serious and urgent the problem is?

Note that there is a difference between 'serious' and 'urgent'. Serious problems have a potentially sizeable impact on the organization's aim and outcomes. Urgent problems are time-sensitive, demanding immediate attention, but their consequences may not necessarily impact significant aims and outcomes. Often, what we assume to be serious (important) problems are really just urgent ones, and not very serious or consequential at all. When we know which problems are both serious and urgent, we can move from firefighting – solving urgent but unimportant problems – to solving 'real' problems.[3]

Is it clear what the major cause(s) of the problem could be?

The key to a good definition of a problem is ensuring that you deal with the real problem – not its symptoms. What we often refer to as causes may actually instead be symptoms or indicators of deeper root causes. For example, a low level of job satisfaction is not the cause of a high employee-turnover rate, but the symptom of an underlying cause, for example underpayment or limited career opportunities. Problem symptoms and problem causes can look very much alike. It is therefore important that you differentiate symptoms from causes, for example by continually asking 'Why is this occurring?' to each explanation and subsequent explanations, until you identify the root cause.

Is it clear what the 'logic model' is?

A **logic model** spells out the process by which an underlying cause leads to a problem and produces certain organizational consequences. It is a short narrative that explains why or when the problem occurs (= cause), and how this leads to a particular outcome (= effect). In the Yahoo example above we might describe the logic model as follows: *People who work at home are often distracted by all kinds of domestic and family issues > thus the speed and quality of their work are often sacrificed > Yahoo has many employees with a work-from-home arrangement > this negatively affects the performance of these employees > the company as a whole therefore performs below the average in the sector.*

Sub-conclusion 1

Based on the answers to these five questions you should be able to conclude whether the problem is sufficiently clearly described. When the answers suggest the problem is unclear, there is no point proceeding with the next step. After all, when a problem is unclear – or possibly non-existent – you cannot solve it, even when you take an evidence-based approach. When the problem is sufficiently clear, you should describe what the problem is, its organizational consequences, its major cause(s) and the PICOC. Use this description as input for step 2: determining whether the problem and underlying cause is supported by the evidence.

 Example

Due to the rapid expansion of our company people have come into management positions for which they were poorly trained. As a result many front-office workers feel they receive too little support from their manager, so their job satisfaction has dropped, which in turn has increased the employee turnover rate by 10 per cent.

P = hotel desk clerks; I = lack of management support; C = good management support; O = job satisfaction, staff turnover; C = fast-growing Canadian hotel chain.

Flowchart 2.2

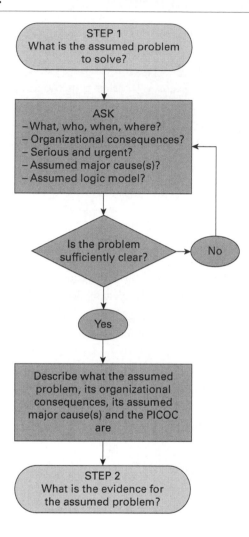

2.5 Step 2: What is the evidence for the problem?

In the previous section we explicitly used the term 'assumed problem'. This is because we don't know (yet) what the evidence is in support of this problem. Thus, the second step is to ask questions to acquire evidence from multiple sources. How to acquire evidence from practitioners, the scientific literature, the organization and the most relevant stakeholders is described in detail in chapters 3, 6, 8 and 10. In this chapter we focus on what questions you can ask.

Evidence from practitioners

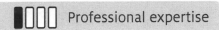 Professional expertise

The professional judgement of experienced practitioners is an essential component for determining whether an assumed problem is indeed a serious problem, whether the assumed cause is indeed the primary or root cause, or whether alternative causes are more plausible. Important questions to ask are:

1 Do you agree with the description of the problem?
2 Do you see plausible alternative causes of the problem?
3 Do you agree that the problem is both serious and urgent?

Evidence from the organization

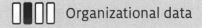 Organizational data

Organizational data can be 'hard' or quantitative indicators such as staff turnover, error rates or productivity levels, but they can also include 'soft' elements such as job satisfaction or attitudes towards senior management. This includes data from governments, international bodies and industry bodies. Organizational data are essential to identify relevant problems and determine possible causes. Important questions to ask are:

1 Do the organizational data confirm the assumed problem?

2 Is there a trend? (Do the data suggest the problem will increase when nothing is done?) Note that three data points are considered the minimum necessary to determine a trend!

3 Do the data confirm the logic model? Is there a correlation between the assumed cause, the perceived problem, and its organizational consequences?

Evidence from the scientific literature

⬜⬜⬛⬛⬜ Scientific literature

When referring to 'scientific literature' we mean empirical studies published in peer-reviewed academic journals. In recent decades, a large amount of research has been published on a wide range of managerial issues such as absenteeism, job satisfaction, improving performance, preventing errors and motivating employees. Many of these studies also provide insight into the most common causes of these issues. Thus, when it comes to tackling these issues in practice, it is important to consult scientific studies. Important questions to ask are:

1 Does the scientific literature confirm the assumed major cause of the problem?

2 Does the literature confirm the logic model? (Is there a correlation between the cause of the problem and its organizational consequences?)

3 Is the evidence generally applicable in the context of the organization (PICOC)?

Evidence from stakeholders

 Stakeholders' view

Stakeholders are individuals or groups who may be affected by an organization's decisions or practices. Internal stakeholders include employees, managers and board members. However, stakeholders outside the organization such as suppliers, customers, shareholders, the government or the public at large may also be affected. As with evidence from experienced practitioners, evidence from stakeholders is an essential component in determining whether a perceived problem is indeed a serious problem. Stakeholders are also important to understanding whose support may be needed in solving the problem. Important questions to ask are:

1 Do you agree with the description of the problem?

2 Do you see plausible alternative causes of the problem?

3 Do you agree that the problem is both serious and urgent?

Sub-conclusion 2

Based on the answers to the questions above you should be able to conclude whether the evidence supports the description of the problem. When the answers suggest that the problem is not supported (or even contradicted) by the evidence, the **probability** that any solution will effectively address the problem is low, and there is no point proceeding to step 3: the preferred solution.

! Note

Before you ask questions to determine whether the solution is clearly described, it is important to determine whether you have considered more than one solution. The reason for this is that the scientific literature suggests that considering multiple solutions tends to lead to better decisions than fixating on 'yes/no' or 'either/or' choices. When we

Flowchart 2.3

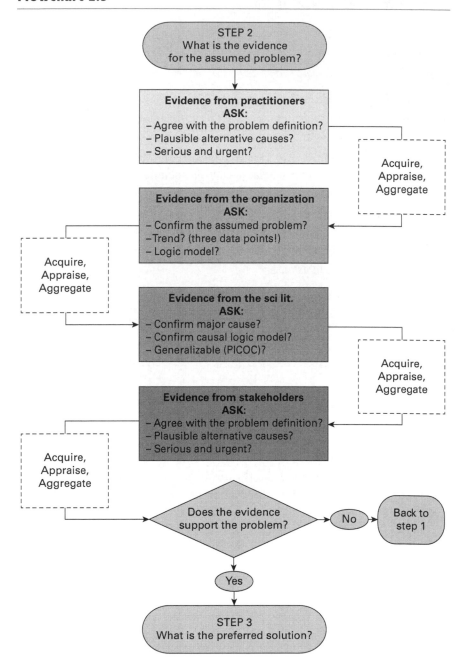

consider only one solution, we tend to ignore evidence contradicting its expected results. Conversely, considering two or more options leads us to gathering more information regarding expected differences in results, and thus leads to a more informed (evidence-based) decision.

2.6 Step 3: What is the preferred solution?

How clearly defined is the preferred solution?

Having a clear description of the preferred solution is a prerequisite to solving the problem. After all, if you don't have a clear idea of what the solution entails and how it is assumed to solve the problem, you cannot implement it. A good description entails at least four elements:

1 The solution itself, stated clearly and concisely. (What? Who? Where? When?)

2 Its (potential) effect on the problem and underlying cause/s (see question 2).

3 Its costs and benefits (see question 3).

4 The PICOC.

Is it clear how the solution would solve the problem?

As explained, a logic model spells out the process by which a solution is assumed to solve the underlying cause that leads to a problem and its unwanted organizational consequences. It is a short narrative that explains how the solution would solve the problem. For example, it is possible to claim that centralization of administrative functions leads to an efficiency gain of X per cent, but to have confidence in this solution you should know HOW centralization would lead to this efficiency gain. In this case, the logic model could be that *centralization of administrative tasks enables > standardization of processes > which eliminates replication of tasks > which reduces costs on labour for duplication of work*. In the Yahoo example above, the assumed logic model is that *flexible working arrangements lower performance > thus eliminating all work-from-home arrangements within the company will increase performance > which will give the company a competitive edge in the market*. Note that in this example it is essential that we first establish that sufficient trustworthy evidence is available to support the assumption that work-from-home arrangements indeed negatively affect performance (evidence from the scientific literature indicates that this is not likely).[4]

How clearly defined are the costs and benefits of each solution?

Even the 'best' solution may come with considerable costs, so a thorough assessment of the expected costs and benefits is a prerequisite to evidence-based decision-making. There are several analytic tools and templates you can use. Some well-designed tools convert the costs and benefits of each solution into a common unit of measurement (usually money) and they then analyse which solution is the most cost efficient. Many analysis tools focused on analysing costs and benefits, however, do a poor job of identifying indirect and intangible costs (for example, a decrease in customer satisfaction or drop in employee morale). Thus, when conducting a costs-benefits analysis, it is important that you consult multiple sources of evidence (organizational data, professionals and stakeholders). In addition, most analyses fail to attach a degree of uncertainty to the estimated costs and benefits. Without having an indication of how certain or uncertain the costs or benefits will be, the outcome of your analysis will be misleading. Thus, a good analysis should explicitly factor in the quality of evidence regarding each cost and benefit and attach an estimate of the degree of uncertainty.

Is it clear what the 'best' and/or 'most feasible' solution is?

Based on the logic model and costs-benefits analyses of each solution your organization should have a clear idea of what the 'best' and/or 'most feasible' solution would be.

Sub-conclusion 3

Based on the answers to these questions you should be able to conclude whether the preferred solution is sufficiently clearly described. Again, when the answers suggest that the preferred solution or its logic model is unclear, there is no point proceeding with the next step. When the solution is sufficiently clear, you should describe in detail what the preferred solution is, its logic model and the PICOC. Use this description as input for the next step: determining whether the preferred solution is supported by the evidence.

Flowchart 2.4

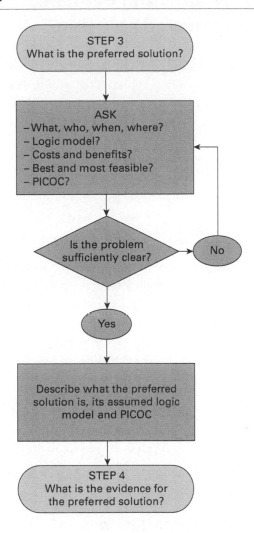

2.7 Step 4: What is the evidence for the preferred solution?

As was the case with the assumed problem, the next step is to ask questions to determine whether the evidence supports the assumed effectiveness of the preferred solution. Again, *how* to acquire evidence is described in chapters 3, 6, 8 and 10 – this section focuses on *what* questions you can ask.

Evidence from practitioners

 Professional expertise

The professional judgement of experienced practitioners inside and outside the organization is an essential component in determining how likely a proposed solution is to work in a particular context. In addition, experienced professionals are often in a good position to rate the solution in terms of implementation costs and other feasibility/risk issues. Finally, experienced professionals may think of alternative solutions that you haven't considered. Important questions to ask are:

1 Do you agree on which solution is the 'best' and/or 'most feasible'?

2 Do you see downsides to or unintended negative consequences of the preferred solution?

3 Do you see alternative solutions to the problem that may work better?

Evidence from the organization

 Organizational data

Ideally you would have organizational data available that could help determine which of the solutions has the highest likelihood of solving the problem. If this is the case, an important question to ask is:

1 Can organizational data be used to monitor the future effectiveness of the preferred solution?

Evidence from the scientific literature

 Scientific literature

As explained earlier, a lot of research has been published on a wide range of managerial issues such as improving performance, preventing errors and motivating employees. Many of these studies also provide insight into which variables or management interventions may have a positive impact. Thus, when it comes to tackling these issues in practice, it is important to consult these studies. Important questions to ask are:

1 What does the scientific literature suggest regarding the effectiveness of the preferred solution?

2 Does the literature suggest other solutions to the problem that may work better?

3 Is the evidence generalizable to the organizational context (PICOC)?

Evidence from stakeholders

 Stakeholders' view

Even the best solution can fail upon implementation if the stakeholders see serious downsides or when they feel an alternative solution may work better. Gathering evidence from stakeholders is therefore an essential component in determining how likely a proposed solution is to work in a particular context. In addition, stakeholders are often in a good position to judge the preferred solution in terms of implementation costs and other feasibility/risk issues. Finally, stakeholders may see alternative solutions that you haven't considered yet. Important questions to ask are:

1   Do you agree on which solution is the 'best' and/or 'most feasible'?

2   Do you see downsides to or unintended negative consequences of the preferred solution?

3   Do you see alternative solutions for the problem that may work better?

4   Are stakeholders supportive of these solutions? How critical is their support for effective solution implementation?

Final conclusion

Based on the answers to the questions above you should be able to conclude whether the evidence supports the decision as to which solution is the 'best' and/or 'most feasible'. Again, when the answers suggest that the preferred solution is not supported (or even contradicted) by the evidence, the likelihood that the solution will effectively address the problem is low. In that case we are left with only one option: to go back to the drawing board. In addition, when you conclude that the available evidence is too limited, you should acquire additional evidence. Only when sufficient (trustworthy) evidence supports the potential effectiveness of the preferred solution we would regard the decision to implement an evidence-based decision.

 Note

Drawing conclusions about whether the evidence supports (or contradicts) the assumed problem and/or preferred solution requires additional evidence-based management skills such as acquiring, critically appraising and aggregating evidence. In the next chapters we will discuss these skills in more detail. The questions formulated in the sections above will thereby serve as a starting point.

Flowchart 2.5

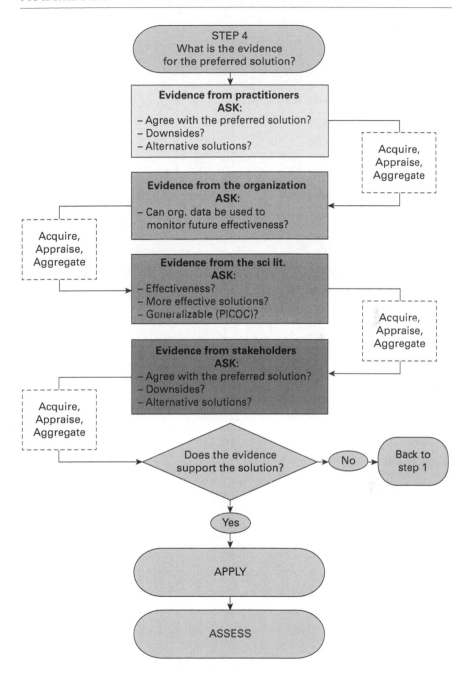

2.8 Developing your capacity to ask questions

As stated at the beginning of this chapter, asking questions kicks off the deliberate search for evidence. In fact, stopping the search process too soon often leads to solving the wrong problem, or settling on a solution before really understanding its possible (side) effects. In a rush to 'get things done', the phase of asking questions, the first step of evidence-based management, can be suppressed and uncertainty glossed over. The resultant lack of evidence and insight leads to solving the wrong problem or pursuing a questionable solution with limited results. Unfortunately, there is no short-cut to a thoughtful start to the evidence-based process, regardless of urgency or the resources poured into a problem. Spending more time assessing the problem means less time required to solve it. This means asking questions – lots of them – to check assumptions, particularly where someone (including ourselves) asserts a belief as a certainty. This habit-forming approach can inform your conversations and deliberations. You will begin to ask yourself and others, 'What's the evidence for that?', as impressions, beliefs and attitudes appear in your conversations about the organization, its practices and the decisions being made. This approach has turned many of our students and course members into the 'evidence squad', and they learn to use it over time in a manner that promotes asking critical questions about evidence without necessarily criticizing. Concern for the evidence behind decisions translates into active questioning and healthy scepticism. Evidence-focused questioning of claims, statements or assertions changes both the conversations and deliberations of emergent evidence-based managers. A must here is for practitioners to learn ways to raise these questions in socially effective ways (read: *civil and persuasive*). To be effective, evidence-based managers need to avoid being dismissed as mere naysayers. Raising questions can be anxiety-provoking for would-be EB managers who fear making waves. This questioning extends to assertions made by professors, consultants and other 'experts'. And, yes, we expect you to question us by critically considering our arguments, reviewing our sources and contacting us, as needs be. Once practised at it, evidence-based managers become comfortable at asking, 'Is this your personal opinion based on your own professional experience, or is there any evidence in support of it?' You may be surprised to learn how much uncertainty really exists regarding the practices your organization uses.

2.9 Checklists

Table 2.2

	Very clear	Fairly clear	Somewhat unclear	Very unclear
Step 1 Determine whether the assumed problem is clearly defined				
1 How clearly defined is the problem? (What? Who? When? Where?)				
2 Is it clear what the organizational consequences of the problem are?				
3 Is it clear how serious and urgent the problem is?				
4 Is it clear what the major cause(s) of the problem is (are)?				
5 Is it clearly defined what the logic model is?				
6 Is it clear what the PICOC is?				

Table 2.3

	All/ most of them	Some of them	Few/ none of them
Step 2 Determine whether the problem is supported by the evidence			
Step 2a: Evidence from practitioners			
1 Do experienced professionals agree with the problem definition?			
2 Do they see plausible alternative causes for the problem?			
3 Do they agree the problem is both serious and urgent?			
Step 2b: Evidence from stakeholders			
4 Do the most important stakeholders agree with the problem definition?			
5 Do they see plausible alternative causes for the problem?			
6 Do they agree that the problem is both serious and urgent?			

Table 2.4

	Yes	Somewhat	No
Step 2c: Evidence from the organization			
7 Do the organizational data confirm the problem?			
8 Is there a trend (do the data suggest the problem will increase if nothing is done)?			
9 Do the data confirm the logic model: is there a correlation between the cause, the problem and its organizational consequences?			
Step 2d: Evidence from the scientific literature			
10 Does the scientific literature confirm the assumed major cause of the problem?			
11 Does the literature confirm the logic model: is there a correlation between the cause, the problem and its organizational consequences?			
12 Is the evidence generalizable to the organizational context (PICOC)?			

Table 2.5

	Very clear	Fairly clear	Somewhat unclear	Very unclear
Step 3 Determine whether the preferred solution is clearly defined				
1 How clearly defined is each solution? (What? Who? When? Where?)				
2 Is it clear how each solution would solve the problem? Is the logic model clear?				
3 How clearly defined are the costs and benefits of each solution?				
4 Is it clear what the 'best' and/or 'most feasible' solution is (and why)?				
5 Is it clear what the PICOC is?				

Table 2.6

	All/ most of them	Some of them	Few/ none of them
Step 4 Determine whether the preferred solution is supported by the evidence			
Step 4a: Evidence from practitioners			
1 Do experienced practitioners agree as to which solution is the 'best' and/or 'most feasible'?			
2 Do they see downsides to or unintended negative consequences of the preferred solution?			
3 Do they see alternative solutions to the problem that may work better?			
Step 4b: Evidence from stakeholders			
4 Do the most important stakeholders agree with the problem definition?			
5 Do they see plausible alternative causes for the problem?			
6 Do they agree that the problem is serious and urgent?			

Table 2.7

	Yes	Somewhat	No
Step 4c: Evidence from the organization			
7 Can organizational data be used to monitor the future effectiveness of the preferred solution?			
Step 4d: Evidence from the scientific literature			
8 What does the scientific literature suggest regarding the effectiveness of the preferred solution?			
9 Does the literature suggest other solutions to the problem that may work better?			
10 Is the evidence generalizable to the organizational context (PICOC)?			

Notes and references

1 Science Weekly Podcast (2016) *The Guardian*, Neil deGrasse Tyson in an interview with Nicola Davis, 7 December

2 Adapted from Saber Tehrani *et al*, 2013

3 Note: well-managed organizations seek to solve serious problems even when they are not urgent. And, an organization with a lot of serious and urgent problems may not be very well-managed.

4 De Menezes, LM and Kelliher, C (2011) Flexible working and performance: A systematic review of the evidence for a business case, *International Journal of Management Reviews*, **13** (4), pp 452–74

PART ONE
Evidence from practitioners

ACQUIRE: Evidence from practitioners

03

What can be asserted without evidence, can be dismissed without evidence

CHRISTOPHER HITCHENS

In organizations, evidence from practitioners is an important source of information. In fact, it may well be the most-used source of information in decision-making processes. In many organizations leadership teams ask employees for their input, managers for their opinion, consultants for their experience, and managers often base their decision on this type of evidence. The quality of decisions will significantly improve when you consider all sources of evidence, including professional expertise, as it can connect external evidence such as scientific research findings to the specific organizational context.

There are many ways in which you can acquire evidence from practitioners. Numerous books and websites are available that can inform you about how to gather evidence in a valid and reliable way, covering important aspects such as sampling procedures, **research designs** and questionnaire development. This chapter therefore does not aim to give a comprehensive and detailed overview of all methods in which you can acquire evidence from practitioners, but rather a quick summary of key aspects that you should take into account.

3.1 What to ask?

Acquiring evidence from practitioners is not a fishing expedition – it starts with an assumed problem, a preferred solution or a deemed opportunity. Before reaching out to practitioners to ask about their take on the matter it is therefore important that you first clearly describe the (assumed) problem that needs to be solved or the opportunity that needs to be addressed. As discussed in Chapter 2, a good definition of the problem entails at least four elements:

1 The problem itself, stated clearly and concisely (What? Who? Where? When?).

2 Its (potential) organizational consequences.

3 Its assumed major cause(s).

4 The PICOC (Population, Intervention, Comparison, Outcome, Context).

The professional judgement of experienced practitioners inside and outside the organization is an essential component in determining whether the assumed problem is indeed a serious problem and in identifying possible causes. Thus, important questions to ask are:

1 Do you agree with the description of the problem?

2 Do you see plausible alternative causes of the problem?

3 Do you agree that the problem is serious and urgent?

In addition, when you need to make a decision that involves whether to implement a proposed solution, having a clear description of that solution is a prerequisite before you consult practitioners. Again, a good description entails at least four elements:

1 The solution itself, stated clearly and concisely (What? Who? Where? When?).

2 Its (potential) effect on the problem and underlying cause/s.

3 Its costs and benefits.

4 The PICOC.

As explained, evidence from practitioners is also an essential component in determining how likely a proposed solution is to work in a particular organizational context. In addition, experienced professionals are often in a good position to rate the preferred solution in terms of implementation costs and other feasibility/risk issues. Finally, experienced professionals may think of alternative solutions that you haven't considered. Thus, important questions to ask are:

1 Do you agree on which solution is the 'best' and/or 'most feasible'?

2 Do you see downsides to or unintended negative consequences of the preferred solution?

3 Do you see alternative solutions to the problem that may work better?

3.2 Whom to ask?

The first step in gathering evidence from practitioners is determining the target audience. Which practitioners in the organization are, given the question or issue at hand, most likely to provide a valid and reliable judgement? Obviously, we want practitioners whose professional judgement is based on a high level of expertise. Expertise refers to skill and knowledge acquired through training and education coupled with prolonged practice in a specific domain, combined with frequent and direct feedback. So, for example, if the question concerns a proposed solution for high levels of staff absenteeism among lawyers in an international accounting firm, then a practitioner who has only a one-time experience with migrant workers picking fruit should obviously not be the first one to invite to give his/her professional judgement. The quality or trustworthiness of practitioner expertise and judgement depends on the relevance of the practitioner's training, education and experience, which we discuss in Chapter 4.

3.3 How many practitioners should I ask?

Sample size

In most cases, it is impossible to ask all practitioners in the organization to give their judgement, so we need a sample – a selection of practitioners chosen in such a way that they represent the total population. But, how many practitioners should your sample consist of? Should you ask 1 per cent, 5 per cent, 10 per cent or even 50 per cent of the practitioners in the organization? This depends largely on how accurate you want your evidence to be. Most researchers use a sample size calculator to decide on the sample size.[1] The required sample size, however, also depends on practical factors such as time, budget and availability. In addition, qualitative methods (for example, focus groups) involve a substantial smaller sample size than quantitative methods (for example, surveys) because for these methods **representativeness** is often more important than accuracy.

Selection bias

Another major concern is **selection bias**. Selection bias, also referred to as sampling bias, occurs when your selection of practitioners leads to an outcome that is different from what you would have obtained if you had enrolled the entire target audience.

Example

In 1936, Democrat Franklin Roosevelt and Republican Alf Landon were running for president. Before the election, the magazine Literary Digest sent a survey to 10 million US voters to determine how they would vote. More than 2 million people responded to the poll; 60 per cent supported Landon (Figure 3.1). The magazine published the findings and predicted that Landon would win the election. However, Roosevelt defeated Landon in one of the largest landslide presidential elections ever. What happened?

Figure 3.1

The Literary Digest
NEW YORK   OCTOBER 31, 1936

Topics of the day

LANDON, 1,293,669; ROOSEVELT, 972,897
Final Returns in The Digest's Poll of Ten Million Voters

Well, the great battle of the ballots in the Poll of ten million voters, scattered throughout the forty-eight States of the lican National Committee purchased THE LITERARY DIGEST?" And all types and varieties, including: "Have the Jews purchased So far, we have been right in every Poll. Will we be right in the current Poll? That, as Mrs. Roosevelt said concerning the Presi-

The magazine used a biased sampling plan. They selected the sample using magazine subscriptions, lists of registered car owners and telephone directories. But that sample was not representative of the US public. In the 1930s, Democrats were much less likely to own a car or have a telephone. The sample therefore systematically underrepresented Democrats, and the result was a whopping error of 19 per cent, the largest ever in a major public opinion poll.[2]

You can prevent selection bias by taking a random sample of the population. However, to get a truly random sample you should not only consider who to ask, but also when to ask. For example, administering a survey on a Monday morning at 9 am to the first 200 employees to start their working day is not random, certainly not when the survey aims to understand the employees' satisfaction with the company's flexible working hours. Employees who start their working day on Monday at 9 am may differ from employees who start their working day at 10 am or even later. In addition, some employees with a part-time contract may have a regular day off on Monday. The survey will therefore most likely yield a sample that is not representative for all employees.

3.4 How to ask?

Walking around and asking

The quickest and easiest way to gather evidence from practitioners is by walking around and asking. Of course, this method is prone to bias, but sometimes wandering around – in an unstructured manner – through the workplace and asking people – randomly – their judgement about an assumed problem or preferred solution, is a good way to start.

Conducting a survey

A survey is a quick and efficient way to ask a large group of people a question (or a series of questions) to gather evidence about their opinion, judgement or attitude towards an assumed problem or preferred solution. Participants in a survey are usually selected in a way that the results are generalizable to a larger population. Most surveys are quantitative in nature, meaning that they place more emphasis on numerical than on narrative data, and are therefore intentionally narrow and specific. For this reason, they typically use questionnaires with closed questions that provide a list of predetermined responses from which the participants can choose their answer. One of the most common formats used in survey questions is the 'agree-disagree' format. In this type of question, respondents are asked whether they agree or disagree with a particular statement. A better practice, however, is to use Likert scales. An example of a close-ended survey question using a Likert scale would be, *'Please rate how strongly you agree or disagree with the following statement: "I receive too many emails." Do you strongly agree, somewhat agree, neither agree nor disagree, somewhat disagree, or strongly disagree?'* An example of an open-ended question would be, *'What do you think is the most important cause(s) for the high level of absenteeism among the lawyers in our firm?'*

When surveying practitioners, it is important to inform them in advance about why you need their input. You also need to set clear expectations regarding anonymity, confidentiality and how information will be used, as this increases the likelihood of honesty. You can administer surveys in several ways, such as through (e)mail, by telephone or face-to-face. In addition, there are several (free) online survey tools available, of which Survey Monkey is probably the best known.

The Delphi Method

The **Delphi Method** is a qualitative, interactive method, involving a group of experts or professionals who anonymously reply to a questionnaire or a set of statements and subsequently receive feedback in the form of a 'group response', after which the process repeats itself. The method is based on the principle that judgements from a group of individuals are more accurate than those from a single person or an unstructured group, provided that the judgements are made independently before being combined.[3, 4, 5, 6] The method is meticulously structured and typically involves the following steps:

1 The facilitator develops a questionnaire.

2 The participants independently and anonymously answer the questionnaire.

3 The facilitator summarizes the responses and develops a feedback report.

4 The participants evaluate the feedback report and revise (any) earlier answers in light of the replies of other participants.

5 The process is stopped after a predefined criterion (for example, number of rounds, consensus, stability of answers).

6 Organizers develop a final summary.

The goal of this method is to reduce the range of responses and converge towards expert/professional consensus. The Delphi Method has been widely adopted and is used by a wide range of organizations across industries, including public policy-making.

Group Decision Room

A Group Decision Room, also known as Acceleration Chamber or Brainbox, is the electronic version of a focus group or the Delphi Method. Participants gather in a meeting room with electronic tools (computer, laptop or tablet) or connect remotely through the internet. Under the guidance of an experienced **moderator** participants can anonymously respond to questions and/or statements, vote on issues or react to topics discussed. The responses are visible (in real time) for all participants, so the outcome can be discussed immediately.

Mobile voting and audience response systems

Mobile voting systems or audio response systems are developed to create live interaction between a presenter/moderator and his or her audience. In educational settings, such systems are often called 'student response systems'. Participants in a management meeting can anonymously vote, answer questions (open ended as well as multiple choice) or give their judgement with any smartphone, tablet or laptop. Results are instantly tabulated and presented on screen in real time for analysis or discussion. Results can also be imported into a database for further evaluation or comparison with other sessions. There are several mobile voting systems available, such as Socrative or VoxVote.

3.5 Developing questions

Perhaps the most important part of gathering evidence from practitioners is the development of questions that accurately measure their opinion, experience or judgement. Irrespective of the data collection method we use, the outcome is useless if the evidence gathered results from ambiguous or **leading questions**. Formulating questions is a process that requires attention to many details. The choice of words in a question is critical to express its meaning and intent – even small wording differences can substantially affect the answers people give. This section provides a number of tips to reduce measurement and comprehension error as a result of the question wording.[7]

3.6 Eight tips for asking valid and effective questions

1 Keep it simple

Although you may feel tempted to build beautiful phrases, questions that are short and use simple and concrete wording are more easily understood. You should avoid academic language (for example, cerebrovascular accident instead of stroke) and unfamiliar abbreviations or jargon (for example, ROI instead of Return on Investment) that can result in respondent confusion. The same counts for complex sentences. For example, the question *'Do you agree or disagree that, controlling for inflation, your income has grown in the last year, where income means your gross household income calculated as the total financial receipts of all adults living in your household'* is far too complex to answer.

2 Avoid double-barrelled questions

Make sure you ask only one question at a time. Questions that ask respondents to evaluate more than one concept are often referred to as **double-barrelled** questions. An example is *'How organized and interesting was the meeting?'* If someone answers 'moderately' to this question, what does that mean? Moderately organized AND moderately interesting? Extremely interesting but only slightly organized?[8] An obvious remedy to this confusion is simply writing two questions instead of one. For example: 1) *'How organized was the meeting?'* and 2) *'How interesting was the meeting?'*

3 Avoid negative, especially double negative questions

For example, *'Do you agree that it is not a good idea not to implement the new IT system?'* will probably confuse respondents what to answer. The use of the double negative causes this confusion. The same may count for a negatively worded question. For instance, how would you interpret an answer to the question *'Should the HR Director not be directly responsible to the CEO?'*

4 Avoid vague or ambiguous terms

You should avoid words such as 'often', 'regularly', 'sometimes', 'normal', 'substantial', 'might', 'could', 'probably', and so on. For example, instead of *'Do you agree that within the Finance and Accounting Department, errors are often being made?'* you should ask *'How many times per week...?'* Don't leave anything to interpretation by respondents. The same counts for abstract terms such as 'moral', 'decent', 'appropriate', because such terms can mean different things to different people. Instead of asking *'Do you agree or disagree that moral values are an important issue in our organization?'* you should define the term 'moral', for instance by asking about a number of specific issues that fall within the 'moral values' umbrella. For example: *'Many issues that involve moral values are prominent in our organization today. Below we have a list of these issues. For each issue, please tell us how important you think it is...'*

5 Define terms very specifically

For example, in the question 'What was your income last year?', the term 'income' is vague. Does it mean personal income or household income? Does it mean income before or after tax? The term income therefore needs more specification. For example, 'What was your total household income before tax in the past year?'

6 Avoid loaded, leading or emotional language

For example, the question 'Do you agree that the organization should immediately stop the failing implementation of the poorly designed IT system?' contains biasing language – immediately stop, failing implementation and poorly designed. These terms can bias respondents towards a certain point of view. These terms should therefore be omitted or replaced with more balanced language.

7 Prevent social desirability bias

Another challenge in developing questions is what is called 'social desirability bias'. Respondents have a natural tendency to want to be accepted and liked, and this may lead respondents to provide 'socially desirable' answers, especially to questions that deal with sensitive subjects such as leadership style, accountability and ethical issues. Research indicates that social desirability bias is more likely to occur when an interviewer is present (for example, during a face-to-face meeting or telephone surveys) than when respondents answer the questions when they are on their own (for example, paper and web surveys). The best option is, of course, to enable respondents to answer the questions anonymously.

8 Always pilot test your questionnaire

Finally, it is important to test your questions before using them to acquire evidence. Pilot testing your questionnaire using a small sample of people from the target population helps you identify ambiguities or questions that are unclear. In addition, you get feedback and an estimate of how much time it will take people to respond to your questions.

Notes and references

1 An example can be found here: http://www.raosoft.com/samplesize.html

2 Squire, P (1988) Why the 1936 Literary Digest poll failed, *Public Opinion Quarterly*, **52** (1), pp 125–33

3 Rowe, G and Wright, G (2001) *Expert Opinions in Forecasting: Role of the Delphi Technique in principles of forecasting: A handbook of researchers and practitioners* (ed JS Armstrong), Kluwer Academic Publishers, Boston

4 Bauer, A *et al* (2003) Forecast evaluation with cross sectional data: The Blue Chip surveys, *Economic Review*, Federal Reserve Bank of Atlanta

5 Armstrong, JS (2001) *Combining Forecasts in Principles of Forecasting: A handbook for researchers and practitioners* (ed JS Armstrong), Kluwer Academic Publishers, New York

6 Yaniv, I and Choshen-Hillel, S (2011) Exploiting the wisdom of others to make better decisions: Suspending judgment reduces egocentrism and increases accuracy, *Journal of Behavioral Decision Making*, **25** (5), pp 427–34

7 Miller, PR (unknown) *Tip sheet question wording*, Initiative on Survey Methodology (DISM)

8 This example is adapted from Survey Monkey [accessed 19 August 2016] Writing Good Survey Questions [Online] www.surveymonkey.com/mp/writing-survey-questions

APPRAISE: Evidence from practitioners

04

It ain't what you don't know that gets you into trouble.
It's what you know for sure that just ain't so.

JOSH BILLINGS

Consider these three real-life examples:

Cisco, a Silicon Valley firm, was once the darling of the new economy. Business analysts praised its customer service, perfect strategy, unique corporate culture and charismatic CEO. In March 2000, it was the most valuable company in the world. When Cisco's stocks plummeted 80 per cent the following year, the analysts reached a different conclusion: poor customer service, a vague strategy, a lame corporate culture and a weak CEO. However, neither the strategy nor the CEO had changed. What had changed was the demand for Cisco's products – and that was through no fault of the firm.[1]

For decades, physicians believed that a stomach ulcer was caused by lifestyle factors, such as severe stress. This was because physicians noticed that men and women with a lot of occupational or personal stress were more likely to develop a stomach ulcer (assuming that stress would lead to more stomach acid, which in turn would damage the stomach's lining). Accordingly, treatment was on neutralizing the secretion of acid, special diets or learning how to deal with stress. However, in the early 1980s it was found that a stomach ulcer was caused by a bacterial infection that could easily be treated with an antibiotic.[2] This meant that the causal relation that physicians have seen for decades turned out to be non-existent.

In 1998, McKinsey – the United States' largest and most prestigious consulting firm – wanted to examine how the top-performing companies differed from other firms. For this purpose, they surveyed and interviewed thousands of managers across the country. When the three consultants who headed the project sifted through the results, they noticed a pattern. To win in business, they concluded, companies must find and hire as many top performers as possible, and then promote their most talented people aggressively. In 2001 the consultants published their insights in a book entitled *The War for Talent*, in which 27 companies were presented as best practices in the industry. Within five years, however, most of these best practices had either disappeared or reported disastrous profitability and investment returns. One of these companies was Enron, considered by McKinsey to be the ultimate 'talent' company. It came to light that Enron's top executives had lied about its profits and had used very clever-seeming but illegal practices to increase revenues. As a result, the company's shares plummeted in value, and, in December 2001, a few months after the publication of McKinsey's book, Enron filed the largest bankruptcy in US history, leaving tens of thousands unemployed and with worthless stock in their pensions.[3]

In organizations, evidence from practitioners is an important source of information. Unfortunately, of the available sources of evidence, professional judgement and expertise are most prone to bias. Therefore, the process of appraising professional expertise and judgement requires explicit assessment as to what extent this evidence may be biased. In this chapter, you will develop a better understanding of the nature of professional expertise and detect common cognitive biases that may negatively affect practitioners' (and your) judgement.

4.1 How to tell whether a practitioner has professional expertise

In general, we would regard business analysts, medical specialists and strategy consultants as highly educated and experienced professionals. However, sometimes even highly educated and experienced professionals hold erroneous beliefs, not because they are ignorant or stupid, but because their judgement is shaped by misreadings of their own personal experience. This leaves us with some fundamental questions: How trustworthy is the judgement of experienced professionals? What constitutes valid and reliable evidence from practitioners?

Professional expertise is the experience and judgement of managers, consultants, business leaders and other practitioners. It is an essential component for determining whether a management issue really requires attention, if the available organizational data are trustworthy, whether research findings apply, or how likely a proposed solution is to work in a particular context.

Professional expertise differs from intuition and personal opinion because it reflects the specialized knowledge acquired by the repeated experience and practice of specialized activities. However, accumulated experience alone does not necessarily result in expertise – we could be doing the wrong thing over and over again.[4] In fact, only under three specific circumstances can professional expertise be considered valid and reliable:[5, 6]

1 When there are numerous opportunities to practise.

2 When practice leads to direct, objective feedback.

3 Within a regular, predictable work environment.

Let's look at a practical example. Within each person's own field, over a five-year period, whose professional expertise would you judge to be more valid and reliable?

- A management consultant specializing in the merger and acquisition of hospitals.
- An orthopaedic surgeon specializing in knee surgery.
- A baker specialized in making sourdough bread.

Given the three conditions for developing expertise, we would argue that the surgeon and baker developed more valid and reliable expertise than the management consultant. After all, the surgeon works in a highly controlled environment (an operating theatre), where the results of his/her actions can be readily determined, and direct feedback is obtained when the surgeon sees the patient the next day and during a follow-up consultation several weeks later. In addition, it tends to be clear whether the surgery was a success: relevant outcome measures such as increased mobility and pain can be measured in a valid and reliable manner. Finally, most orthopaedic surgeons perform a specific surgical procedure several times a week. A baker's professional expertise can also be considered valid and reliable: a baker works in a bakery, which can be regarded as a very regular and predictable work environment. In addition, the baker bakes many loaves of bread each day, so there is lots of opportunity to practise and receive direct feedback. Finally, it is very clear whether the baker was successful: it is self-evident whether the bread baked was a success, and otherwise the customers would certainly be able to tell the baker.

The opposite is true for a management consultant specializing in mergers and acquisitions. Firstly, the consultant is involved in a merger or acquisition only a few times per year. As a result, there are not many opportunities to practise. Secondly, it is often not immediately clear whether a merger has been a success or a failure: results may be difficult to determine and what is regarded as a success by one person may be seen as a failure by another. Finally, the consultant does not typically operate in a regular and predictable environment: the outcome of a merger is often influenced by numerous contextual factors such as organizational differences, power struggles and the economic situation, which make it hard to determine whether the outcome was the direct result of the consultant's actions or the indirect outcome of contextual factors.

4.2 Why is it so hard to develop valid and reliable professional expertise?

As explained, the management domain is often not favourable to developing valid and reliable professional expertise.[7] There are, of course, exceptions. One good example is a sales agent. In general, sales agents work within a relatively steady and predictable work environment, they give their sales pitch several times a week (or even daily), and they receive frequent, direct and objective feedback: the deal is accepted or not. But even having many opportunities in which to practise, the receipt of direct and objective feedback and a controlled, predictable environment are no guarantee that our experience is valid and our judgement sound.[8]

It was long believed that human beings base their judgement on experience, knowledge acquired through education or other sources of information. However, in the past 50 years an abundance of research has repeatedly demonstrated that our judgement is highly susceptible to systematic errors – cognitive and information-processing limits make us prone to biases that have negative effects on the quality of the decisions we make.[9] Notably, there were four Nobel Prizes awarded to researchers whose scientific work demonstrates that human judgement systematically deviates from rationality (Herbert Simon, Daniel Kahneman, Robert Shiller and Richard Thaler). These systematic errors are the result of the way our brain is wired: we are predisposed to see order and causal relations in the world, we are overly optimistic, we are overly confident, and we process information in a way that confirms our existing beliefs, expectations and assumptions. As a result, cognitive biases are more influential than you think, and they are the secret authors of many professional judgements.[10]

4.3 Two modes of thinking

We make judgements every day – whether we can trust a person, if we should do something (or not), which route to take, how to respond to someone's question – the list is endless. If we carefully considered and analysed every possible outcome of these judgements, we would never get anything done! Thankfully, our mind makes things easier by using efficient thinking strategies known as heuristics.

Heuristics

A **heuristic** is a mental shortcut that helps us make judgements quickly without having to spend a lot of time researching and analysing information. They allow unconscious mental processes to make up for the lack of information and lead us to 'routine' decisions that are often correct. Most of the time this happens below the radar of our conscious awareness and so we are often oblivious to the impact of heuristics on our judgements. They are learned or hard wired in our brain by evolutionary processes.

 Example

- **Authority heuristic:** 'This man has a degree from Harvard in botany, so if he says this flower is not a dandelion but a salsify, I better trust his judgement.'

- **Wisdom of the crowd:** 'If this many positive reviews have been written about the hotel, and if this many people recommend it, then it must be good.'

- **Representativeness heuristic:** 'This woman loves to listen to New Age music and faithfully reads her horoscope each day. So, she's more likely to be a yoga teacher than a bank cashier.'

- **Halo effect:** 'This candidate looks very professional – he wears a nice Italian suit and has a warm, confident smile, so he's probably a great manager.'

- **Educated guess:** 'This house has a garden, so I guess it's more expensive than the one with only a balcony.'

- **Familiarity heuristic:** 'When I'm on vacation and I have to buy some groceries, I always buy products from a brand I recognize.'

However, this does not mean that we always form our judgement or make decisions by using heuristics. Sometimes we take the time to make deliberate, mindful decisions based on a careful weighing of all the information available. In his book *Thinking, Fast and Slow*, Nobel Prize winning psychologist Daniel Kahneman refers to these two modes of processing as 'System 1' and 'System 2' thinking.

System 1 and System 2 thinking

System 2 is slow, effortful, deliberate and rational. It is the slow, effortful reasoning system that draws heavily on our cognitive resources and requires attention and concentration. In fact, all thinking that demands mental effort tends to be classified as System 2. In contrast, **System 1** is fast, intuitive, associative and emotional. It is the fast, effortless thinking system that operates automatically with little voluntary control and that uses intuition or heuristics to make decisions fast. In daily life System 1 is our dominant mode of thinking, because this way of information processing is necessary for survival. When driving a car System 1 automatically makes us hit the brakes when the brake light of the car in front comes on – we don't have time for System 2 to process all information and figure out whether the other driver foresees a real dangerous situation or is just an extremely nervous person with limited driving experience. In addition, when a number of students suddenly jump up and leave the room, System 1 triggers other students to follow suit. From an evolutionary point of view this makes perfect sense: there could be a dangerous situation, such as a fire, that made the students decide to leave the room. After carefully processing, weighing and judging all information System 2 may come to the conclusion that their decision was wrong (there is no fire – it's just the air conditioning leaking a foul-smelling water vapour), but in life-and-death situations there is often no time for careful judgement. However, while System 1 with its heuristics can speed up our judgement and decision-making process, it can introduce serious cognitive biases that impair the quality of the decisions we make.

 Example

A consultant gives a presentation that looks very professional: the slides and graphics are very well designed and the model he recommends has a logical structure and appears to make sense. The organization's senior managers therefore decide to hire the consultant and adopt the model.

In this example, it appears that the senior managers have fallen prey to the halo effect heuristic: the presentation looks professional and the proposed model is taken at face value rather than critically evaluated. This suggests that their decision to hire the consultant and adopt the model was based on System 1 rather than System 2 thinking.

 Example

A large academic hospital loses revenues because patients don't show up for their scheduled appointment. The IT director therefore suggests implementing a text-messaging system that sends a reminder to patients 24 hours before their appointment. Most physicians think this is a great idea that will certainly reduce the number of no shows. The hospital's administrator, however, decides to first find out what the experiences are of hospitals that have already implemented the system.

The administrator could have fallen prey to the wisdom of the crowd heuristic: if most physicians think the new system is a good idea it will probably work. It is unknown, however, whether the physicians have any experience with the system or that their judgement is based on only an assumption. The administrator's decision to find out what the experiences are of other hospitals is therefore an example of System 2 thinking.

It is the interaction between System 1 and System 2 that defines how we think. However, we rely on System 2 much less than we think we do. Often when we presume we are thinking rationally and systematically – when we think we have a sound reason for our judgement – in effect our judgement is tainted by the heuristics and biases that are dictated by our System 1. So, why don't we use System 2 more? According to Daniel Kahneman this is because using System 2 is hard work. 'The law of least effort applies. People are reluctant – some more than others, there are large individual differences. But thinking is hard, and it's also slow. And because System 1 thinking is usually so efficient, and usually so successful, we have very little reason to work very hard mentally.'[11]

4.4 Cognitive biases

Cognitive biases are errors in thinking that affect how we make decisions. They directly stem from our System 1. There are many different types of cognitive biases. For example, Wikipedia provides a page that lists more than 100 different biases, some of them labelled with exotic names such as the 'Cheerleader Effect' and the 'Gambler's Fallacy'. Some cognitive biases, however, are more relevant for the domain of management than others, three of which we describe on the following pages along with other cognitive biases.

Patternicity and illusion of causality

Our System 1 is predisposed to see order, pattern and causal relations in the world. As a result, we tend to see meaningful patterns, some of which are meaningful and others are but meaningless noise. This **cognitive bias** is often referred to as 'patternicity' or 'illusion of causality'. We seek patterns and assume causal relations by connecting the dots: A appears connected to B, so we assume there is a causal link. Our System 1 is also very good in recognizing images of animals, faces or objects in blurry pictures. However, our System 1 can easily be fooled: it also recognizes images when they are not there. That's why we sometimes see images of animals or UFOs in clouds, or the face of Jesus on the surface of a grilled cheese sandwich.

Sometimes A is really connected to B, but sometimes it is not. For instance, when someone eats a poisonous berry (A) and then gets sick (B), he assumes it was the berry that made him sick. However, the baseball player who forgets to shave before the game (A) and hits his first home run (B) may falsely assume that not shaving before the game made him hit a home run. This is how people become superstitious. When a pattern or association is real, we learn something valuable from the environment, so we can make predictions that help us to survive. This process is also known as association learning and is fundamental to all human behaviour. Unfortunately, our System 1 is not very good in distinguishing false and real patterns and causal relations. In fact, human brains are inclined to believe that a perceived causal relation is real until proven otherwise.

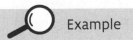

Example

An insurance company introduces a decentralized organization structure where autonomous business units make their operational decisions and are fully responsible for their own profit and loss. However, after two years it turns out that the company's overhead is too high and the profit margin cut in half. The company's executive board jumps on the idea that a recent change is at fault: autonomous business units were introduced two years before and now profit margins have declined. They therefore decide to establish a new financial control system and reduce the autonomy of the business units.

Confirmation bias

Due to the dominance of our System 1 thinking, we are predisposed to confirm our existing beliefs. By selectively searching for and interpreting information in a supporting fashion while ignoring information to the contrary we reinforce our existing beliefs. In other words, we 'see what we want to see'. This phenomenon is known as confirmation bias and is one of the most important biases.

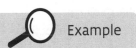

Example

Traditionally, women have been underrepresented in major symphony orchestras. Even renowned conductors claimed for a long time that female musicians have 'smaller techniques' and are 'more temperamental' and are thus unsuitable for orchestras. As a result, orchestral selection committees tended not to hire women, because their members were convinced (and thus heard during the audition) that men were better musicians. In fact, some orchestras did not hire women at all. Confirmation bias, however, is hard to prove. But in 1997 a landmark study confirmed the existence of biased hiring by major orchestras and illustrated the value of blind auditions, which have been adopted by most major orchestras.[12] Using data from audition records, the researchers found that blind auditions increased the likelihood of a female musician being hired sevenfold. As a result, blind auditions have had a significant impact on the face of symphony orchestras. About 10 per cent of orchestra members were female around 1970, compared with about 35 per cent in the mid-1990s.

In his book *You Are Not So Smart*, David McRaney explains that decades of research have placed confirmation bias at the top of all cognitive biases and among the most important mental pitfalls.[13] For this reason, journalists who want to tell an objective story must actively search for evidence contradicting their initial beliefs. Without confirmation bias, conspiracy theories would fall apart. Did the United States really put a man on the moon? McRaney argues that if you are looking for evidence they didn't, you will find it. In this age of the internet, people are bombarded with information. However, our System 1 tends to filter out information that does not confirm our existing beliefs. In making an evidence-based judgement, we therefore need to actively search for evidence that challenges our judgement.

 Example

If you believe that techniques such as Six Sigma are likely to make business processes more efficient, it won't be difficult to find evidence confirming your belief. A wide range of companies claim to have successfully implemented Six Sigma, such as Motorola, General Electric, Amazon, Ford and even the United States Army[14] – a sufficient number to make your System 1 automatically jump to the conclusion that your belief is right. However, if you would suspend your judgement and actively search for evidence to challenge your belief, you would find several examples of companies where the implementation of Six Sigma was less successful. For instance, 3M, one of the world's most innovative companies, lost its innovative edge when it began using Six Sigma to try to improve its operational efficiency. James McNerney, the CEO named in 2000, introduced Six Sigma as soon as he took the helm of the firm. But when he applied Six Sigma to 3M's research and development processes it led to a dramatic fall-off in the number of innovative products developed by the company during those years.[15] In fact, Fortune Magazine reported in 2006 that 91 per cent of the large corporations that had implemented Six Sigma had fallen behind the growth rate of the S&P 500, blaming this poor result on a significant decline in innovation at these firms.[16]

Suspending your judgement in order to actively search for contradicting evidence is an effective way to prevent confirmation bias. In this particular case, we would probably conclude that there are indeed many examples that indicate that Six Sigma may have benefits in terms of cost-efficiency and quality-control benefits, but that there is also evidence that suggests that it may seriously hamper innovation.

Group conformity

Group conformity is the tendency to conform to the others in a group, even if doing so goes against your own judgement. Human beings are very social creatures and are very aware of what people around us think. Therefore, our System 1 is strongly inclined to conform to the group: we strive for consensus and avoid confrontations, even when we don't agree with what people are saying.

 Example

A disturbing example of how people are naturally inclined to conform to the group is the Asch experiment, a study that was first conducted in the 1950s but that has been repeated over and over again with exactly the same outcome. In this experiment, a volunteer is told that he is taking part in a visual perception test. What he doesn't know is that the other participants are actors. The leader of the experiment places two cards before the participants: the card on the left contains one vertical line, the card on the right displays three lines (A, B and C) of varying length. Each participant has to state aloud which of the three lines on the card on the right (A, B or C) has the same length of line as the card on the left.

The actors give a variety of answers, at first correct, to avoid arousing suspicion in the volunteer, but then with some incorrect responses added. The results are very interesting. When surrounded by participants giving an incorrect answer, over one-third of the volunteers also give an incorrect answer.

In fact, at least 75 per cent of the volunteers give the wrong answer to at least one question.[17]

In a professional context group conformity can have devastating effects on the outcome of a decision-making process. In fact, there are numerous examples of conformity bias affecting a professional judgement made by clever people, the most (in)famous may be the Challenger disaster in 1986, when the NASA Space Shuttle Challenger broke apart 73 seconds into its flight, leading to the deaths of its seven crew members. In the corporate world similar examples exist, such as the collapse of Swiss Air,[18] Enron,[19] and the global financial crisis of 2008.

We can see another example of group conformity in the context of management and organizations in popular management techniques. When you look at a chronological overview of popular techniques, it is hard to get a sense of scientific progress: Management by Objectives, Business Process Reengineering, Total Quality Management, Learning Organizations, Knowledge Management, Lean Management, Six Sigma, Talent Management, Employee Engagement, Agile. Though many of these techniques once enjoyed the enthusiastic support of managers and consultants, all but the most recent have fallen from favour, replaced by the new flavour of the month. As such, the ebb and flow of popular management techniques are similar to that of a fashion cycle.[20, 21] The impact of group conformity in the domain of management is strikingly worded by Geoffrey Colvin: 'And there we see the power of any big managerial idea. It may be smart, like quality, or stupid, like conglomeration. Either way, if everybody's doing it, the pressure to do it too is immense. If it turns out to be smart, great. If it turns out to be stupid, well, you were in good company and most likely ended up no worse off than your competitors.'[22] The message here is clear: Practitioners, like all human beings, are social creatures who are very much aware of what other practitioners think. As a rule, they don't want to be seen as the person 'that rocks the boat', so in many cases they will conform to the group.

Other common cognitive biases

The effect of cognitive biases on human judgement is one of the most widely studied topics in the field of psychology. As a result, an overwhelming number of scientific publications are available. One could argue that all cognitive biases are relevant to the domain of management. However, apart from the three cognitive biases discussed above, we consider the following biases as particularly relevant:

- **Availability bias:** the tendency (of our System 1) to rely on examples that spontaneously come to mind when evaluating a specific topic, method or decision. As a result, we are more likely to believe something is true, effective or commonplace if we know an example of it, and we are less likely to believe in something that we've never seen or heard before. However, the examples that are 'available' in our memory are largely determined by how recent the examples are or how unusual or emotionally charged they may be. For example, a manager who has just read an article on the benefits of Lean Six Sigma in a popular magazine will more likely suggest (or accept) this as a solution for a managerial problem than a model he or she has never heard of.

- **Authority bias:** the tendency to over-value the opinion of someone who is seen as an authority. As a result, we tend to be less critical when an 'authority' makes a claim or a suggestion. For example, consultants from a large, renowned, international consulting firm tend to get less critical questions when making a recommendation than a consultant from a small, relatively unknown, local firm. The same counts for the so-called 'HIPPO' – the Highest Paid Person Opinion – a term coined by Avinash Kaushik.[23] In meetings HIPPOs are often deemed to be more valuable and important than the judgement of a practitioner on a lower pay grade.

- **Outcome bias:** the tendency to evaluate the quality of a management decision, technique or practice on the basis of its outcome. This bias occurs even when the outcome is determined by chance. For example, when Steve Jobs was fired from Apple in 1985 over a disagreement regarding how to save the company during a period of declining sales for the Apple II computer, he was publicly regarded as a bad leader who had seriously damaged the organization with his emotional swings and immature behaviour. However, after his return in 1996 and Apple's success with the iPod and the iPhone he was regarded as one of the most influential and innovative leaders of his time.

- **Overconfidence bias:** the tendency to have an unwarranted faith in one's own knowledge, judgements, cognitive abilities or skills. Research has demonstrated that 93 per cent of US drivers rate themselves as better than the median.[24] Professionals, such as physicians, economists, lawyers and managers, are by no means immune to this tendency either – research has demonstrated they all tend to overestimate their knowledge and ability. Physicians, for example, frequently underestimate the proportion of negative outcomes among patients in their caseload.[25]

- **Social desirability bias:** the tendency to answer questions in a manner that will be viewed favourably by others. Management practitioners, like all human beings, want to be accepted and liked. As a result, they are more likely to answer questions in a manner that will be viewed positively by their peers and bosses, especially to questions that deal with sensitive subjects such as leadership style, accountability and ethical issues.

4.5 Avoiding or reducing bias

Due to the dominance of our System 1, human judgement is highly susceptible to systematic errors. The fundamental question is: How can we make professional judgements without falling prey to our biases? Awareness that decisions can be biased is an important first step. Still, being aware that human judgement suffers from cognitive biases does not prevent them from occurring. Even Daniel Kahneman, the world's leading authority on this subject, stated: 'I've been studying this stuff for 45 years, and I'm no better than when I started. I make extreme predictions. I'm over-confident. I fall for every one of the biases.' Thus, you may accept that you have biases, but you cannot eliminate them in yourself. However, as Kahneman also points out, 'There is reason for hope when we move from the individual to the collective, from the decision maker to the decision-making process, and from the executive to the organization'. As researchers have documented in the realm of management, the fact that individuals are not aware of their own biases does not mean that biases can't be neutralized – or at least reduced – at the organizational level.[26] As an evidence-based professional you can add tremendous value to your own and others' decision-making by checking the judgements people make by acquiring, appraising and applying multiple sources of evidence. In addition, you can take some practical measures to prevent cognitive biases from clouding your own judgement (or that of other practitioners); some of them were mentioned earlier:

1 **Consider multiple options:** the scientific literature suggests that considering multiple solutions tends to lead to better judgement than fixating on 'yes/no' or 'either/or' choices.[27] When we consider only one solution, we tend to ignore evidence contradicting its expected results, and as a result we fall prone to confirmation bias. Conversely, considering two or more options leads to gathering more information regarding expected differences in results, and thus leads to a more informed judgement.

2 **Get the evidence before forming an opinion, not after:** as Sherlock Holmes once stated: 'It is a capital mistake to theorize before one has data. Insensibly one begins to twist facts to suit theories, instead of theories to suit facts.'[28] If you nevertheless have a strong opinion or preference (for example, regarding a specific solution, intervention or management model) it may help making your beliefs explicit, for instance by writing it down. This way you remind yourself that you may be biased against alternative options and take this into account when making a judgement.

3 **Blind assessment:** as described above, an effective method to prevent confirmation bias, halo effect and authority bias is **blinding**. For example, hiding all information in a person's CV and application letter that could induce bias allows making a more objective assessment of a candidate's qualities. The same counts for the source of the evidence when evaluating its trustworthiness, such as the title of the journal where a scientific study was published, the name of the consulting firm that provided the data, or the seniority or status of the professional who provided his or her judgement. After all, we are interested only in the evidence itself, not the status or authority of its source.

4 **Falsify views and judgements:** as mentioned earlier, actively looking for evidence that contradicts your (or your colleagues'/clients') beliefs and opinions can lead to a more objective and balanced judgement. In addition, it may help to actively seek out people with contradictory beliefs and judgements. Our System 1 strongly favours our own ideas, so we need others to provide balance; however uncomfortable, it'll pay off longer term. Herbert Simon, a founder of modern organizational science, artificial intelligence and robotics, recognized the importance of decision processes for overcoming bias. He championed a practice still used today at Carnegie Mellon University in evaluating faculty for promotion and tenure. The discussion of all faculty cases begins with a presentation by two faculty members, one chosen to develop the pro case, why the candidate should be promoted or tenured, and another chosen to give the con case, why tenure or promotion should be denied. After the pro and con

have each presented their respective cases, the assembled faculty members ask them questions first 'with hats on' (answering the question from the pro or con perspective) and then with 'hats off' (their own personal views of the case). The result is a thoughtful, rich discussion of the candidate's case.

5   **Seek disagreement:** Alfred Sloan, the former president of General Motors strongly believed decisions should not be made until someone had brought forward why the 'preferred' option might be wrong. 'If we are all in agreement on the decision – then I propose further discussion of this matter until our next meeting to give ourselves time to develop disagreement and perhaps gain some understanding of what the decision is all about.'[29] Encouraging people to disagree and to be as open as possible may help prevent groupthink and authority bias from occurring. If needed, you could assign someone to play **devil's advocate.**

6   **Playing devil's advocate:** a devil's advocate is a person who expresses an opinion that disagrees with the prevailing point of view, for the sake of debate or to explore the thought further. By taking an opposite view (which he or she may not actually hold) and playing the devil's advocate role, he or she seeks to engage others in an argumentative discussion process. The purpose of this process is to determine the **validity** of the original point of view and identify biases in its argumentation, in order to increase the quality of the decision-making process. When applied to a project team, the devil's advocate should be a different person for each meeting.

7   **Install a red team:** the concept of a **red team** was originally developed by the US Army during the Cold War, using a team of officers taking a Soviet ('red') perspective to penetrate the US defenses. Nowadays red teams are used by companies – for example IBM, SAIC, Microsoft, and the CIA – to challenge assumptions, unearth preconceived notions and identify symptoms of bias (especially confirmation bias and groupthink) that could affect professional judgement.

Aside: Can you debias other people (or yourself)?

As stated earlier, being aware that your judgement suffers from cognitive biases does not prevent them from occurring. Many scholars therefore doubt that lone individuals can 'debias' themselves. Some scholars, however, suggest that everyday reasoning can be improved – to a certain extent– through experience and education.[30] In his chapter 'Debiasing' Richard Larrick provides an overview of what personal strategies we as individuals can apply:[31]

- **Motivational strategies:** there is little empirical evidence that incentives improve decision-making. A more viable approach is to hold people accountable for their decisions. Under certain circumstances, accountability leads to greater effort and use of evidence, which may lead to improved decision-making.

- **Cognitive strategies:** teaching people to 'consider the opposite' or to ask oneself 'What are possible reasons that my initial judgement might be wrong?' has been shown to be effective at reducing over-confidence, hindsight bias and anchoring effects. Training in specific thinking rules, logical principles or decision rules has also shown some (moderate) effect.

- **Technological strategies:** decision support systems have the potential to improve individual decision-making, but the research on this topic is still in its early stages.

4.6 Critical appraisal of evidence from practitioners

This chapter may leave you with a sense of disappointment. It shows that human judgement is inherently flawed – we see patterns and causal relations where they don't exist, we selectively search for and interpret evidence in a way that confirms our prior beliefs, we conform to others in a group (even when we don't agree), we over-value the opinion of authorities, we are over-confident, and so on. And there is not much we can do about it. Your conclusion may therefore be that evidence from practitioners is always unreliable and thus we should ignore it. This conclusion, however, would be incorrect. As stated at the beginning of this chapter, professional expertise/ judgement is an important source of evidence, especially as it can connect evidence from other sources (for example, scientific research findings and organizational data) to the specific organizational context. In addition, professional expertise is the most widely used source of evidence for the simple reason that it is easily obtainable. So, the message here is don't throw away the baby with the bathwater. Practitioner judgement/expertise too can, under specific conditions, be a valid and reliable source of evidence, provided that we critically appraise its trustworthiness before we apply it to the decision-making process.

Three preliminary questions

Especially when it comes to questions that assume a certain level of professional expertise on the matter (for example, 'Will this solution solve the problem?' or 'What are the possible downsides or unintended consequences of this solution?'), it is important that the three criteria for valid and reliable expertise are met:

1 Numerous opportunities to practise. Does the practitioner have extensive experience with the matter (problem, preferred solution)?

2 Direct, objective feedback. Was the practitioner able to evaluate the outcome, and, if so, was direct, objective feedback available?

3 A regular, predictable work environment. Can the organizational context in which the practitioner gained his or her experience with the matter be regarded as regular and predictable?

As explained at the beginning of this chapter, this means that the trustworthiness of a manager's experience regarding mergers and acquisitions is limited, whereas the trustworthiness of a sales agent's experience regarding effective sales pitches is rather high.

Has an effort been made to reduce bias?

As discussed, we can take some practical measures to reduce or prevent cognitive biases from affecting our judgement, especially in the context of group judgement. Relevant appraisal questions you can ask are:

• Were multiple options considered?

• Was the available evidence assessed blind from information that could induce bias?

• Was an attempt made to falsify views and judgements (for example, by actively seeking for contradictory evidence)?

• Was an attempt made to actively seek disagreement (for example, from other practitioners)?

• Was an opposite view brought into the judgement process (for example, a devil's advocate)?

Could there be bias?

Even when we made a serious effort to reduce bias, it could still have affected people's judgement. As explained, cognitive biases are, by definition, implicit, meaning that bias is not a deliberate process but something that unwittingly sneaks into someone's judgement. This means that you should always check if – and to what extent – cognitive bias could have affected a practitioner's judgement, such as social desirability bias, confirmation bias, availability bias or group conformity.

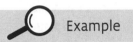

Example

A CEO of a large insurance company is very enthusiastic about a new IT system that is said to provide valid and reliable information regarding the organization's performance on relevant outcome metrics. She and a group of five senior managers therefore pay a visit to a company that has successfully implemented this new system, so they can learn from their experiences. In a board meeting the CEO reports that the other company's CEO and financial director are very positive about the IT system, and that she was impressed by the system's user-friendly interface. The senior managers who have accompanied the CEO on her visit agree that the IT system is exactly what the company needs.

Our System 1 strongly favours our own ideas, so by paying a visit to a company that has successfully implemented the IT system the CEO falls prone to confirmation bias. Instead, the CEO should have also looked for evidence that may contradict her view, for example by visiting a company where the implementation was NOT successful. In addition, it is unclear whether an effort has been made to prevent the senior managers from authority bias and group conformity, and whether multiple options were considered. Finally, the other company's CEO and financial director are 'very positive' about the IT system, but it is unclear whether this judgement is based on direct, objective outcome measures (and whether other practitioners agree). We would therefore argue that in this example the trustworthiness of the evidence (the judgement of the CEO and the senior managers) is rather low.

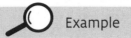

Example

Senior executives in a large, international investment bank are concerned by the number of transactional errors made in processing trades. They strongly believe that a significant proportion of these errors are preventable and feel that this is due to a lack of risk awareness among employees in the back office. Before they make a final judgement, however, they decide to interview some middle managers who may have a different view and ask the employees in the back office what they consider to be the major cause of the errors being made. Finally, the executives decide that they should reach a conclusion independently of each other and they anonymously write down their final judgement.

In this case, clearly an attempt is being made to reduce bias. As a result, the executives' judgement will be more trustworthy than the judgement of the CEO and senior managers in the first example. However, given the fact that the executives 'strongly believe' that the errors are due to a lack of risk awareness makes them prone to confirmation bias. We would therefore argue that they should have tried to falsify their beliefs, for example by consulting the scientific literature to see whether lack of risk awareness is indeed a common cause of people making mistakes or whether other causes are more likely. We would therefore argue that in this case the trustworthiness of the evidence (the executives' judgement) is moderate.

Was the evidence acquired in a valid and reliable way?

The trustworthiness of evidence from practitioners is not only determined by factors such as experience, feedback and susceptibility to bias, but also by the way in which the evidence was obtained. This means that, when critically appraising evidence from practitioners, we should also account for the method used to acquire the evidence. For example, wandering around through the workplace and asking practitioners their opinion on an assumed problem or preferred solution is more prone to bias than conducting a survey with a large random sample or a Delphi panel. In addition, a major concern when obtaining evidence from practitioners is selection bias. This occurs when your selection of practitioners leads to an outcome that is different from the one you would have expected had you enrolled the entire target audience. Finally, we must consider the wording of the questions when acquiring the evidence, especially when a survey questionnaire is used.

 Example

The following three statements are from a survey questionnaire that was used by a large banking firm. The respondents were asked to what extent they agreed or disagreed with the following statements:

1 Roles and responsibilities for managing risk in my area are clear and consistent.

2 In the team meetings I attend, risk management is a regular agenda item.

3 In our department, there is an open environment that is receptive to challenge and improvement.

All three statements are inadequately formulated. The first statement is 'double-barrelled', because roles/responsibilities and clear/consistent are different things. An option would be to split the statement into two or more separate statements. In the second statement the term 'regular' is imprecise and should be avoided – it would be better to ask 'In the past month, how many times was risk management...?' The third statement is very vague and uses abstract terms such 'open environment' and 'receptive to challenge'. It would be better to define these terms or illustrate them with an example.

As explained in the previous chapter, the choice of words in a question is critical to express its meaning and intent – even slight wording differences can substantially affect the answers practitioners give. In Chapter 3 we provide tips for writing valid and effective survey questions.

4.7 Checklist

Table 4.1

	Yes	No	Unclear
Does the practitioner have extensive experience with the matter (problem/solution)?			
Was the practitioner able to evaluate the outcome, and, if so, was direct, objective feedback available?			
Can the organizational context in which the practitioner gained his or her experience be regarded as sufficiently regular and predictable?			
If applicable, has an effort been made to reduce bias by taking measures, such as: • Blind assessment • Falsification of views and judgements • Seeking disagreement • Introducing an opposite view (eg devil's advocate)			
To what extent could cognitive bias have affected the practitioner's judgement, such as: • Social desirability bias • Patternicity/illusion of causality • Confirmation bias • Group conformity • Availability bias • Authority bias • Outcome bias • Over-confidence bias			
Was the evidence acquired in a valid and reliable way? Were the questions worded adequately?			

Notes and references

1 This example is adapted from Dobelli, R (2015) *The Art of Thinking Clearly*, HarperCollins, New York, NY

2 Ford, L (2005) Australian Pair Wins Nobel Prize for Stomach Ulcer Research, *The Guardian*, Monday, 3 October

3 This example is partly adapted from Gladwell, M (2002) The Talent Myth, are smart people overrated? *The New Yorker*, **22** (2002), pp 28–33

4 Tracey, TJ, Wampold, BE, Lichtenberg, JW and Goodyear, RK (2014) Expertise in psychotherapy: An elusive goal?, *American Psychologist*, **69** (3), p 218

5 Harvey, N (2011) Learning judgment and decision making from feedback, *Judgment and decision making as a skill: Learning, development, and evolution*, pp 199–226

6 Kohler, DJ, Brenner, L and Griffin, D (2002) The calibration for expert judgment: Heuristics and biases beyond the laboratory in *Heuristics and biases: The psychology of intuitive judgment*, ed Gilovic, T, Griffen, D and Kahneman, D, Cambridge University Press, New York, NY, pp 686–715

7 Hamori, M and Koyuncu, B (2015) Experience matters? The impact of prior CEO experience on firm performance, *Human Resource Management*, **54** (1), pp 23–44

8 Spengler, PM and Pilipis, LA (2015) A comprehensive meta-reanalysis of the robustness of the experience-accuracy effect in clinical judgment,' *J Couns Psychol*, **62** (3), pp 360–78

9 Tversky, A and Kahneman, D (1974) Judgment under uncertainty: Heuristics and biases,' *Science*, **185** (4157), pp 1124–1131

10 Kahneman, D (2011) *Thinking, Fast and Slow*, Penguin Group, London

11 Schrage, M and Kahneman, D (2003) The Thought Leader Interview, *Strategy & Business*, **33** (6)

12 Goldin, C and Rouse, C (1997) Orchestrating impartiality: The impact of 'blind' auditions on female musicians (No w5903), *National Bureau of Economic Research*

13 McRaney, D (2011) *You Are Not So Smart*, Penguin Group Inc, New York

14 Pande, PS, Neuman, RP and Cavanagh, RR (2000) *The Six Sigma Way*, McGraw-Hill

15 Peppers, D (2016) *How 3M Lost (and Found) its Innovation Mojo*, published on the Inc. website in May 2016

16 Morris, B (2006) New rule: Look out, not in, *Fortune Magazine*, 11 July

17 Larsen, KS (1990) The Asch conformity experiment: Replication and transhistorical comparisons, *Journal of Social Behavior & Personality*

18 Hermann, A and Rammal, HG (2010) The grounding of the 'flying bank,' *Management Decision*, 48 (7), p 1051

19 O'Connor, MA (2003) The Enron board: the perils of groupthink, *University of Cincinnati Law Review*, 71 (4), pp 1233–1320

20 Abrahamson, E (1991) Managerial fads and fashions: The diffusion and rejection of innovations, *Academy of Management Review*, 16 (3), pp 586–612

21 Staw, BM and Epstein, LD (2000) What bandwagons bring: Effects of popular management techniques on corporate performance, reputation, and CEO pay, *Administrative Science Quarterly*, 45 (3), pp 523–56

22 Colvin, G (2004) A Concise History of Management Hooey: For every Six Sigma quality initiative, there's an inkblot test. Why FORTUNE 500 companies fall prey to boneheaded fads and fashions, *Fortune Magazine*, 28 June

23 Kaushik, A (2007) *Web Analytics: An hour a day,* Wiley Publishing Inc, Indianapolis, IN

24 Svenson, O (1981) Are we all less risky and more skillful than our fellow drivers?, *Acta Psychologica*, 47 (2), pp 143–8

25 Lambert, MJ (2010) Prevention of treatment failure: The use of measuring, monitoring, and feedback in clinical practice, *American Psychological Association*, Washington, DC

26 Kahneman, D, Lovallo, D and Sibony, O (2011) Before you make that big decision, *Harvard Business Review*, 89 (6), pp 50–60

27 Nutt, PC (1999) Surprising but true: Half the decisions in organizations fail, *The Academy of Management Executive,* 13 (4), pp 75–90

28 Sherlock Holmes quote in Doyle, AC and Holt, R (1999) *A Scandal in Bohemia*, Pearson Education

29 Sloan, AP (1964) *My Years with General Motors*, Crown Business

30 Nisbett, RE (ed) (1993) *Rules for Reasoning,* Erlbaum, Hillsdale, NJ

31 Larrick, RD (2004) Debiasing in *Handbook of Judgment and Decision Making,* ed Koehler, J and Harvey, N, Blackwell, Malden, MA

PART TWO
Evidence from the scientific literature

A short introduction to science

05

Science is a way of thinking much more than it is a body of knowledge.

CARL SAGAN

5.1 What is science?

What comes to mind when you hear the term 'science'? Laboratory workers in white coats? The Large Hadron Collider in Geneva? Memories of exciting and seemingly dangerous chemistry experiments at school? Or mice in a cage? These are widespread and popular ideas of science. So, is it any surprise that many managers and leaders, when confronted with the term 'scientific research', wonder what it has got to do with them or their work? Of course, science isn't only about what might be called 'hard science'. As a method and way of thinking about how to understand the world, science can be applied to almost anything, including organizations, management, workers and business.

The basic purpose of science is to acquire information that will help us to *describe, explain, predict and control* phenomena in the world. Science distinguishes itself from other human pursuits by its power to examine and understand phenomena on a level that allows us to predict with varying degrees of accuracy, if not sometimes control, the outcomes of events in the natural and human-made world.[1] However, for science to do so, we need trustworthy information or data, acquired in ways that minimizes bias and other misleading factors.

Still as human beings, we are inclined to use the most easily accessible source of information – ourselves. We rely on what we remember from our own experiences; what we think; and what we believe to be true. Our self-centred approach to information saves time and effort – and probably works reasonably well for simple day-to-day decisions. For more complicated decisions in business and management, however, relying solely on our own experience and judgement may well lead to poor decisions. As you have learned in Chapter 4, we are prone to cognitive biases in our thinking, and this causes us to make mistakes in analysing and interpreting our own experience and judgement. Science emerged partly as a response to the twin problems of relying solely on personal information and the biases inherent in interpreting it. A core activity of science is therefore gathering objective, *external* information, rather than relying solely on the subjective *internal* knowledge in our heads. Even the smartest people can easily be fooled into believing something that is not true, so we need to put some safety checks into place when we acquire and appraise external information. Below we discuss three safety checks.

The scientific method

One of these safety checks is the **scientific method,** a defining feature of science since the 17th century. The scientific method can be summarized in one sentence: *Do whatever it takes to avoid fooling yourself into thinking something is true that is not, or that something is not true that is.*[2] Scientists use it as a procedure to ensure the trustworthiness of their findings usually by:

1 Asking a question about something they observe (How? What? When? How many? Who? Why? or Where?).

2 Formulating a hypothesis (an assumption about how things work or a prediction about what will happen).

3 Testing the hypothesis by doing an experiment or making systematic observations.

4 Collecting the data.

5 Analysing the data.

6 Drawing a conclusion as to whether and the extent to which the hypothesis is likely to be right.

When scientists find discrepancies between the hypothesis and the outcome of the test, they modify the hypothesis and repeat steps 3 to 6. The scientific method is used in all scientific fields – including chemistry, physics and psychology – but scientists in these disciplines ask different questions and perform different kinds of tests.

Organized scepticism (peer review)

Another safety check that lies at the core of science is that the evidence generated by scientists is subject to 'organized scepticism'. This means that the scientific community collectively scrutinizes findings from a position of distrust: the burden of proof is on the scientist with a novel claim. In this sense, science is intrinsically cautious. As Naomi Oreskes states in her TED-talk *Why we should trust scientists*, it is hard to persuade the scientific community to say, 'Yes, we know something, this is true'.[3] So, another way to think of science is to see it as the consensus of scientific experts, who – through a process of collective scrutiny – have judged the evidence and come to a conclusion about it. Organized scepticism does not mean unanimity – we expect scientists to continue to question and raise alternative explanations to pursue deeper understanding. However, consensus means that a general agreement exists without strong arguments or evidence to the contrary. In science, consensus typically reflects the best available scientific evidence. Note: the organized scepticism of science means that we *never* prove a theory, as we must always consider the possibility of disconfirming evidence. However, we can have higher confidence and lower uncertainty where scientific consensus about the body of evidence is strong.

Replication

The final safety check to ensure the trustworthiness of scientific claims is **replication**. In fact, exactly repeating studies to see if the same result is obtained is a cornerstone of science. If novel findings from scientific research can be replicated, it means they are more likely to be correct. Multiple replications of scientific findings may turn a hypothesis into a more formal statement or theory. On the other hand, if the findings cannot be replicated, they are likely to be incorrect or oversimplified (due to some error or even chance). The following example shows why replication is essential in science.[4]

 Example

In 1998, a British researcher published an article in a medical journal reporting that he had found a link between a common childhood vaccine and autism. According to the article, children in his study developed autism soon after receiving the vaccine.[5] Following publication of the article, many parents refused to have their children vaccinated. Several epidemics occurred as a result and some children died. Soon after the original study was published, other researchers failed to replicate its findings: no other studies could find a link between the vaccine and autism. Eventually, researchers found that the original study was a fraud.[6] The author had received a large amount of money to find evidence that the vaccine caused autism, so he faked his results. If other scientists had not tried to replicate the research, the truth might never have come out.

 Note

Pseudo-science

Do you know what **pseudo-science** is? Disciplines such as astrology and parapsychology are regarded as pseudo-sciences. You know from our discussion above that science is a method used to test hypotheses in a way that takes account of coincidence, bias and other misleading factors. It follows that if we can't test a hypothesis or theory, we can't subject it to scientific investigation. One of the people who has thoroughly examined the difference between science and pseudo-science is the philosopher Karl Popper. He states that it is easy to obtain evidence in favour of virtually any theory. (This seems even more true in the internet era, where an array of evidence and ideas for almost any claim or theory can be found via a brief online search.) According to Popper, a theory should only be considered scientific if it is the positive result of a genuinely 'risky' prediction, which might conceivably have been found to be false. Put differently, a theory or model is scientific only if it can be tested and falsified. Take for example Uri Geller, a famous psychic who repeatedly demonstrated on television and on stage that he could bend keys and restart watches by using 'mental energy'. However, when his assumed psychic abilities were tested scientifically, Geller stopped the experiment by claiming that the scientific setting interfered with his mental energy, making it impossible to refute or falsify his claim.

5.2 Science is not about 'truth' or 'proof'

Developing a scientific understanding of the trustworthiness (validity and **reliability**) of information is important. But equally important is the realization that science is not about truth or proof. Science is about gathering information and testing assumptions (hypotheses) in ways that allow us to estimate how *likely* it is that something is true. We can never know for sure. Our uncertainty stems from three main sources.

First, it is always possible that *new* information will cast serious doubt on a well-established model or theory. For example, more rigorous research may demonstrate that the underlying assumptions are incorrect or that previous research was flawed in ways that produced biased or even false results. To claim something is 'true' or 'proven' is to miss the point of science: research can deliver only the best current evidence and calculate a probability, but, when new evidence becomes available, this probability may change. The job of an evidence-based manager is to make decisions on the basis of best available evidence at a given time while remaining open to new, better evidence that may emerge.

Second, even when something seems very close to being proven, it will still be subject to boundary conditions – it always depends on the situation. Even though a lot of data may support a particular theory, there may be other data from other settings to suggest that this theory does not hold true everywhere. Goal-setting theory – which proposes that setting moderately difficult goals leads to higher performance – for example, holds up well in some contexts and less so in others.[7]

Last, as we find out more and more about something, we sometimes discover that our original findings were not quite correct – or at least not specific enough. Take the concept of organizational commitment: when first developed, it was a general and one-dimensional construct that suggested that employees were just more or less committed to their jobs. However, subsequent research has shown there are at least three *different* and *specific forms* of commitment, which have *different* and *specific effects* on outcomes.[8] To claim, therefore, that commitment in general has some effect on outcomes no longer holds water, as it depends on which *form* of commitment we are looking at.

If you dig into scientific findings looking for absolute truth and proof, then you will be disappointed. If you look for evidence about likelihoods and probabilities, then research findings can be very useful to overcome the limitations of human judgement. We describe five of these limitations in detail below.

5.3 Limitation 1: Coincidence

The first limitation of human judgement that science aims to overcome is coincidence: could our observation of a phenomenon be due simply to chance? For example, when we notice that a person becomes ill after eating wild berries, we are inclined to conclude that the person became sick because of eating the berries. However, this could also just be coincidence. To rule out chance we therefore apply the scientific method: based on our observations we formulate a hypothesis (in this case, that eating wild berries makes you sick), and then test our hypothesis by doing an experiment. However, as you just have learned, science is not about 'proof' or 'the truth', but about probabilities and likelihoods. Thus, before we run our experiment – or conduct any other type of study – we should first determine what degree of uncertainty we are willing to accept. Should we accept a probability of 10 per cent that our experiment's outcome was due to chance, or should we be more lenient and accept a threshold of 20 per cent? Or an even higher value?

Statistical significance: p-value

In 1925, the English statistician Ronald Fisher suggested that, within the realm of science, this threshold should be set at 5 per cent (1 in 20).[9] This threshold was – unfortunately – later referred to as the *significance* level, and the corresponding probability (p) as *p*-value.[10] Fisher argued that if the *p*-value is higher than 0.05, then the probability that a study's outcome is due to chance should be considered too high. From that moment onwards the significance level of $p = 0.05$ became the most widely used but also most misapplied and misunderstood statistic in science. This is because, from an evidence-based perspective, there are two very serious problems with this metric.

Statistical significance versus practical relevance

In the realm of science, a 'significant' outcome is often interpreted as a finding that was most likely not due to chance.[11] In daily life, however, significant means 'sufficiently great or important to be worthy of attention'. However, *statistically* significant research outcomes are sometimes *insignificant* from a practical perspective (and vice versa). This is because statistical significance, outcome and sample size are interlinked. If the effect found is small but the sample size is very large, the *p*-value can be statistically significant. Similarly, if the effect is large and the sample size is small, the *p*-value can also be significant. Thus, when you make a sample size large enough, even highly trivial outcomes can be statistically significant.[12]

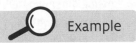 Example

Imagine that someone has developed a training programme that aims to increase the IQ of young children. With only 4 children enrolled in the programme, an increase of 10 IQ points would be a statistically significant outcome. However, with 25 children enrolled, an increase of 4 IQ points would also be significant, and with 10,000 children even an increase of 0.2 IQ points would be significant (see Table 5.1). However, would you send your child to this training programme? Probably not, as an increase of 0.2 IQ points almost certainly has no practical relevance. This means that the fact that a study's outcome is statistically significant has limited meaning and is of limited value, because it doesn't tell us if that outcome is of practical relevance.

Table 5.1

Sample size (number of children)	Effect size ('significant' increase in IQ)
4	10
25	4
100	2
10,000	0.2

 Note

From a practical perspective, a significance level of $p = 0.05$ is often too strict

Imagine the following scenario. A study reports a 10 per cent lower rate of production-line errors in manufacturing companies that use a particular quality management model. The p-value for the difference in error rate (compared with companies that have not implemented the model) is 0.07. The common interpretation of this p-value is that there is a probability of 7 per cent that this outcome is due to chance. Now, imagine that every 1 per cent error decrease yields a profit increase of $50,000, which equates to a total sum of $500,000. Let's also assume that the cost of implementing the model is quite low. Would you implement the model? You probably would. In fact, even if the p-value were 0.10 or 0.30, the odds on making a profit increase of half a million dollars might be too good to ignore. What we can learn from this is that the scientific thresholds of 0.05 or even 0.01 may sometimes be too stringent from a practical perspective.

5.4 Limitation 2: Methodological bias

The second limitation of human judgement that science aims to overcome is **methodological bias**: could our observation be due to personal preference or prejudice? In Chapter 4 you learned that human judgement is prone to a wide range of cognitive biases, such as the illusion of causality, confirmation bias, availability bias and outcome bias. As a result, people (including researchers and scientists) can be easily fooled into believing something that is incorrect. Thus, when researchers study a phenomenon or test a hypothesis, they need to put a 'safety measure' into place: the scientific method. Unfortunately, even the scientific method – or the way science in general is practised – is prone to all kinds of methodological biases. Some of the most common are described below.

Selection bias

Also referred to as sampling bias, selection bias occurs when the particular choice of participants in a study leads to an outcome that is different from the outcome that would have occurred if the entire population were studied. For example, if we want to know something about people's attitudes towards sex outside marriage, surveying people in a nightclub on a party island resort would likely yield a result different from a survey of churchgoers in the US Bible Belt. Researchers use 'probability sampling' (or 'random' sampling) to prevent selection bias. Note that random means the people in the sample are chosen by chance (thus, each person in the population has the same probability of being chosen). When you pick a truly random sample, you reduce the chances of selection bias.

Social desirability bias

This bias occurs when research participants answer questions in ways that they think are more socially acceptable. Social desirability reflects the concern people may have about how others view them. It is a difficult bias to overcome because people are inclined to report inaccurately on sensitive or personal topics in order to present themselves in accordance with other people's expectations. It can be reduced in several ways such as by assuring confidentiality or anonymity, by observing behaviour directly, or by using qualitative methods that build trust between researcher and study participants.

Halo effect

The halo effect describes the basic human tendency to make generalized inferences based on a few pieces of information. In his article 'The halo effect and other business delusions', Phil Rosenzweig gives the following example: 'When a company is doing well, with rising sales, high profits, and a surging stock price, observers naturally infer that it has a smart strategy, a visionary leader, motivated employees, excellent customer orientation, a vibrant culture, and so on. When that same company suffers a decline – when sales fall and profits shrink – many people are quick to conclude that the company's strategy went wrong, its people became complacent, it neglected its customers, its culture became stodgy, and more.'[13] This bias is also often present in employee performance ratings and employee selection. In good scientific research we can minimize the halo effect by blinding (or hiding) the characteristics of the participants, such as name, age and gender in the case of individuals, or reputation, brand and profitability in the case of organizations.

5.5 Limitation 3: Confounders

The third limitation of human judgement that science aims to overcome is confounding: the idea that a third **variable** distorts (or confounds) a relationship between two other variables. For instance, when factor A causes disease B, that relationship could be confounded by factor X that has a causal influence on both factor A and disease B. In that case, X would be an alternative explanation for the observed relationship between A and B. This can be illustrated using the following example.

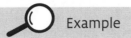 Example

It was long believed that when more ice cream is sold, more children who go swimming drown, because when children eat ice cream, their stomach gets cold, thus their body reacts by withdrawing blood from their limbs to their abdomen. So, when children go swimming after eating ice cream, their arms and legs are less saturated with blood, causing a shortage of oxygen in their muscles, which causes muscle fatigue, and, as a result, they are more likely to drown. This explanation is, of course, nonsense. When we take a closer look at the relationship between children eating ice cream (A) and children drowning (B), we will see that this relationship is distorted by a **confounder**: hot sunny weather (X). When the weather is nice and the sun is shining, more children will eat ice cream, but also more children will go swimming; when more children go swimming, a larger number of children will drown. So, despite the initial explanation of this relationship above, eating ice cream (A) does not lead to more children drowning (B); nice, sunny weather (X), however, does.

By applying rigorous research methods we can prevent confounders from distorting our observations. For various reasons, however, such methods are not always applied, and as a result research can produce very misleading results. Here are some other examples. Research has shown that:

- at primary schools, children with a large shoe size have better handwriting;
- people who drink alcohol are more likely to die of lung cancer (the same is true for gambling);
- children who use a night-light are more likely to develop myopia (short-sightedness).

You probably easily worked out what the confounder is in the first example: age. When children are older, their feet are larger, but because they are older they have also spent more time practising writing, thus the quality of their handwriting is better. In the second example the confounder is smoking: people who drink alcohol (or who gamble) are also more likely to smoke, and people who smoke are more likely to die of lung cancer.

The third example is a little more complicated. It was long assumed that children who use a night-light are more likely to develop short-sightedness (myopia). This assumption was investigated in a scientific paper that received a lot of publicity.[14] The findings were that exposure to night-time light before the age of two was indeed related to the incidence of myopia. Nearly a year later other researchers – who used a more rigorous research design – failed to replicate the findings. They did, however, find another result: myopic parents were more likely to leave the lights on at night. The explanation for this phenomenon is simple: myopic parents can't see well at night, and because young children often require night-time visits, they thus prefer to leave a night-light on in the bedrooms. We know, however, that genetic factors play an important role in the development of myopia, therefore the relationship between night-time lighting during early childhood and the later development of myopia is based on a confounding variable: parental myopia.[15]

5.6 Limitation 4: The placebo effect

In medicine a great deal of research has been done on a phenomenon that for a half century has been known as the placebo effect: a genuine effect, which is attributable to a patient receiving fake treatment or an inactive substance (for example, a sugar pill or an injection with distilled water). The treatment has no medical or healing power, so its effect is therefore due to other factors, such as a patient's hope and expectations, or his or her trust in a positive outcome. Due to the placebo effect sugar pills often have the same medical effect as a 'genuine' pill, and even fake operations can sometimes improve a patient's health simply because the person expects that it will be helpful. The placebo effect can be quite substantial.[16]

The placebo effect is not only present in medical treatments, but also in any intervention that aims to influence human behaviour, including management interventions. Among notable examples of this are the Hawthorne experiments, conducted between 1924 and 1933 by Elton Mayo and Fritz Roethlisberger, who examined the relationship between the productivity and working conditions of factory workers.[17, 18] When the researchers increased the level of light that the workers were subjected to, productivity improved. The same happened when the working conditions were changed in other ways, such as the introduction of rest breaks. However, when the researchers decreased the level of light, the productivity increased even more. In fact, when all working conditions were restored to how they had been before the experiments began, productivity at the factory was at its highest level! What happened was that the placebo effect had affected the outcome:

productivity gain did not increase because of the intervention (improving the employees' working condition), but due to a psychological factor: the motivational effect on the workers caused by the researchers showing interest in them.[19] Such a placebo effect can occur in organizational interventions that provide special treatment or attention to the participant and requires careful research design in order to rule it out.

The placebo effect is considered to be a special type of confounder that is present in all scientific studies in which an effect on human beings is involved. As we will see, however, using an appropriate research design can minimize the chance of the placebo effect or other confounders affecting the outcome.

5.7 Limitation 5: Moderators and mediators

Finally, another important influence on findings that science seeks to understand is the effect of moderators and mediators. Human beings are very good at detecting the presence of an effect, but they do less well when it comes to identifying (process or contextual) factors that may have caused or influenced that effect. In fact, in many cases, researchers are not as interested in whether something works, but rather in whether there are factors that (positively or negatively) influence the outcome. In science we refer to these factors as moderators and mediators.

A moderator is a variable that affects the direction and/or strength of the relationship between a predictor (for example intelligence) and an outcome (for example work performance). Put differently, moderators indicate when or under what conditions a particular effect is likely to be stronger or weaker. A well-known example is the effect of intelligence on job performance.[20] In general, intelligence is a good predictor of work performance: the higher a person's IQ, the higher his/her performance. However, this effect is moderated by the level of job complexity. The extent to which intelligence has an effect on job performance depends on the level of job complexity: When a highly intelligent person has to perform relatively simple tasks, his/her performance may not be much different than a less intelligent person's. On the other hand, when the task is complex the highly intelligent person is likely to outperform those of lesser ability. Thus, the positive effect of intelligence on performance is moderated by (or depends on) job complexity (Figure 5.1).

Figure 5.1

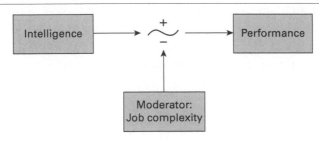

Figure 5.2

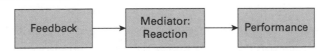

A **mediator**, on the other hand, is a variable that specifies how or why a particular effect or relationship occurs. Thus, if you remove the effect of the mediator, the relationship between the predictor and the outcome will no longer exist. For example, as early as the 18th century it was found that eating vegetables prevents sailors from getting scurvy. It was, however, not until the early 20th century that scientists found the specific mediator: vegetables only prevent scurvy when they contain vitamin C. A similar example can be found in management. In general, feedback has a positive effect on a person's performance. This effect, however, is mediated by a person's reaction to the feedback.[21] Put differently, it is a person's reaction to feedback, and not feedback per se, that determines the extent to which his or her performance will improve (Figure 5.2).

5.8 Qualitative versus quantitative research

Qualitative research is research that uses data that are not expressed in numbers. These data are usually obtained from interviews, focus groups, documentary analysis, narrative analysis or participant observation. Qualitative research is often *exploratory* research: we use it to gain an understanding of underlying reasons, opinions, motivations or mechanisms, or to generate hypotheses and/or theories that we can test through quantitative research. **Quantitative research,** on the other hand, is research that uses data that are quantified in various ways, that is, measured and expressed using numbers. These data are usually obtained from surveys, tests, financial reports, performance metrics or statistics. We often use this type of research to generalize results to a larger population, uncover patterns and relationships between variables, or measure the size of an effect of an intervention on an outcome.

Quantitative research is widely considered to differ fundamentally from qualitative research. In fact, a common prejudice is that quantitative research is 'objective' and concerns 'hard' data, whereas qualitative research is 'subjective' and concerns 'soft' data. Often people take sides and favour qualitative research over quantitative research or vice versa. A pro-qualitative research person might say: 'Quantitative research is useless because it is all about numbers and averages. But people are not numbers and employees and organizations are never average. If you want to get a better understanding of phenomena in an organization you should talk to the people who work there, observe closely, and experience what's happening for them. Subjectivity and interaction are key.' A pro-quantitative person might respond: 'Qualitative research is totally subjective, and thus biased and flawed. You should instead focus only on measurable outcomes, discovering general patterns and explanatory laws that can be translated to the local context. What can't be measured can't be managed, so objectivity and quantitative measures are key.' This is, of course, something of a nonsensical discussion, just as it would be nonsensical to discuss which car is better: a Formula 1 car, a small Fiat or a Range Rover? If you wanted to travel fast from A to B and the road was straight, the Formula 1 would most likely be the best car. However, if you wanted to drive through the old centre of Naples, this would be a bad choice. The same counts for an off-road adventure in the inlands of Guatemala. The small Fiat would be good for the streets of Naples and the Range Rover ideal for off-road driving. This means that the answer to which car is better always depends on the situation. The same is true of whether qualitative research is 'better' than quantitative research (or any other type of research): it depends on what you want to know and, hence, the research question. This principle is also known as **methodological appropriateness,** which we will discuss later in more detail.

5.9 Research designs

A research design is the 'blueprint' of a study that describes its steps, methods and techniques used to collect, measure and analyse data. Examples of study designs we frequently use in management are cross-sectional studies, experiments, case studies and meta-analyses. However, in our field all kinds of study designs are used, sometimes with exotic names that make it difficult to fathom exactly which research methods were used. Table 5.2 describes he elements of common research designs in the social sciences.

Table 5.2

Name	Description	Elements
Systematic review	A study that aims to identify as thoroughly as possible all the scientific studies of relevance to a particular subject and to assess the validity and quality of the evidence in each study separately. As the name indicates, a systematic review takes a systematic approach to identifying studies and has their methodological quality critically appraised by multiple researchers. Sometimes a systematic review includes a meta-analysis.	Depends on the studies included. Uses a systematic and transparent search process that specifies the criteria used to include or exclude studies.
Meta-analysis	A study that summarizes a large number of studies on the same topic in which statistical analysis techniques are used to combine the results of individual studies to get a more accurate estimate of the effect. Sometimes a meta-analysis includes a systematic review.	Depends on the studies included. Averages effect sizes of quantitative studies on a given topic.
Randomized controlled study (also referred to as randomized controlled trial, RCT, experiment, true-experiment)	A study in which participants are randomly assigned to a group in which an intervention is carried out (experimental group) and a group where no (or an alternative) intervention is conducted (control group), and the effect is measured after (and also often before) the intervention.	Random assignment, control group, before–after measurement

(continued)

Table 5.2 *(Continued)*

Name	Description	Elements
Controlled before-after study (also referred to as NRCT, non-randomized controlled trial, CBA, quasi-experiment, observational study, controlled longitudinal study, comparison group before–after study, non-equivalent control group design)	A study in which participants are (not randomly) assigned to a group in which an intervention is carried out (experimental group) and a group where no (or an alternative) intervention is conducted (control group), and the effect is measured both before and after the intervention.	Control group, before–after measurement
Cohort study (also referred to as panel study, observational study, longitudinal study)	A study where large groups of participants (also referred to as a cohort or panel) are followed over a long period (prospectively) to see whether differences arise among the groups.	Control group, before–after measurement (prospective)
Case-control study (also referred to as observational study)	A study in which one group of participants with a particular outcome is compared (retrospectively) with a group that did not experience this outcome. The starting point of the study is the outcome (dependent variable) rather than the intervention or exposure (independent variable).	Control group, before–after measurement (retrospective)
Interrupted times series (also referred to as repeated measures quasi-experimental study)	A study that measures participants repeatedly on a particular outcome (dependent variable). Data are collected (or variables measured) at three or more points both before and after the intervention or exposure.	Before–after measurement

(continued)

Table 5.2 (Continued)

Name	Description	Elements
Controlled study (also referred to as controlled post-test only, comparison group design)	A study in which subjects are (not randomly) assigned to a group in which an intervention is carried out (experimental group) and a group where no (or an alternative) intervention is conducted (control group), and the effect is measured only after the intervention.	Control group, after measurement
Before–after study (also referred to as single group before-after study)	A study in which data are obtained or particular variables are measured before and after an intervention/ exposure/event.	Before–after measurement
Post-test only (also referred to as pre-experimental design, one-shot survey, or one-shot case study)	A study in which data are obtained or particular variables are measured only after an intervention/exposure/ event.	After measurement (prospective)
Cross-sectional study (also referred to as survey or correlational study)	A study in which a large number of data or variables are gathered at one point in time, and the intervention or exposure (independent variable) and outcome (dependent variable) are measured simultaneously. It provides a 'snapshot' of the current situation.	Cross-sectional (retrospective)
Case study (sometimes referred to as field study)	A study in which a large number of aspects of a single case (organization or team) are investigated in depth over a long period within the case's own context. A case study is often used to narrow down a broad field of research into an easily researchable practical example. It is a useful design when not much is known about an issue or phenomenon. Researchers using a case study design often apply a variety of (often qualitative) methodologies and rely on a variety of information and data sources.	Often qualitative methods are used

(continued)

Table 5.2 (*Continued*)

Name	Description	Elements
Action research (also referred to as community-based research, participatory action research or collaborative inquiry)	A study carried out during an activity or intervention to improve the methods and approach of the people involved. The research is conducted by (and for) those taking the action: it is typically designed and conducted by practitioners who analyse their own data to improve their own practice. Action research follows a characteristic cycle whereby an exploratory stance is adopted. Often a variety of (qualitative and quantitative) methodologies are applied.	Often a variety of methods are used
Ethnographic study (also referred to as field research or naturalistic inquiry)	A study in which researchers completely immerse themselves in the lives, culture, context or situation (eg merger between two organizations) that they are studying. The study is designed to explore cultural phenomena where the researcher observes the organization from the point of view of the participants (eg employee or manager) in the study.	Qualitative methods
Mixed methods study (also referred to as a triangulation design)	A study that involves collecting, analysing and integrating quantitative (eg experiments, surveys) and qualitative (eg focus groups, interviews) research.	Both qualitative and quantitative methods are used

It is by no means comprehensive, but it provides a basic frame of reference.

In addition to the research designs listed above we use several other classifications and dichotomies, of which the following are the most common.

Descriptive versus exploratory versus causal research

Descriptive research describes events or states and aims to find out 'what is', so we frequently use observational and survey methods to collect the data. Exploratory research aims to generate new questions and hypotheses, investigating underlying reasons or gaining a better understanding of a certain topic. Qualitative methods are often used. Causal research aims to discover causal relationships, hence we often use research designs with a **control group** and a pre-measure and designs that assess or measure at multiple time points.

Prospective versus retrospective research

Many studies are prospective: first a research question or hypothesis is developed, then a representative sample of participants is selected and a baseline measure obtained, and finally, after an intervention (or exposure to a variable), the data about the participants are analysed to examine the effect. In 'retrospective studies', researchers investigate an intervention or exposure by looking back at events that have already happened. Such studies can yield important scientific findings without taking a long time following the participants to find out the outcome.[22]

Experimental versus observational research

Experimental research refers to studies where the researcher manipulates one or more variables and controls the other variables to determine whether there is a causal relationship between the manipulated variable and the outcome. Observational research refers to studies where the researcher merely observes but does not intervene, with the intention of finding associations among the observed data.

Experimental versus correlational research

In this case experimental research typically refers to studies that are regarded as 'true' experiments (ie randomized controlled studies) that allow drawing causal conclusions, whereas correlational research concerns studies (such as non-randomized or non-controlled studies) that only allow conclusions about correlations or associations.

Cross-sectional versus longitudinal research

Longitudinal research concerns studies that involve repeated observations (measurements) of the same variable(s) over a certain period of time (sometimes even years), for example cohort studies or interrupted times series. Cross-sectional research refers to studies – such as a survey – in which a large number of data or variables are gathered only at one point in time. It provides a 'snapshot' of the current situation.

5.10 How to read a research article

Research findings are reported on TV, in newspapers and in magazines. However, those sources often provide information that is too limited to critically appraise or judge a study's trustworthiness. In order to do that we need to find and read the original research article.

Non-academics often consider research articles difficult to read. Practitioners and students sometimes complain that research articles are too lengthy and use too much jargon. They also complain that too many of these articles are dedicated to theory. As a result, non-academics tend to lose track of what the authors are saying, or lose interest after a few pages. We should realize, however, that the target audience for academic journals is made up of academics, not practitioners or students. The authors therefore assume that their readers are familiar with academic conventions as well as technical jargon. In other words, research articles are pieces of technical writing whose purpose is to communicate research ideas and findings between researchers.

The most common and important mistake you can make is thinking that a research article is the same as an interesting short story or a newspaper article and you can therefore read it in the same way. The truth is that research articles are a particular type of writing that requires a specific approach in order to fully appreciate or understand them. Research articles are not typically intended for you to read from the beginning to the end in a linear way. They often require jumping back and forth between the different sections, tables and appendices. For this reason, reading a research article requires specific skills. Since developing skills requires practice, the more you read research articles, the better you should get at it. To quickly get the most important elements out of a research article, try the following approach:

Step 1: Read the abstract

Start by trying to find out what the article is generally about. What claim(s) is it making? Sometimes the abstract is unclear, but often it provides a summary of the research question, the design, key methods, results and conclusions of the study.

Step 2: Skim the introduction

Quickly skim the first few sections of the introduction, then skim theory and discussion of previous research.

Step 3: Skim the middle section

Skim the subtitles. Find out what the research questions or hypotheses are. What is the purpose of the research? What are the researchers trying to find out and why?

Step 4: Read the 'method' section

Find out what kind of research design the authors used. Did they use a control group and was there a before and after measurement? Try to find which variables and/or outcomes they measured and see if valid and reliable measurement methods were used. Exactly how do they propose to answer their research questions or test their hypothesis?

Step 5: Skim the 'outcome' or 'results' section

Skip all elaborate statistical information and focus on outcomes that are expressed in frequencies, percentages, correlations or other effect sizes. Sometimes the main outcomes are summarized in the first part of the results. More often outcomes are reported separately for each research question or hypothesis. Tables can be very helpful. Search for a correlation matrix or a table with outcome measures or effect sizes.

Step 6: Read the conclusion

Find out what the authors consider to be the most important outcomes of their study. Are their conclusions justified by the data they presented? Remember that the conclusions authors reach about their research and what it means may not be the same as the conclusions others would draw from their study.

In general

Don't let yourself be taken in by scientific jargon or complex use of language! Focus on the research question, study design, possible **weaknesses** and the most relevant outcomes.

Notes and references

1 deGrasse Tyson, N (2016) *What Science Is – and How and Why It Works*, The Blog, *Huffington Post*, 18 November

2 Ibidem

3 Oreskes, N (2014) *Why we should trust scientists*, TED-talk, posted June

4 This example is adapted from CK-12 [accessed 12 June 2017] Replication in Science [Online] https://www.ck12.org/book/ CK-12-Physical-Science-Concepts-For-Middle-School/section/1.24/

5 Wakefield, A *et al* (1998) RETRACTED:—Ileal-lymphoid-nodular hyperplasia, non-specific colitis, and pervasive developmental disorder in children, *Lancet*, 351 (9103), pp 637–41

6 Deer, B (2011) [accessed 25 January 2018] How the case against the MMR vaccine was fixed, *BMJ*, **342** (c5347)

7 For example, when employees must first acquire requisite knowledge or skills to perform the task, specific and challenging goals can have a negative effect on performance.

8 Allen, NJ and Meyer, JP (1990) The measurement and antecedents of affective, continuance and normative commitment to the organization, *Journal of Occupational and Organizational Psychology*, 63 (1), pp 1–18

9 Fisher, RA (1925) *Statistical Methods for Research Workers*, Oliver and Boyd, Edinburgh, UK, p 43

10 Neyman, J and Pearson, ES (1933) The testing of statistical hypotheses in relation to probabilities a priori, *Mathematical Proceedings of the Cambridge Philosophical Society*, 29, pp 492–510

11 Unfortunately, this interpretation is not accurate. You may be surprised, because this is probably what you learned in class or read in textbooks. So, what does a p-value or the term 'significant' mean? Unfortunately, it is very hard to explain what it really means. The official definition looks like this: 'The probability of getting results equal or even more extreme as the ones you observed, if the **null hypothesis** would be true.' In other words, it is the probability of your data, *given* your hypothesis. Still confused? Don't worry about it. As you can see in this video, not even scientists can easily explain what a p-value really means: http://fivethirtyeight.com/features/not-even-scientists-can-easily-explain-p-values/

12 Kühberger, A, Fritz, A, Lermer, E and Scherndl, T (2015) The significance fallacy in inferential statistics, *BMC research notes*, **8** (1), p 84

13 Rosenzweig, P (2007) Misunderstanding the nature of company performance: the halo effect and other business delusions, *California Management Review*, **49** (4), pp 6–20

14 Quinn, GE, Shin, CH, Maguire, MG and Stone, RA (1999) Myopia and ambient lighting at night, *Nature*, **399** (6732), pp 113–14

15 Andrade, C (2007) Confounding, *Indian Journal of Psychiatry*, **49** (2), pp 129–31

16 Stewart-Williams, S and Podd, J (2004) The placebo effect: Dissolving the expectancy versus conditioning debate, *Psychological Bulletin*, **130** (2), p 324

17 Mayo, E (1993) *The Human Problems of an Industrial Civilization*, Macmillan, New York

18 For a more complete discussion of the Hawthorne effect, see Olson, R, Verley, J, Santos, L and Salas, C (2004) What we teach students about the Hawthorne studies: A review of content within a sample of introductory IO and OB textbooks, *The Industrial-Organizational Psychologist*, **41** (3), pp 23–39

19 It should be noted that while the Hawthorne effect is plausible more recent research has described the Hawthorne effect found in these original studies as something of a myth and a re-analysis of the data from one of the original studies shows that the effects were not as strong or straightforward as was claimed. See, for example: Kompier, MA (2006) The 'Hawthorne effect' is a myth, but what keeps the story going?, *Scandinavian Journal of Work, Environment & Health*, pp 402–12 and Levitt, SD and List, JA (2011) Was there really a Hawthorne effect at the Hawthorne plant? An analysis of the original illumination experiments, *American Economic Journal: Applied Economics*, **3** (1), pp 224–38.

20 Schmidt, FL and Hunter, J (2004) General mental ability in the world of work: occupational attainment and job performance, *Journal of Personality and Social Psychology*, **86** (1), pp 162–73

21 See CIPD (2017), *Could do better? What works in performance management*, [Online] www.cipd.co.uk/knowledge/fundamentals/people/performance/what-works-in-performance-management-report

22 Note that sampling on the dependent variable can invite serious problems –see Rosenzweig's (2007) *Halo Effect* for in-depth discussion.

ACQUIRE: 06
Evidence from the scientific literature

Our duty is to believe that for which we have sufficient evidence, and to suspend our judgement when we have not.

JOHN LUBBOCK

Consider the following real-life example. A consulting firm developed a framework to ensure better accountability, conduct and culture in banking firms. When asked about the scientific evidence underlying the framework, they provided the following answer:

Our framework is grounded in the work of Professor X on trust and trustworthiness. In addition, we explored the seminal work of Professor Y, Professor Z on the role of culture in financial services, Professor A and others on biological drivers, Professor B on culture and dishonesty in banking, Professor C on measuring and assessing culture in healthcare, Professor D on psychological safety, and Professor E on moral disengagement and unethical behaviour.

After developing an initial set of survey questions, we conducted cognitive testing with employees at six different firms, and we used the results to refine the questionnaire from this year's assessment exercise.

So, would you consider this to be a good example of an evidence-based approach, in particular consulting the evidence from the scientific literature? After all, they did consult several academics and asked for their views on the evidence and probably looked at some of the scientific literature too.

Consulting some well-known professors from well-known universities and looking at just some of the scientific literature, however, is not technically an 'evidence-based' approach. The entire purpose of evidence-based management is both to get away from consulting experts about evidence and their opinion of such (which is regarded as low-quality evidence in evidence-based management) and away from dipping into the scientific literature. We consult the scientific literature, which should be done in a systematic, transparent and verifiable way – after all our aim is to minimize bias by having an explicit search strategy and clear criteria for judging the **methodological quality** of the scientific evidence we find. In this sense, it has nothing to do with the opinions of experts or the work of particular researchers, but is a search for **all** the relevant scientific evidence, which we then judge using objective criteria.

So, yes, we agree that the consulting firm consulted the scientific literature, but this is not the same as taking an evidence-based approach. To bring evidence from the scientific literature into your decisions, you need to know how to search for empirical studies in online research databases. This chapter will therefore teach you the skills necessary to successfully conduct a systematic, transparent and verifiable search in online research databases such as ABI/INFORM Global, Business Source Premier and PsycINFO.

6.1 The scientific literature

Peer-reviewed journals

When we refer to evidence from the scientific literature we mean empirical studies published in **peer-reviewed** academic (scholarly) journals. The articles submitted to these journals are first evaluated and critiqued by independent, anonymous scientists in the same field (peers) to determine whether they merit publication in a scientific journal. This way an author can revise the article to make corrections and include any peer reviewers' suggestions that will make the article stronger, such as incorporating previously overlooked ideas and addressing methodological concerns. If the author cannot or will not take the peer reviewers' advice, the article may be rejected, and, as a result, it will not be published. Peer review ensures that an article – and therefore the journal and the discipline as a whole – maintains a high standard of quality, accuracy and academic integrity. Of course, this sounds good in theory, but in practice this is unfortunately not always the case – poor-quality studies suffering from methodological flaws, bias and incomplete conclusions are also rife in peer-reviewed journals. The same counts for so-called 'top' journals with a high 'impact factor' – a measure reflecting that the articles in the journal are often cited by other researchers.

Such journals can also contain articles that report on studies that are seriously flawed. For this reason, an evidence-based approach always involves critically appraising the studies found, even when they are published in a well-known, highly reputed, peer-reviewed journal.

The easiest way to find peer-reviewed articles is to search in an online research database. To make sure your results come from peer-reviewed (also referred to as 'scholarly') journals, you just simply check the box that allows you to limit your results to peer-reviewed only.

Online research databases

As you just have learned, when we search for empirical studies we first look for studies in peer-reviewed journals. In the past, this meant asking an academic or a business librarian for titles of journals that would most likely publish studies relevant to your question, and then going to the library and sifting through tens to hundreds of issues until you found a sufficient number of studies. Nowadays a visit to the library is no longer necessary, because most published research is retrievable through the internet. In addition, online research databases make it possible to simultaneously conduct a search in thousands of peer-reviewed journals. In fact, you can now conduct a search for studies from any place at any time, for example at home, in your favourite coffee shop, or during the break of an important business meeting.

In the first instance, you should conduct your search in the two most relevant databases for the field of management: ABI/INFORM Global from ProQuest and Business Source Elite or Premier from EBSCO. Depending on your question, you may also need to search in databases that are aimed at neighbouring disciplines such as psychology (PsycINFO), education (ERIC) or healthcare (PubMed). In addition, you can easily find research articles through **Google Scholar**.

 Tip

How do I get access to research databases?

In order to search for empirical studies published in peer-reviewed journals, it is essential that you have access to online research databases. Some databases, such as Google Scholar, ERIC and PubMed, are open to the general public and are easily accessible through the internet. However, most research databases, such as ABI/INFORM, Business

Source Elite and PsycINFO, are only accessible to students, faculty or staff of universities or other educational institutions. This means that you can access these databases only through the website of a university or educational institution. If you are not affiliated to a university you can get access to ABI/INFORM and Business Source Elite by becoming a member of the Center for Evidence-Based Management (CEBMa, see www.cebma.org).

PICOC

Before you start your search, it is important to make explicit the professional context that should be taken into account when answering your question. For example, questions such as 'Does team-building work?' or 'Does 360-degree feedback increase performance?' may be relevant, but they are also very broad. For example, you may be specifically interested to know whether team-building improves product quality in a German manufacturing company that just has undergone restructuring, or whether 360-degree feedback is effective as a tool for improving governmental managers' service to the public. To make your question more context-specific you can formulate a so-called **PICOC**. A PICOC is a mnemonic to help you find studies that are relevant to your professional context. The PICOC acronym is shown in Table 6.1.

Your PICOC will help you to determine whether the findings of a study will be generalizable and applicable to your organizational context. More specifically, your PICOC helps to answer the question whether your population, outcome of interest and organizational characteristics are so different

Table 6.1

Population	Who?	Type of employee, subgroup, people who may be affected by the outcome
Intervention	What or how?	Management technique/method, factor, independent variable
Comparison	Compared to what?	Alternative intervention, factor, variable
Outcome	What are you trying to accomplish/improve/change?	Objective, purpose, goal, dependent variable
Context	In what kind of organization/ circumstances?	Type of organization, sector, relevant contextual factors

from those in the study that its results may be difficult to apply. After all, some psychological principles are generalizable to all human beings, but sometimes what works in one narrowly defined setting might not work in another.

6.2 Determining your search terms

The act of determining your search terms is the most important step when searching for empirical studies in an online research database. As you can imagine, here too the rule 'garbage in, garbage out' (GIGO) applies. Research databases just process the search terms you enter. Good, clear, specific search terms generally result in good outputs (ie relevant to your question), whereas unclear, vague, ambiguous or incorrect search terms will most certainly result in bad outputs (ie those that are not). The following four steps will therefore help you to identify search terms that will yield studies relevant to your question.

Step 1: Determine the two most important terms of your PICOC

The first step in finding relevant empirical studies is to determine the two most relevant PICOC terms. In most cases this will be the intervention (management technique, independent variable) and the outcome (objective, outcome measure, dependent variable). Other PICOC terms such as population and context may also be important, but their specificity tends to lead to them excluding relevant studies, so as a rule we leave them out.

Step 2: Finding alternative and related terms

In some cases, the two most important terms of your PICOC will suffice to find relevant studies. In most cases, however, you will need to identify alternative and related terms. For example, if you want to know whether cultural diversity has a positive effect on the creative performance of a product development team, the PICOC terms 'diversity' (intervention) and 'performance' (outcome) may be enough to find relevant studies. But what if you would like to know whether 360-degree feedback will be effective as a tool for improving the performance of physicians? Will the terms '360-degree feedback' and 'performance' suffice, or should you also use other related terms? To find out, we searched the internet for the term '360 degree feedback'. A Google search with the term "360 degree feedback" (with the term contained within double quotation marks – see Searching with Google below) yields a large number of results, and listed at the top is a Wikipedia page dedicated to this topic. Although the content is not always accurate, Wikipedia pages can be very helpful, especially with identifying alternative and related terms. In this case the first sentence on the page states '360-degree feedback, also known as multi-rater feedback, multi-source feedback or multi-source assessment…' This means that if we only searched for the term '360 degree feedback' in a research database, we would miss relevant studies using alternative terms such as 'multi-source feedback' or 'multi-rater feedback'. Another example is the term 'merger'. When you do a Google search for this, you will learn that 'fusion', 'acquisition' and 'take-over' are relevant related terms. This means if you conduct a search for empirical studies on the effect of mergers, you should also use these related terms. It is therefore important that, before you start your search for studies in a research database, you check Google to see if alternative or related terms exist. Other good places to identify alternative terms are websites such as Thesaurus.com, www.powerthesaurus.org and online dictionaries.

 Tip

Searching with Google

Think you know how to search with Google? Did you know that if you search for a specific phrase or composite term such as cultural diversity, you must enclose your words in double quotation marks: "cultural diversity"? If you don't do this, you will find websites or documents that mention EITHER of these two words (and end up with a large number of irrelevant results). There are several tools Google provides via regular and advanced searches that can help find what you're looking for faster and easier. Therefore, even if you think you know how to search with Google, we would strongly recommend everyone to have a look at this six-minute video, since you are likely to discover things that are new to you: www.youtube.com/watch?v=RODQfwc72PM.

Step 3: Identifying corresponding academic terms

People often state that managers and academics live in very separate worlds. This is particularly true for the terms and jargon they use. For instance, for managers performance is often just performance, whereas academics distinguish between many different types of performance, such as task performance, contextual performance, counterproductive work behaviour, extra role performance, organizational citizenship behaviour and so on. The same counts for terms that managers widely use, which sometimes have corresponding, but different, names in academia. As a result, searching for studies with only managerial – that is, non-academic – terms most probably won't yield relevant results.

 **Example**

As a change consultant, I am expected to contribute to the realization of organizational change. The outcomes of an organizational change intervention can be both positive and negative, depending on the type of change and the specific individual or group affected. Especially when the change has predominantly negative outcomes (for example, lay-offs), it is assumed to be important that the change process is perceived by the employees to be fair. My question therefore is: what is known in the research literature about the impact of a fair process on the way employees perceive the outcomes of organizational change?

In the example above the term 'fair process' yields many results on Google, including some pages where alternative terms are mentioned. In addition, a search for alternative or related terms on the website Thesaurus.com yields terms such as 'honest', 'trustworthy' and 'objective'. However, we are not sure whether these terms are also used in academia, so we need to check whether there are corresponding or alternative academic terms.

Thesaurus

A quick and easy method to find corresponding or alternative academic terms is the **thesaurus** or subject index of a research database. All online research databases have developed their own controlled vocabulary, which is listed in a database's thesaurus. By scanning the thesaurus, you will get a sense of the academic terminology used, and to view broader, narrower and related search terms. To browse the thesaurus of terms available in the database Business Source Elite, click the Thesaurus link at the top of the (advanced) search screen. Enter your search terms in the Browse field, and then select from: Term Begins With, Term Contains, or Relevancy Ranked radio buttons and click Browse. A list of headings is displayed and your search terms are retained in the Browse field. To browse the hierarchy of a subject term and see its broader, narrower and related terms, click the hyper-linked term from the result list.

Google Scholar

Another good place to find corresponding or alternative academic terms is Google Scholar (scholar.google.com), a search engine developed by Google that provides a simple way to broadly search for scholarly literature, including research articles. If you search for 'fair process' on Google Scholar, you will get many results. However, the results listed at the top suggest that there is a specific academic term for fair process: 'procedural justice'. When you skim through the first pages of the articles listed at the top, you will see that 'procedural justice' is indeed a term (**construct**) that academics and researchers widely use. This means that if we searched for the term 'fair process' in a research database, we would find only a limited number of studies, while we would miss important, relevant studies using the academic term 'procedural justice'.

Step 4: Determining whether there is a broader underlying principle

As explained, sometimes the two most important terms of your PICOC will suffice to find relevant empirical studies, but in most cases, you will need to identify alternative terms and/or corresponding academic ones. In some cases, it also pays to examine whether a broader general principle is underlying your term(s) of interest. For example, 360-degree feedback is a process in which someone receives feedback about his or her performance from several other people. Thus, the general underlying principle is performance feedback. This means that it would make sense to search additionally for studies on the effect of feedback on people's performance in general.

Identifying broader underlying principles is particularly useful in the case of popular management techniques. For example, a search with the term 'balanced scorecard' will yield numerous studies, but most of them may be of low quality. However, when skimming through some of the articles found, it becomes clear that this popular management technique is all about setting strategic goals and measuring indicators of performance. The broader underlying principle is therefore goal setting and, again, performance feedback.

The best way to examine whether there is a broader underlying principle is to search for articles in Google Scholar. The introduction section of a research article often contains an extensive explanation of the underlying principles, and is therefore a good starting point.

Tip

Snowballing

When you are looking for academic terms or the broader underlying principle in Google Scholar, it pays to unsystematically browse through the results, read the abstracts and 'snowball' – starting from one article, you search for other articles on the same topic. This way you get a general understanding of the topic and quickly learn about what the topic entails, common definitions, core elements and so on. In Google Scholar, your search results are sorted by relevance, based on the number of times an article is cited by other authors. To find newer articles you can click 'Sort by date' in the left sidebar. By clicking on the 'Related articles' link you can snowball to other articles that may be relevant and search for related terms. This technique is also referred to as **'pearl growing'**.

6.3 Searching in research databases: Some basic search techniques

Title and/or abstract

In contrast to Google and Google Scholar, research databases such as ABI/ INFORM, Business Source Elite and PsycINFO provide you with several options to specify your search. Firstly, the interface of a research database allows you to search for keywords in the title and/or the abstract. You can do this by entering your search terms in the search field and clicking the drop-down menu on the right. In addition, it is possible to search with multiple search terms.

Boolean operators

Research databases make use of so-called **Boolean operators** (AND, OR and NOT), which allow you to use search terms in different combinations (Figure 6.1). The Boolean operator OR increases the number of results you retrieve and is used to combine synonyms or related terms to make your results more comprehensive. For example, searching for "360-degree feed-back" OR "multi-source feedback" finds articles that mention EITHER of these topics in the title or abstract. Conversely, AND reduces the number

Figure 6.1

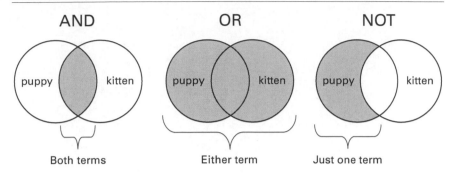

of results you retrieve and is used to combine PICOC terms or methodological filters to make your results more relevant. For example, searching for "cultural diversity" AND "performance" finds articles that mention BOTH topics in the title or abstract. The Boolean operator NOT reduces the number of results you retrieve by excluding a search term. For example, searching for "diversity" NOT "cultural" finds articles that mention diversity in the title or abstract but removes any articles that mention cultural.

Truncation

Most research databases allow you to use the **truncation** symbol * for finding singular and plural forms of words and variant endings. For example, typing work* into the search field will find articles containing any of the following words in the title or abstract: works, worker, workers, working, workforce or workplace.

Using the search history to combine searches

Another great feature that all research databases have, is the search history. All searches performed during your search session are available from the Search History screen (in some databases the term 'Recent Searches' is used). In the screenshot below (Figure 6.2) you can see that we have searched in the database Business Source Elite for the search terms "multi-source feedback", "multi-rater feedback" and "360 degree feedback" in the title or the abstract. We can now combine all our search queries with OR to create one big bucket with all articles that may be relevant. We can do that in two ways: either we select all search queries by clicking the checkboxes and then click the button 'Search with OR', or we can just type in S1 OR S2 OR … etc in the search field. In the screenshot below you can see this yields about 480 results.

Figure 6.2

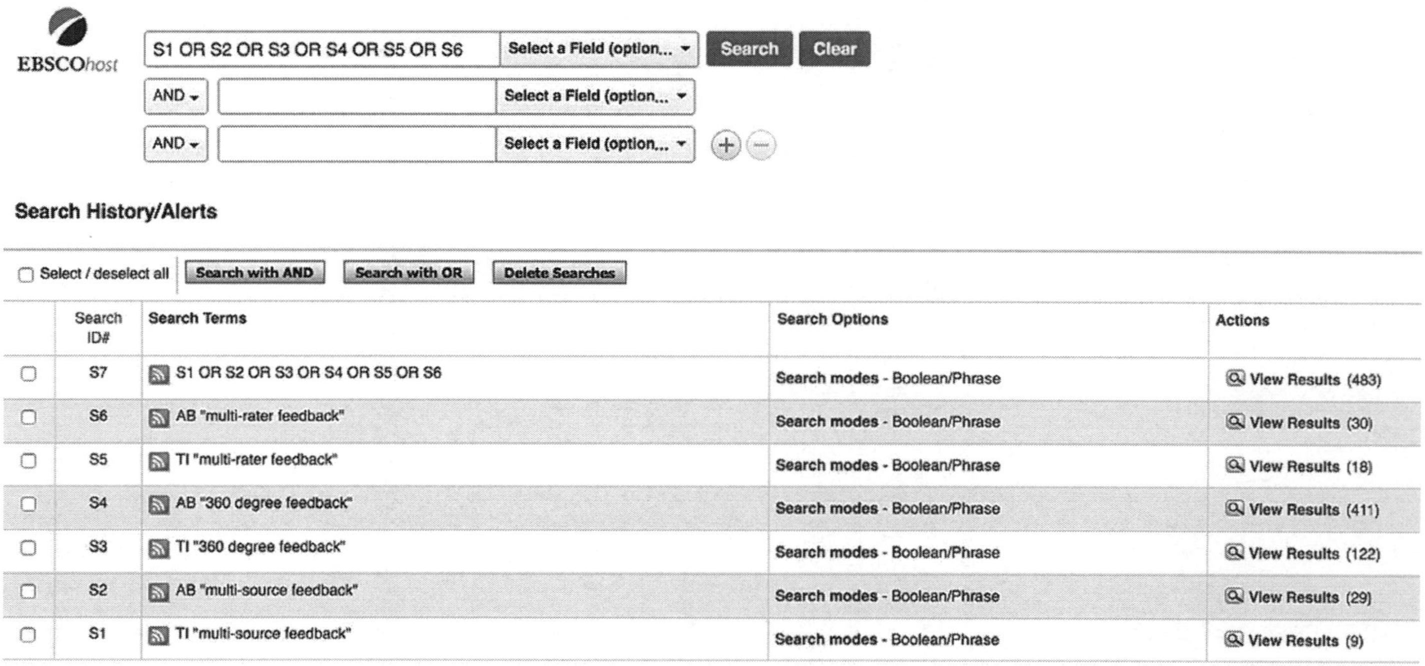
EBSCOhost
S1 OR S2 OR S3 OR S4 OR S5 OR S6
Select a Field (option...
Search
Clear
AND
Select a Field (option...
AND
Select a Field (option...
Search History/Alerts
Select / deselect all
Search with AND
Search with OR
Delete Searches

	Search ID#	Search Terms	Search Options	Actions
	S7	S1 OR S2 OR S3 OR S4 OR S5 OR S6	Search modes - Boolean/Phrase	View Results (483)
	S6	AB "multi-rater feedback"	Search modes - Boolean/Phrase	View Results (30)
	S5	TI "multi-rater feedback"	Search modes - Boolean/Phrase	View Results (18)
	S4	AB "360 degree feedback"	Search modes - Boolean/Phrase	View Results (411)
	S3	TI "360 degree feedback"	Search modes - Boolean/Phrase	View Results (122)
	S2	AB "multi-source feedback"	Search modes - Boolean/Phrase	View Results (29)
	S1	TI "multi-source feedback"	Search modes - Boolean/Phrase	View Results (9)

It is important that you thoroughly understand how to use the basic search features of a research database, such as the use of Boolean operators, truncation and the search history to combine search queries using AND or OR. You can find many tutorial videos are available explaining these features on YouTube. The best way, however, to improve your search skills is by learning through play: just try all the buttons, make lots of mistakes and have fun!

6.4 Pre-testing your search terms

After you have identified alternative terms and corresponding academic terms it is important to pretest your search terms: see which of the terms you have identified yield the most relevant results in the research databases you have selected. In general, a pretest in just one research database will already give you a good impression of which search terms yield the most relevant results (sensitivity) while minimizing the number of irrelevant results (specificity).

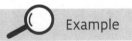 Example

In 2015, McKinsey & Company, a prestigious international consulting firm, published a research report entitled *Why Diversity Matters*, in which it claimed that companies with an ethnically diverse workforce outperformed other non-diverse companies. Based on this report the HR director of a Danish manufacturing company specializing in children's furniture considered setting up a project to increase the diversity of its workforce. Before making a decision, however, she first wanted to find out what was known in the scientific literature about the effect of ethnic diversity on workplace performance. After she had formulated her PICOC (P = manufacturing workers; I = ethnic diversity; C = no diversity; O = performance; C = Danish company specializing in the production of children's furniture) she decided that 'ethnic diversity' and 'performance' were the two most important PICOC terms. After a search on Google and Google Scholar she found several related terms, such as 'cultural diversity', 'demographic diversity', 'heterogeneity', 'minority', 'multiformity' and 'variation'. When she pretested her search terms in the research database ABI/INFORM Global she got the following results (Table 6.2):

Table 6.2

Search term	Results	Search term	Results
TI diversity	4,880	TI heterogeneity	2,268
AB diversity	21,334	TI (heterogen* AND work*)	131
TI (ethnic* AND divers*)	224	TI (heterogen* AND organization*)	29
AB (ethnic* AND divers*)	1,832	TI minority	2,386
TI (cultur* AND divers*)	458	TI (minorit* AND work*)	75
AB (cultur* AND divers*)	5,169	TI (minorit* AND organization*)	20
TI (demograph* AND divers*)	65	TI (multiformity AND work*)	0
AB (demograph* AND divers*)	1,303	TI (variation AND work*)	90

When she skimmed through the titles and the abstracts of the articles found, she noticed that a search with a combination of the terms 'divers*', 'ethnic*', 'culture*' and 'demograph*' in the title yielded the most relevant results, while other terms resulted in many articles that were irrelevant.

 Note

Pretesting is important not only for relevance, but also for spelling!

When it comes to spelling, even for native speakers English is a difficult language. For example, should we search for 'multisource feedback', 'multi-source feedback', or 'multi source feedback'? For example, the terms 'multi-source feedback' and 'multi source feedback' both yield 29 results in Business Source Elite, whereas the term 'multisource feedback' yields 73 (different) results. This means that you should always test whether a different spelling yields different results.

6.5 Searching for empirical studies: Systematic, transparent and reproducible

As you noticed we have dedicated quite some time to identifying the right search terms. We explained above why this was important: Garbage In, Garbage Out – good search terms result in good outputs, and unclear, ambiguous or incorrect search terms result in bad outputs. Whereas the phase of finding the right search terms is characterized by a trial-and-error approach and a rather associative and explorative search process, the search for empirical studies in a research database is highly systematic. In general, we typically follow these six steps:

1 Conduct a search with your (pretested) search terms and combine the outcome.

2 Filter the combined outcome for meta-analyses and/or systematic reviews.

3 Filter the combined outcome for high-quality primary studies.

4 If necessary: filter the combined outcome for low-quality primary studies.

5 If necessary: limit the number of results by adding a second or third PICOC term.

6 Screen the articles found for relevance.

Step 1: Enlarge the pie – conduct a search with your (pretested) search terms and combine the outcome with OR

Figure 6.3

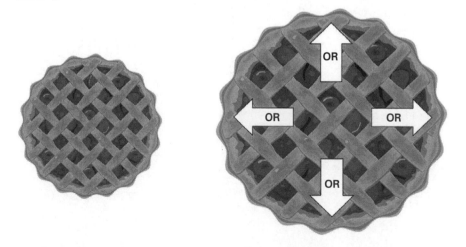

Figure 6.4

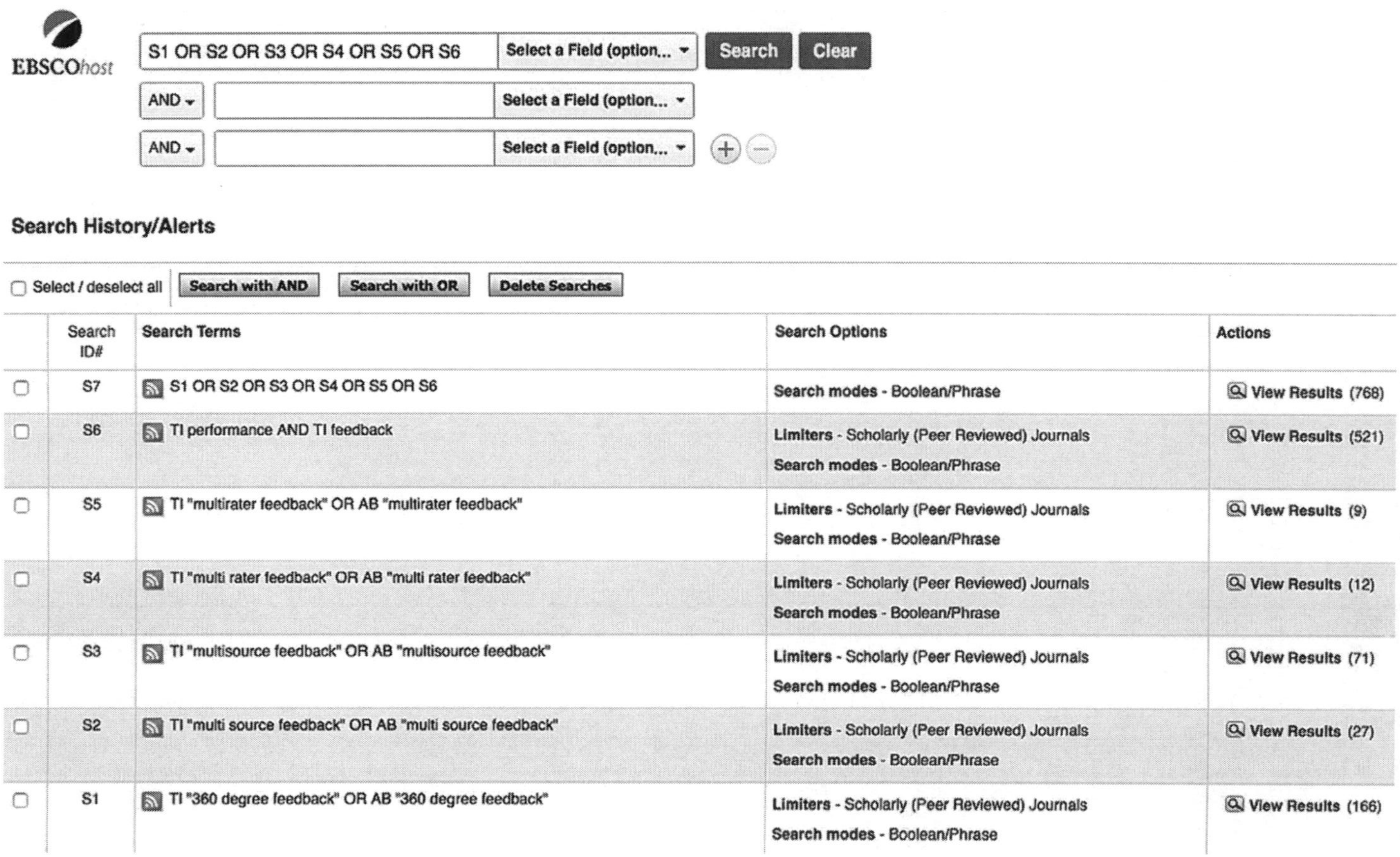

EBSCOhost

| S1 OR S2 OR S3 OR S4 OR S5 OR S6 | Select a Field (option... ▸ | Search | Clear |

AND ▸ | | Select a Field (option... ▸ |

AND ▸ | | Select a Field (option... ▸ |

⊕ ⊖

Search History/Alerts

☐ Select / deselect all | Search with AND | Search with OR | Delete Searches

	Search ID#	Search Terms	Search Options	Actions
☐	S7	🔊 S1 OR S2 OR S3 OR S4 OR S5 OR S6	Search modes - Boolean/Phrase	🔍 View Results (768)
☐	S6	🔊 TI performance AND TI feedback	Limiters - Scholarly (Peer Reviewed) Journals Search modes - Boolean/Phrase	🔍 View Results (521)
☐	S5	🔊 TI "multirater feedback" OR AB "multirater feedback"	Limiters - Scholarly (Peer Reviewed) Journals Search modes - Boolean/Phrase	🔍 View Results (9)
☐	S4	🔊 TI "multi rater feedback" OR AB "multi rater feedback"	Limiters - Scholarly (Peer Reviewed) Journals Search modes - Boolean/Phrase	🔍 View Results (12)
☐	S3	🔊 TI "multisource feedback" OR AB "multisource feedback"	Limiters - Scholarly (Peer Reviewed) Journals Search modes - Boolean/Phrase	🔍 View Results (71)
☐	S2	🔊 TI "multi source feedback" OR AB "multi source feedback"	Limiters - Scholarly (Peer Reviewed) Journals Search modes - Boolean/Phrase	🔍 View Results (27)
☐	S1	🔊 TI "360 degree feedback" OR AB "360 degree feedback"	Limiters - Scholarly (Peer Reviewed) Journals Search modes - Boolean/Phrase	🔍 View Results (166)

The first step is to 'enlarge the pie': Conduct a search with each of your (pretested, most relevant) search terms and combine the outcomes with the Boolean operator OR. This 'pie' will be the basis for the next steps of your search. In the screenshot on the previous page (Figure 6.4) you can see how we did this in the case of the example of the question regarding the effectiveness of 360-degree feedback. Note that we have conducted a search for both 'multi-source feedback' and 'multisource feedback' as we know from our pretest that this yields different (but relevant) results. The same counts for 'multi rater' and 'multirater'. Because we found that 'performance feedback' is an underlying construct, we have also conducted a search with the terms 'performance' and 'feedback' in the title. Finally, we have combined the six search queries with OR which resulted in a large 'pie' with 768 peer-reviewed papers.

Step 2: Filter for meta-analyses and/or systematic reviews

Figure 6.5

A **systematic review** or meta-analysis is a research paper in which the authors systematically searched for and summarized the findings of relevant studies on the same topic (see Chapter 5). In fact, systematic reviews or meta-analyses often provide the best available scientific evidence on a topic. Thus, if we find a systematic review or meta-analysis we can save ourselves a lot of time and effort. However, it is too time-consuming to read 768 abstracts

Figure 6.6

Search History/Alerts

	Search ID#	Search Terms	Search Options	Actions
Select / deselect all		Search with AND	Search with OR	Delete Searches
☐	S9	🔊 S7 AND S8	Search modes - Boolean/Phrase	🔍 View Results (6)
☐	S8	🔊 TI(meta-analy*) OR AB(meta-analy*) OR TI("systematic review") OR AB("systematic review")	Limiters - Scholarly (Peer Reviewed) Journals Search modes - Boolean/Phrase	🔍 View Results (6,720)
☐	S7	🔊 S1 OR S2 OR S3 OR S4 OR S5 OR S6	Search modes - Boolean/Phrase	🔍 View Results (768)

to find out whether an article concerns a meta-analysis or systematic review, so we have to find a clever way to filter them out. We therefore apply a methodological search filter. You can copy and paste the filter below directly in the search box of the database. Don't select a specific field (for example, title or subject term) in the drop-down list, as this will negatively affect your search.

Filter to identify meta-analyses and systematic reviews

TI(meta-analy*) OR AB(meta-analy*) OR TI("systematic review") OR AB("systematic review")

If we run a search with this filter and combine the outcome in the search history with our 'pie' of 768 papers by using AND we get 6 results (Figure 6.6).

Step 3: Filter for high-quality single studies

Figure 6.7

If you found one or more relevant meta-analyses, you may already have sufficient scientific evidence to answer your question. Unfortunately, for many topics, meta-analyses or systematic reviews are not available. In that case, your search will not yield any (or only irrelevant) articles, and you will have to look for high-quality primary studies – that is controlled and/or longitudinal

Figure 6.8

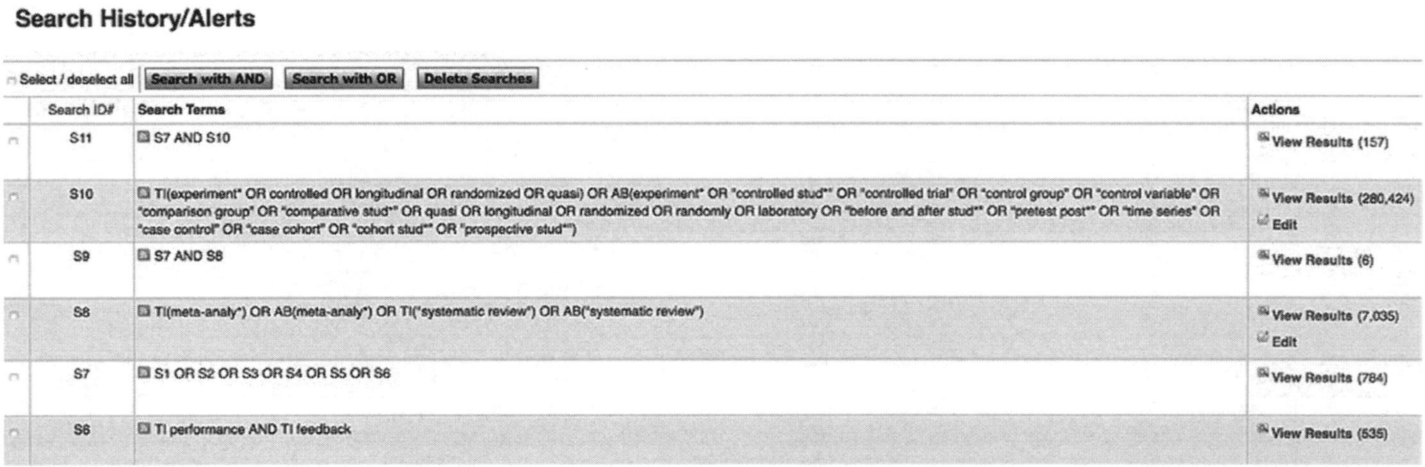

Search History/Alerts

Select / deselect all | Search with AND | Search with OR | Delete Searches

	Search ID#	Search Terms	Actions
	S11	S7 AND S10	View Results (157)
	S10	TI(experiment* OR controlled OR longitudinal OR randomized OR quasi) OR AB(experiment* OR "controlled stud*" OR "controlled trial" OR "control group" OR "control variable" OR "comparison group" OR "comparative stud*" OR quasi OR longitudinal OR randomized OR randomly OR laboratory OR "before and after stud*" OR "pretest post*" OR "time series" OR "case control" OR "case cohort" OR "cohort stud*" OR "prospective stud*")	View Results (280,424) Edit
	S9	S7 AND S8	View Results (6)
	S8	TI(meta-analy*) OR AB(meta-analy*) OR TI("systematic review") OR AB("systematic review")	View Results (7,035) Edit
	S7	S1 OR S2 OR S3 OR S4 OR S5 OR S6	View Results (784)
	S6	TI performance AND TI feedback	View Results (535)

studies (see Chapter 5). To find high-quality single studies, first, enlarge the pie: Conduct a search with your (pretested) search terms and combine the outcome with OR. This search query is probably still present in the search history. We then cut the pie by applying a second methodological search filter to find controlled and/or longitudinal studies (Figure 6.7). Again, you can copy the filter below and paste it directly into the search box of the database.

CEBMa filter to identify controlled and/or longitudinal studies

TI(experiment* OR controlled OR longitudinal OR randomized OR quasi) OR AB(experiment* OR "controlled stud*" OR "controlled trial" OR "control group" OR "control variable" OR "comparison group" OR "comparative stud*" OR quasi OR longitudinal OR randomized OR randomly OR laboratory OR "before and after stud*" OR "pretest post*" OR "time series" OR "case control" OR "case cohort" OR "cohort stud*" OR "prospective stud*")

Please keep in mind that the sensitivity (true positive rate) and specificity (true negative rate) of these filters are limited. As a consequence, your search results may still contain low-quality or theoretical studies while some high-quality studies may be missed. In the example below, we have applied this filter to our search for empirical studies on 360-degree feedback, you can see our search yielded 157 studies (Figure 6.8).

Step 4: Filter for low-quality single studies (if necessary)

Figure 6.9

For some topics, even controlled and/or longitudinal studies are not available. In that case, we are left with no other option than to search for low-quality studies. In the first example above (360-degree feedback) we could go through all the titles and abstracts of all articles we have retrieved with the combined search query (see Figure 6.8), but most of these articles may concern non-empirical studies such as essays and theoretical papers. For this reason, we conduct a final search query that selects only articles that mention the word 'study' in the abstract. This method, however, is not very reliable and you should only use it when no (or only a limited number of) meta-analyses or high-quality studies are available.

Step 5: Limiting your search result by adding extra PICOC terms

When you search for meta-analyses and/or systematic reviews often one PICOC term (with or without its alternative and related terms) may suffice to yield relevant studies. The same may count for controlled and/or longitudinal studies. When your intervention or topic of interest concerns a construct that is well defined (for example, '360-degree feedback' or 'virtual team'), then your search often yields a manageable number of meta-analyses or high-quality studies. In those cases, it doesn't make sense to limit the results by adding another PICOC term, as you will most probably end up with too few (or even zero) studies. In some cases, however, the number of results is very large, and reading all the titles and abstracts to see whether the study is relevant is just too

Figure 6.10

time-consuming. For example, when we searched for controlled and/or longitudinal studies on virtual teams we found more than 80 results. When we search for low-quality studies the outcome is often much higher, sometimes more than 1,000. In those cases, we should add a second PICOC term (usually the O – outcome, or the P – population). By doing this we not only limit the number of results, but we also increase the relevance of the studies found.

Example

A hospital administrator wants to know what is known in the research literature about the effect of 360-degree feedback on the performance of physicians. She has defined the following PICOC:

P: physicians
I: 360-degree feedback
C: no feedback
O: performance
C: large university hospital in the United States

She conducts a quick search with the terms "360-degree feedback" and "multisource feedback" in the title and the abstract. When she filters the combined outcome for meta-analyses and/or systematic reviews she finds

Figure 6.11

Search History/Alerts

Select / deselect all | Search with AND | Search with OR | Delete Searches

	Search ID#	Search Terms	Search Options	Actions
○	S12	S3 AND S11	Search modes - Boolean/Phrase	View Results (6)
○	S11	S8 OR S9 OR S10	Search modes - Boolean/Phrase	View Results (93,221)
○	S10	TI clinic* OR AB clinic*	Limiters - Scholarly (Peer Reviewed) Journals Search modes - Boolean/Phrase	View Results (29,921)
○	S9	TI hospital* OR AB hospital*	Limiters - Scholarly (Peer Reviewed) Journals Search modes - Boolean/Phrase	View Results (31,553)
○	S8	TI healthcare OR TI "health care" OR AB healthcare OR AB "health care"	Limiters - Scholarly (Peer Reviewed) Journals Search modes - Boolean/Phrase	View Results (46,488)
○	S7	S3 AND S6	Search modes - Boolean/Phrase	View Results (18)
○	S6	TI(experiment* OR controlled OR longitudinal OR randomized OR quasi) OR AB(experiment* OR "controlled stud*" OR "controlled trial" OR "control group" OR "control variable" OR "comparison group" OR "comparative stud*" OR quasi OR longitudinal OR randomized OR randomly OR laboratory OR "before and after stud*" OR "pretest post*" OR "time series" OR "case control" OR "case cohort" OR "cohort stud*" OR "prospective stud*")	Search modes - Boolean/Phrase	View Results (363,609)
○	S5	S3 AND S4	Search modes - Boolean/Phrase	View Results (4)
○	S4	TI(meta-analy*) OR AB(meta-analy*) OR TI("systematic review") OR AB("systematic review")	Search modes - Boolean/Phrase	View Results (7,429)
○	S3	S1 OR S2	Search modes - Boolean/Phrase	View Results (230)
○	S2	TI "multisource feedback" OR AB "multisource feedback"	Limiters - Scholarly (Peer Reviewed) Journals Search modes - Boolean/Phrase	View Results (71)
○	S1	TI "360 degree feedback" OR AB "360 degree feedback"	Limiters - Scholarly (Peer Reviewed) Journals Search modes - Boolean/Phrase	View Results (166)

four studies, of which only one seems relevant. A search for controlled and/ or longitudinal studies yields 16 results, of which four seem relevant. None of the studies, however, concern physicians or hospitals. She, therefore, decides to add a second PICOC term: "hospital*". Because this term may be too narrow she decides to include the related terms "healthcare" and "clinic*". When she runs the searches and combines the outcome with AND she gets six results of which three seem relevant.

Tip

Limiting your search result by limiting the date range

Another way to limit the number of results is by limiting the date range. You can limit the range by adjusting the date slider. After executing your search, the date slider feature is under 'Limit To' to the left of the result list. To set a start date for your results, drag the left slider bar towards the middle, and the results are refreshed. To set an end date, drag the right slider bar towards the middle, and the result list is refreshed. You can return to your original date range by clicking the x icon in the Current Search box to remove the date range limiter.

Step 6: Screening the articles found for relevance

In general, a search will yield many studies, some of which will not be relevant to your question and PICOC. The next step is hence to screen the articles to check whether they are relevant. Screening for relevance is usually a two-stage process. First, compare each title and abstract against your question and PICOC. Unfortunately, not all abstracts will contain the information you need to determine whether the article is relevant. In that case, you need to retrieve the full text and skim through it.

As mentioned earlier, your PICOC will help you to determine whether the findings of a study will be generalizable and applicable to your professional context. Keep in mind though that sometimes what works in one narrowly defined setting might not work in another, but that some psychological principles are generalizable to all human beings. For example, what if you would like to know whether 360-degree feedback will be effective as a tool for improving the task performance of physicians in a Dutch university hospital, and the outcome of your search yields only high-quality studies in which the effect was examined on the performance of US lawyers and German teachers? Would you consider the outcome of these studies, given your question and PICOC, to be relevant? Unfortunately, there are no general guidelines to help you to evaluate the **generalizability** of research findings, so this is where your professional judgement comes in.

Retrieving full-text articles

When you run a search query, the database will provide a list with results and indicate whether the full text is available. In the example below (Figure 6.12) the full text can be retrieved by clicking the little icon and link 'PDF Full Text' at the bottom of the description. When you access a database through a university network, the full text can often be retrieved by clicking a special icon. In the example below the databases were accessed through the network of New York University and, as a result, an NYU icon is displayed.

In some cases, however, the full-text article is not available. Full-text journal subscriptions are very expensive – sometimes US $10,000 a year for a single journal – and universities buy subscriptions based on the number of likely users. For this reason, small educational institutions provide access to only a limited number of journals. When the full text is not available, you can first try finding a copy through Google Scholar, as many researchers make the full text of their article available through their personal or university's web page. In addition, some full-text articles are available through the websites of professional bodies, research groups or

Figure 6.12

1. The influence of cultural context on the relationship between gender diversity and team performance: a meta-analysis.

Academic Journal

By: Schneid, Matthias; Isidor, Rodrigo; Li, Chengguang; Kabst, Rüdiger. International Journal of Human Resource Management. Mar2015, Vol. 26 Issue 6, p733-756. 24p. 1 Diagram, 6 Charts. DOI: 10.1080/09585192.2014.957712.

Subjects: Personnel management research; Task performance; Human Resources Consulting Services; Administration of Human Resource Programs (except Education, Public Health, and Veterans' Affairs Programs); **Diversity** in the workplace -- United States; Equality research; Collectivism (Social psychology); Social psychology

PDF Full Text (189KB)   NYU   Find Full Text

non-profit organizations such as CEBMa. If the full text of an article is freely available somewhere on the internet, Google Scholar will most probably find it.

If the full text of an article is not available through the internet, your only option is to go to a large library. There you can use the library's computers to search for the desired article and print it, download it onto a flash drive, or e-mail it to yourself. In some cases, if you simply become a member of the library, you can even access some journals and databases online from home.

6.6 Finally, some tips

If you find no (or limited) results, try searching for terms in the abstract (instead of only the title). In addition, see if a search with a broader term will yield more results. For example, if you conduct a search for 'collaboration' and 'multi-disciplinary teams', try also the broader term 'teams'.

- Split up word combinations. Instead of searching with the term "performance feedback" (between quotation marks), search for 'performance' AND 'feedback'. In ABI/INFORM Global the first option yields 125 results, whereas the second option yields 351 results. Always try to imagine how authors may have used the search terms in the title or the abstract. For example, if you only search for the term 'cultural diversity' in the title, you would miss the meta-analysis 'Unravelling the effects of cultural and gender diversity in teams'.

- Don't use too many search terms. In the example above a search for articles with the terms 'cultur* OR diversity AND performance' in the title would also leave out the meta-analysis, because the term 'performance' is not mentioned in the title. Keep in mind that, in general, meta-analyses and systematic reviews do not mention all outcome measures in the title or abstract, so when your search yields no (or limited) results, consider leaving out a search term.

- When there are no (relevant) meta-analyses or systematic reviews, try to search for articles with the word 'review' in the title. This will usually yield several review studies that don't meet the quality criteria of true systematic reviews or meta-analyses, but they can nevertheless be useful.

- Do not panic when your search yields a large number of studies. Skimming through, say, 80 to 100 titles or abstracts can be done pretty quickly. In addition, the chances are that most of the studies will not be relevant to your question, so your final selection will most probably be much smaller.

- If your search yields too many studies, you can limit the number of studies by adding another PICOC term. An alternative would be to limit the time frame of your search (for example, looking only for studies that were published in the past 10 years).

- Document your search process. As explained in the introduction, it is important that your search is systematic, transparent and verifiable, so that other people can check or reproduce your search. For this reason, you should clearly document the search process, preferably in the form of a table that shows the search terms used, how search terms were combined, and how many studies were found at every step. In addition, the table should specify the date on which the search was conducted and the search filters that were applied. In most cases, however, it suffices to provide a screenshot of your search history, as in the examples above.

- Keep in mind that searching for relevant empirical studies is an iterative process. Although this chapter presents the search process as highly systematic and linear, in practice you will most probably jump back and forth between the steps, especially when your initial search yields unsatisfactory results.

- Finally, let the evidence find you. Other than Google and Google Scholar, research databases have several features that make the life of an evidence-based practitioner much easier. For example, for topics that are important to you, you can set up a 'search alert'. A search alert sends you an e-mail when new research that fits your search criteria becomes available. To make use of this service you need to set up a personal account (in some databases it's called Research Account or My Research) by establishing a username and password – usually there is no fee involved. To set up a search alert, execute your search, then click on 'Create Alert', then simply follow the instructions on the screen.

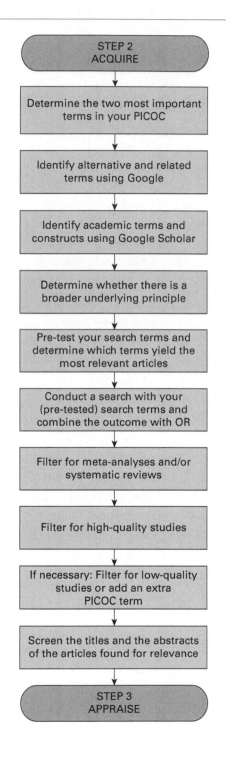

APPRAISE: 07
Evidence from the scientific literature

> To be scientifically literate is to empower yourself to know when someone else is full of shit.
>
> NEIL DEGRASSE TYSON

In 2001, Jim Collins, a former faculty member at Stanford University's Business School, published *Good to Great*.[1] In this book, Collins claims to reveal the principles behind company growth, financial performance and shareholder value. The book focuses on 11 companies that were just 'good', and then transformed themselves into 'great' performing companies – where 'great' is defined as a sustained period of 15 years over which the cumulative total stock return dramatically outperformed the general market and its competitors. It took Collins five years to establish how 'good' companies became 'great'. In this period, he and his team of researchers reviewed annual reports, company records and financial analyses for each company, totalling 980 combined years of data; they conducted 84 interviews with senior managers and board members, and they finally scrutinized the personal and professional records of 56 CEOs.

Collins' research indicated that every 'great' company had at the helm *an ambitious leader combining personal humility with professional will* – referred to by Collins as 'level 5 leadership'. In addition, his research found seven principles that make 'great' companies different from 'good' or 'average' ones. All principles are described in detail in his book, in which he presents them as a framework for success.

The book became a bestseller, selling 4 million copies and going far beyond the traditional audience of business books. Because the principles of *Good to Great* were based on research, they were considered highly trustworthy, and a large number of managers, business leaders, executives, policymakers, hospital administrators and CEOs used the framework as a blueprint for their own organization.

But over time what happened with the companies praised in *Good to Great*? You might not be surprised to hear that quite a few have since fallen from grace. In fact, within a few years after the book's publication, all the 'great' companies fell into decline. Moreover, some of them even filed for bankruptcy, and one company, Fannie Mae, was bailed out by the US government. Pointedly, if you had bought Fannie Mae stock around the time that *Good to Great* was published, you would have lost over 80 per cent of your initial investment.

So, what can we learn from this? The obvious answer might be that there is little value in business books that claim to contain a recipe for dramatic success. The less obvious answer is that, when meticulously collecting and analysing external evidence, even well-trained and experienced people such as a Stanford professor and his team can come to flawed conclusions if they don't follow the methodological rules of science. This chapter will help you to learn how to critically appraise the trustworthiness of external evidence such as journal articles, business books, newspaper articles or textbooks based on scientific research.

7.1 Critical appraisal: Three preliminary questions

Before we discuss the two elements that determine a study's trustworthiness – methodological appropriateness and methodological quality – we first need to ask three questions. Only when we can answer these questions positively does it make sense to go through the process of critical appraisal.

Question 1: Are the findings of the study of practical relevance?

Academics are scientific practitioners, not management practitioners. In fact, it is often suggested that academics and management practitioners live in very separate worlds and are interested in different aspects of management and organizations. As a result, the research produced by academics is often of limited relevance to the daily practice of managers. This is especially the case for quantitative studies. As we explained in Chapter 5, the fact that a study's outcome is statistically significant has limited meaning, because it doesn't tell us whether that outcome is of practical relevance. To determine practical relevance, one of the things we need to consider is the *effect size*. An **effect size** is a *standardized* measure of the magnitude (impact) of the effect. The fact that the measure is 'standardized' means that we can compare effects or differences across different studies, regardless of the variables, measurements or statistical tests that were used.[2] For example, we could compare an effect size based on customer satisfaction in study A to an effect size based on number of customer complaints in study B.

There are many different measures of effect sizes, but most effect sizes can be grouped into one of two 'families': the difference between groups (also known as the *d* family) and measures of association (also known as the *r* family).[3] To determine the magnitude of an effect found in a study, you can apply **Cohen's rules of thumb** (see below).[4] According to Cohen, a 'small' effect is one that is only visible through careful examination. A 'medium' effect, however, is one that is 'visible to the naked eye of the careful observer'. Finally, a 'large' effect is one that anybody can easily see because it is substantial. Table 7.1 provides an overview of how this rule of thumb applies to different measures of effect sizes.

Note, however, that Cohen's rules of thumb were meant to be exactly that – 'rules of thumb' – and are for many reasons arbitrary.[5] For example, a *d* of 0.20 may be regarded as 'small' when the outcome concerns job satisfaction but 'large' when the outcome concerns fatal medical errors. When assessing impact, we need to relate the effect size directly to the outcome measured and its relevance, importance and meaning in each specific context.

Effect sizes would be typically provided in the Results section of a research paper and/or a separate table. Don't let yourself be taken in by the huge amount of numbers and symbols – just scan through the text and see if you can identify one of the effect sizes listed in the table below. In addition,

Table 7.1

Effect size	Small	Medium	Large
Standardized mean difference: d, Δ, g	≤ .20	.50	≥ .80
ANOVA: $\eta2$, $\omega2$	≤ .01	.06	≥ .14
Chi-square: $\omega2$	≤ .10	.30	≥ .50
Correlation: r, ρ	≤ .10	.30	≥ .50
Correlation: r2	≤ .01	.09	≥ .25
Simple regression: β	≤ .10	.30	≥ .50
Multiple regression: β	≤ .20	.50	≥ .80
Multiple regression: R2	≤ .02	.13	≥ .26

Table 7.2 *Specific goals: Effect sizes and moderators*

Variable	k	d	SE	95%CI Low	95%CI High
Overall effect	49	0.56	0.095	0.37	0.75
Goal difficulty					
Easy (1)	8	0.23	0.111	0.01	0.45
Moderate (2)	15	0.53	0.145	0.25	0.81
Difficult (3)	23	0.80	0.180	0.45	1.15
Task complexity					
Low (1-2.75)	22	0.50	0.092	0.32	0.68
Moderate (3-4.75)	21	0.52	0.163	0.20	0.84
High (5-7)	6	0.94	0.440	0.08	1.80

Note Findings (k = 49) are based on 739 groups, consisting of 2,954 individuals. k = number of effect sizes; CI = confidence interval.

if you have two studies that use different effect sizes, you can use the table to make a comparison. For example, if the first study finds a difference of $d = 0.20$ between the job satisfaction of two groups, and the second study has a difference of $\eta2 = 0.01$, you can conclude that the differences found in both studies are small. The same counts for effect sizes within a study. Take, for example, Table 7.2.

In the table, you can see that the overall effect of goal setting on performance is $d = 0.56$, which we consider a medium effect. When you look under 'Goal difficulty', however, you can see that easy goals have a small effect ($d = 0.23$), whereas difficult goals have a large effect ($d = 0.80$). Both effects are statistically significant, but only the impact of difficult goals is practically relevant. Therefore, we can conclude that difficult goals have a large effect on performance.

Most quantitative studies include a so-called correlation matrix, which is an overview of the correlation coefficients between all of the variables measured in a study. An example is provided in Table 7.3. As you can see, in this study a significant correlation was found between sales training A, sales training B, sales training C and sales performance (-0.07, 0.62 and 0.11 respectively), but only the effect of sales training B is of practical relevance.

Obviously, in newspapers, business books and popular magazines, effect sizes are not normally provided, which makes them an inappropriate source of scientific evidence. However, you may be surprised to learn that many

Table 7.3 Correlation matrix for study variables

No	Variable	1	2	3	4	5	6	7	8	9	10
1	gender	1									
2	age	−0.15*	1								
3	education	−0.32*	−0.02	1							
4	firm size	0.03*	0.20*	0.21	1						
5	firm age	0.07	0.02	0.19	0.34	1					
6	sales training A	−0.02	0.12	0.02	0.02	0.02	1				
7	sales training B	0.12	0.09*	0.04*	0.03	0.05	0.03	1			
8	sales training C	0.09	0.48	0.01	0.22	−0.06	0.05*	0.16	1		
9	experience	0.07	0.39	0.24	0.27	−0.05	0.11*	0.05	0.32	1	
10	sales performance	0.06	0.01	0.21	0.19	−0.07	−0.07*	0.62*	0.11*	0.13	1

Note *Significant at 0.05 level

scientific papers published in academic journals also fail to report effect sizes. If this is the case, and no other information is provided regarding the magnitude of the effect or difference found, your conclusion must be that the study provides insufficient information to determine whether it might be relevant for practice.

Question 2: How precise are the findings?

Researchers are never able to include all the elements that may be relevant to the outcome of interest in their study. For example, sometimes the population is too large (for example, surveying all US citizens will cost too much time and effort) or doesn't yet exist (for example, in the case of a new educational method we are interested in the population of *future* students). In those cases, researchers need to rely on a sample – a smaller group that is representative of the whole population. Effect sizes, however, will differ across samples, meaning that they are only an *estimate* of the 'true' effect size. The same counts for other parameters, such as a mean, a percentage or proportion. So, when an effect size is reported, we also want to know how *precise* the effect is. We can determine the precision of the effect size (or any other point estimate) by looking at the **confidence interval**. A confidence interval provides the upper and lower boundaries between which we expect – usually with a 95 per cent certainty – the true value to fall. A confidence interval is stated as *95% CI*. If the 95% CI is fairly narrow, then the estimated effect size is a more precise reflection of the 'true' effect size. A 95% CI is considered *too wide* if the decision you would make based on the value of the lower boundary of the interval would be different from the decision you would make based on the value of the upper one.

When you look at Table 7.2 you can see that the estimated overall effect of goal setting is $d = 0.56$, and that the 95% CI is between 0.37 and 0.75, meaning that we are 95 per cent certain that the true effect size falls somewhere between these two values. This can be considered sufficiently precise. When we look at the effect of easy goals ($d = 0.23$), however, we can see that the 95% CI is between 0.01 (which suggests no or only a negligible effect) and 0.45 (which suggests a medium effect). We consider this confidence interval to be rather wide, because it is less likely that you will decide to implement when the effect is close to zero than when the effect size is near 0.45.

Question 3: How were the findings measured?

The trustworthiness of a study is first and foremost determined by the way in which the outcome and other variables are measured. When critically appraising a study, we start by asking, 'How was the outcome measured and is that a reliable way of measuring?' In general, the measurement of direct/objective variables (for example, production errors, staff turnover rate) is more likely to be valid and reliable than that of self-reported/subjective variables (for example, trust, employee engagement or organizational culture).[6] In addition, when a study makes use of a questionnaire, you should always check if the questionnaire has been validated or used in previous studies. In most studies, you can find this information in the 'Method' section, usually under 'Measurements' or 'Tools'.

 Note

If the outcome of a study is not relevant to practice, lacks precision, or is measured in a flawed or highly subjective way, critical appraisal of its trustworthiness is often pointless.

7.2 Critical appraisal: Methodological appropriateness

When we find a study that appears to answer our question, we need to know how trustworthy that answer is. How confident can we be that the findings uncovered in the study are valid and reliable? Alternatively, what is the chance that alternative explanations – also known as confounders, as we explored in Chapter 5 – for the observed effect are possible? In other words, to what extent should we trust the findings of a study? As a rule, a study's trustworthiness is largely determined by its *methodological appropriateness*. A study's appropriateness is high when its design reflects the best way to answer our question.

Types of research questions

In the domain of management there are different types of research questions. These questions can be classified in different ways, but for practitioners the distinction between cause-and-effect and non-effect questions is perhaps the most relevant:

Cause-and-effect questions

Cause-and-effect questions concern the causal relationship between an action or intervention and an outcome. Examples are:

- Does A have an effect/impact on B?
- Does A work?
- Does A work better than B?

Non-effect questions

Non-effect questions concern aspects other than cause and effect, such as attitude, frequency or procedure. Examples are:

- How often does A occur?
- How many people prefer A over B?
- Is there a difference between A and B?
- How do people feel about A?
- Why are people dissatisfied with A?

7.3 Methodological appropriateness: Cause-and-effect studies

Questions about cause and effect can be difficult to answer. As we will explain in this section, controlling the independent variable (cause) and separating it in time from the dependent variable (effect) can be very difficult. In addition, many confounding factors may affect the outcome. This means that if we find a study that appears to answer a cause-and-effect question, we need to make sure that the results of the study are not affected by confounders, alternative factors that might account for the observed effect. In the realm of science how well a research design addresses potential confounders is referred to as **internal validity**. Internal validity indicates the extent to which the results of a study rule out or control for confounding factors or bias and is thus a comment on the degree to which alternative explanations for the outcome found are possible. In the example of the Hawthorne study, which we used in Chapter 5, confounding factors affected the outcome. This means that the internal validity of the Hawthorne study and thus the trustworthiness of its findings are both low. As we will see in the next section, internal validity is a great concern for cause-and-effect questions.

About cause and effect

Many claims, assumptions and hypotheses in management and leadership are about cause and effect. In fact, cause-and-effect relationships are usually of the greatest interest and relevance to management as much management is about making decisions on the basis that it is likely to have an effect on the organization or people within it. Some practical examples include:

- Participative decision-making (A) will lead to higher job satisfaction among our employees (B).
- The Balanced Scorecard (A) is an effective tool to implement our organization's strategy (B).
- Implementing activity-based costing (A) will lead to better financial control of our organization (B).
- If we introduce virtual teams (A), the organization's performance will improve (B).

How can we judge the extent to which these claims are likely to be true? Put differently, how sure can we be that it is the cause (A) that leads to the effect or outcome (B), rather than some confounder (C)? Or will the outcome simply be due to the placebo effect? You probably won't be surprised to learn that this question has preoccupied people since ancient Greece. In fact, it wasn't until the 18th century that the Scottish philosopher David Hume came up with an answer – one that is still used in modern science today. Hume suggested that we should first determine which characteristics a relationship (between A and B) must have before we can call it 'causal'. These characteristics were adapted 200 years later by Paul Lazarsfeld, who described the three criteria for a causal relationship.[7]

The three criteria for causation

1 Covariation: The two variables A and B are empirically correlated with one another.

2 Temporality: If variable A is the cause and variable B the effect, then A must occur before B.

3 No plausible alternative explanations: The observed empirical correlation between A and B cannot be explained as a result of a third variable that causes both A and B.

Criterion 1: Covariation

Before researchers can demonstrate that there is a causal relationship, they first must show that there is *some* relationship. This relationship is referred to as **covariation**: when the value of one variable changes, the value of the other one will alter as well. This change may be large or small, or even negative (for example, an increase in one variable leads to a decrease in the other), but there must nevertheless be an empirical (observable, measurable) relationship between the two. Covariation is expressed through a simple metric: a correlation coefficient – a numerical index that reflects the strength of the relationship between two variables.[8] The value of this coefficient ranges between -1 and +1. As you can see in Figure 7.1, when the correlation coefficient is high, the points in the figure are closely aligned, indicating covariation. Conversely, when the correlation coefficient is low, the points in the figure are dispersed, indicating limited covariation. There are different types of correlation coefficients, depending on the type of variables that are measured, but they can all be considered an effect size: a *standardized* measure of the *strength* of the relationship. Thus, a correlation of $r = 0.60$ is stronger than a correlation of $r = 0.30$.

Figure 7.1

| Strong positive correlation $r = +1$ | Moderate positive correlation $r = +0.75$ | No correlation | Strong negative correlation $r = -1$ | Moderate negative correlation $r = -0.6$ | Curvilinear relationship |

You have probably heard many times before, however, that correlation is not causation. Therefore, when a study describes a correlation between two variables, it only means that they were able to demonstrate 'some' relationship. In fact, correlation doesn't even mean that the two variables are directly related. As we have seen in the example with the sales of ice cream and the number of children drowning (Chapter 5), these two variables closely covary. Moreover, if you were to calculate a correlation coefficient, you would find a strong correlation between the two. It would not matter, either, how many times you measured this relationship: it would always be there. We can learn from this example that the mere fact that two variables correlate does not mean that there is a causal relation, even when the correlation is strong and consistent. In fact, when we measure only whether two variables covary, we can find the most exotic and bizarre relationships. For example, in Figure 7.2 you can see that eating cheese highly correlates with the number of people who died by becoming tangled in their bedsheets![9]

Nevertheless, covariation is the first criterion for an assumed cause-and-effect relationship. This means that – if a correlation or effect is found – our next question should be: How was the effect measured (and is that a reliable way to measure it)? This also means that if no correlation or effect is found, we can safely conclude that a cause-and-effect relationship is not likely.[10]

Criterion 2: Temporality

When there is a correlation or effect, we then must demonstrate that the cause (A) happened before the effect (B). After all, it could also be the other way around: B causes A. For example, research has demonstrated that

Figure 7.2

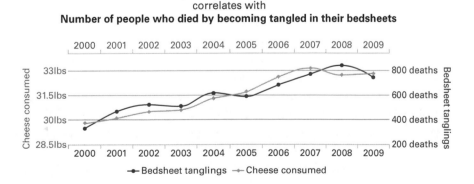

married people are, on average, happier than single people.[11] This suggests that getting married makes you happy. But maybe it is the other way around: if you are a grumpy, unhappy person, you are less likely to get married. For this reason, we need to make sure the effect was not already present before the cause. This means we need a so-called '**baseline**' measurement: a calculation of the variables of interest at the beginning of a study that are compared to later measurements to judge the outcome. The baseline measure is usually referred to as the 'before' measurement, whereas the one taken at the outcome is referred to as the 'after' measurement.

In athletics, for example, a baseline is essential. Without being sure that all athletes in a running event start at the same time, we can't be certain that the winner was indeed the fastest. But a baseline is also essential in studies examining a cause-and-effect relationship between two variables. Consider the following example. A study has demonstrated that youngsters who smoke tend to have better lung capacity than youngsters who don't smoke. You may wonder how that can be. After all, we know that smoking is very damaging to our health, especially our lungs, so how is it possible that young smokers tend to have better lung capacity? Could it be that they compensate their unhealthy habit with sports and other physical activities? What if we tell you that this study did not have a 'before' measure? This means that we can't rule out that the outcome (bad lung function) may have been already present before the cause (smoking). This makes the explanation for this bizarre outcome rather simple: youngsters with a serious lung condition such as asthma are less likely to start smoking than healthy youngsters, so there is an over-representation of youngsters with poor lung function among non-smokers. The lesson here is obvious: When we don't know whether subjects (groups or individuals) are comparable at baseline, we can't say with certainty that there was a cause-and-effect relationship.

Criterion 3: No plausible alternative explanation

Once researchers have demonstrated that the assumed cause (independent variable) and effect (dependent variable) covary and that the effect does not precede the cause in time, they have to rule out plausible alternative explanations. One of the ways to do that is through a study's research design, the 'blueprint' of a study that describes its steps, methods and techniques used to collect, measure and analyse data. We already learned that in order to demonstrate causality a study needs to include a before and after measurement, but to rule out other explanations for the effect found researchers need to include two additional components into the research design: a control group and **random assignment**.

Control group

In a 'controlled' study, one group (sometimes referred to as an 'intervention', 'treatment' or 'experimental' group) that is exposed to a condition or situation expected to have an effect (the assumed cause) is compared with another group (known as the 'control' or 'comparison' group) that is not. Thus researchers expose just one group to the variable they expect to have an effect and then compare that group to another which is not exposed to help rule out alternative explanations. In addition, the control group can serve as a **benchmark** for comparison against the intervention group. Imagine that researchers want to know whether a new fertilizer makes potted plants grow faster. They make two groups. One group of plants receives the fertilizer (the intervention group) and one group does not (the control group). If they make sure that the lighting, water supply, size of the pot and all other factors are held constant for every plant in both groups – and thus the only thing that differs between the two groups is the fertilizer given to the plants – only then can the researchers be certain that the new fertilizer causes the difference in growth.

Random assignment

Even when researchers use a control group, they still can't be 100 per cent certain that there were no (unknown) confounders that affected the outcome. For example, in the case above, factors such as lighting, water supply and size of the pot were equal in both groups. But what if the plants in the control group were obtained from a different grower than the ones in the experimental group? Or what if the plants in the control group were in the left-hand side of the greenhouse and those in the experimental group were on the right? The researchers can't rule out that the plants might be different in terms of nutritional benefits, DNA or factors of which they are unaware. For this reason, they must use random assignment when creating an intervention and control group.

Random assignment is a method used to create different groups that include subjects (organizations, units, teams or individual employees) with similar characteristics, so that the groups are similar at the start of the study. The method involves assigning subjects to different groups 'at random' (by chance, like the flip of a coin), so that each subject has equal chance of being assigned to each group, and any possible distorting factor is equally spread over both groups. Thus, the researchers can more confidently attribute any differences between the groups measured at the end of the study to the variable that is expected to have an effect (the assumed cause).

Note

Random assignment is not the same as random sampling!

Random sampling refers to selecting subjects in such a way that they represent a larger population, whereas random assignment concerns assigning subjects to a control group and experimental group in such a way that they are similar at the start of the study. Put differently, **random selection** ensures high representativeness, whereas random assignment ensures high internal validity. This means that if a study uses the term 'random' or 'randomized', you should always determine whether this concerns random selection (as in a survey) or random assignment (as in a controlled study).

The gold standard

Based on the elements described above, we can now determine the 'best' – that is, the most appropriate – study to answer a cause-and-effect question with the lowest chance of confounders. Let's consider the example of a researcher who wants to examine the effect of a stress-reduction programme using on-site chair massage therapy. The first criterion of causality is demonstrating that the cause and effect correlate using valid and reliable measurements. The researcher has already determined that the most valid and reliable way to measure stress reduction would be to measure the cortisol levels (a stress hormone) in the saliva of employees. The second criterion of causality, temporality, states that he or she must demonstrate that the cause (chair massage therapy) preceded the effect (stress reduction). The researcher therefore measures the employees' cortisol level both before and after the chair massage therapy.[12] The third criterion concerns ruling out plausible alternative explanations for the effect found, so he or she randomly assigns employees to a control or an intervention group. The researcher first takes a representative sample of the employees and then randomly assigns them to the two groups by flipping a coin. Then the researcher needs to determine what the control group should do to create a valid and reliable benchmark: Continue working, take a break, or 'fake' massage therapy? After some discussion, he or she decides that continuing working is an unfair comparison and a fake massage therapy is hard to realize, so the control group will take a break during which they do something to relax. This means that the research design would be as depicted in Figure 7.3. This design is known as a randomized controlled study or randomized controlled trial (RCT), the gold standard to answer cause-and-effect questions.

It should be noted, however, that randomized controlled trials are sometimes conducted in an artificial (lab-type) setting – with students carrying out prescribed work tasks – which may restrict their generalizability. Non-randomized trials in a field setting – with employees carrying out their normal tasks within an organizational setting – on the other hand, have a lower level of trustworthiness, but can still be informative for management practice.

 Note

Don't worry about statistics!

Cause and effect can be established only through the proper research method: valid and reliable measurement methods; a before and after measurement; a control group; and random assignment. No amount of statistical hand waving can turn correlations into conclusions about causation!

7.4 Methodological appropriateness: Non-effect studies

Non-effect questions and cause-and-effect questions are answered in different ways. For example, the question 'How many hospitals in Denmark have applied Lean Management to their surgery department for outpatients?' is best answered by taking a random, representative sample of all Danish hospitals and asking them by phone, e-mail or letter (ie survey research) whether they have applied Lean Management. The same is true of questions regarding nurses' feelings towards the use of Lean Management in their hospitals. In that case, focus-group research could be a good choice. The question of whether Lean Management has a positive effect on the performance of surgical teams, however, can't be answered with a survey or a focus group, because this question is about cause-and-effect and therefore needs – as a minimum – a control group, and a before and after measurement.

Figure 7.3

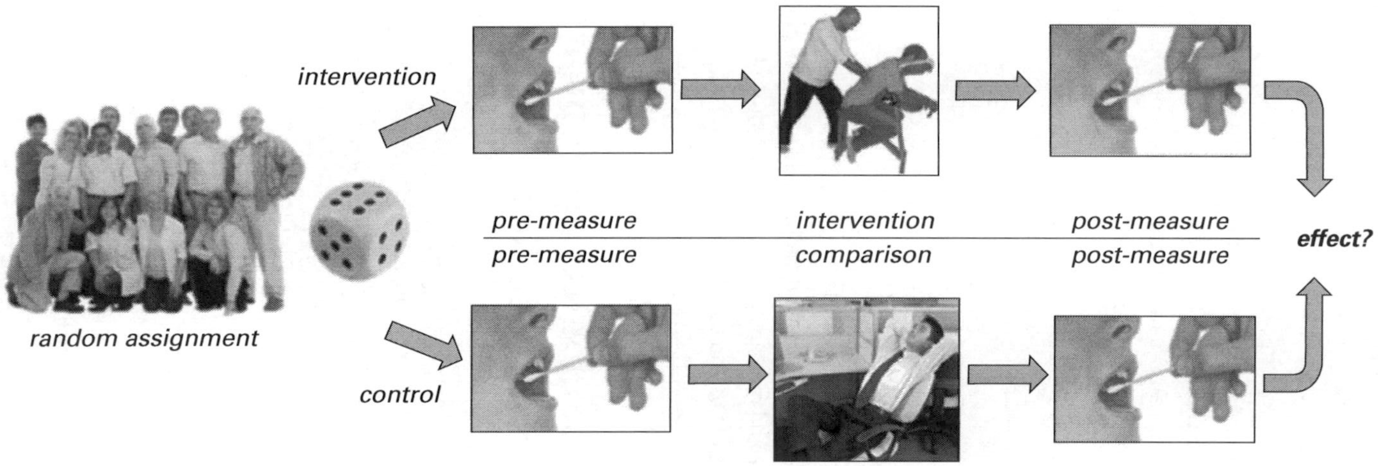
intervention
control
random assignment
pre-measure
pre-measure
intervention
comparison
post-measure
post-measure
effect?

As discussed in the previous sections, the main concern in cause-and-effect studies is internal validity, the extent to which a study's results may be affected by confounders. In non-effect studies **external validity** rather than internal validity is often a bigger concern. External validity is the extent to which the results of the study can generally be applied to other situations (for example, organizations) and to other people (for example, employees). For instance, in the example above we want to make sure that our sample of hospitals and nurses accurately represents all Danish hospitals and nurses, and the findings from our survey and focus group are generalizable to the whole population. This, and other concerns for non-effect studies, means that a randomized controlled trial, the gold standard for cause-and-effect questions, is not an appropriate design for non-effect studies. Below we provide an overview of common non-effect questions and the corresponding appropriate study designs.

Questions about frequencies

In organizations, questions concerning frequencies are common. In hospitals, for example, common questions would be the number of patients admitted today, how many hip replacements the surgical team performed this week, or how many medical errors were made last month. The same is true of questions regarding the number of employees who are absent, the number of employees who are satisfied with their working conditions, or the number of employees who will retire within the next five years – all common questions for an HR manager. Not surprisingly many scientific studies also address research questions about frequencies. Control groups and pre-measures are not needed to answer these questions. The most appropriate research design for answering a frequency question is a cross-sectional survey, as this type of study obtains information on counts.

Questions about differences

Related to frequency questions are questions concerning differences. When the hospital manager has determined how many medical errors were made on average, he or she may also want to know whether there are differences between the medical departments. Likewise, an HR manager may want to know whether satisfaction with working conditions differs among divisions or types of employees. In the scientific literature, differences between organizations, teams or employees are also often the focus of research. For example, a large number of studies is available on the (assumed) differences between entrepreneurs and managers, knowledge workers and manual labourers, virtual teams and collocated groups, and private companies and public organizations and so on. Usually these differences concern productivity or performance, but differences regarding attitudinal, motivational or behavioural factors are also common. Questions concerning differences – as with questions relating to frequency – are best answered with a study that uses a cross-sectional design. Note that a **cross-sectional study** is a very appropriate design for establishing whether there is a difference, but it does a poor job of determining the cause of this difference. When a difference has occurred over time, a longitudinal (before–after) study is the more appropriate design.

Questions about attitudes and opinions

For some managers, questions about frequencies or differences often relate to attitudes or opinions. In the example of the HR manager, the frequency and possible difference involved an attitudinal factor: employees' satisfaction with their working conditions. Other examples of workplace-related attitudes are organizational commitment, turnover intention and trust in management. When we have – in advance – a clear idea about the attitude we want to measure, and this attitude is quantifiable, a cross-sectional study is the most appropriate design. If, however, we want to more deeply explore and better understand the attitudes and opinions of people, a study with a qualitative design, such as focus-group research, may be a more appropriate option.

Questions about experiences, perceptions, needs and feelings

In general, experiences, perceptions, needs and feelings can be difficult to quantify. For example, the answers to questions such as 'How do you feel about the introduction of flexible work arrangements in this company?' or 'What do you think you need to optimally function within a virtual team?' can be a challenge to express in numbers. Data relating to experiences, perceptions, needs or feelings are therefore usually obtained from interviews, focus groups, narrative analysis or participant observation, in other words: qualitative methods.

Questions about associations or relationships

Questions concerning associations fit into a special category. For example, the hospital manager may want to know whether medical errors are related to the time of the day or a specific weekday. Determining whether there is a (co)relation – also referred to as association – between two variables is, as discussed earlier, often the first step in identifying a causal relationship. Thus, a cross-sectional study is an appropriate design to determine whether there is an association between two variables. Clearly, study designs that use a before–after measurement, a control group, and/or random assignment are also appropriate for measuring the extent of an association, but such designs are used mainly to determine whether the association could be causal.

 Note

Beware of single studies!

As we explained in the introductory chapter, an important 'safety check' to ensure that scientific claims are trustworthy is replication. If novel findings from scientific research can be reproduced, it means they are more likely to be valid. On the other hand, if the findings cannot be replicated they are likely to be invalid. Therefore, no single study (not even a randomized controlled trial) can be considered to be strong evidence – it is merely indicative. For this reason, we prefer meta-analyses or, even better, systematic reviews. As explained earlier, a systematic review is a summary of studies that aims to identify all relevant studies on a specific topic. A meta-analysis is a summary of studies in which statistical analysis techniques are used to combine the results of individual studies to get a more accurate estimate of the effect. Thus, irrespective of the type of question, meta-analyses and/or systematic reviews are often the most appropriate research designs. In other words, it is the body of evidence that is important – not single studies.

Methodological appropriateness: Summary

To summarize, when answering questions about cause-and-effect, we need studies with a research design suited to answering cause-and-effect questions; that is, a study that includes both a control group (preferably randomized) and before and after measurements. When we want to answer non-effect questions, such as questions about predictions, associations, frequencies, differences or attitudes, a cross-sectional survey would be better. Finally, when we want to explore feelings, perceptions, needs or experiences, qualitative methods are likely to be most appropriate. In Table 7.4 we provide an overview of the methodological appropriateness of research designs for different types of research questions.

When we critically appraise the trustworthiness of a study's findings, we need to consider its methodological appropriateness to the type of question that it aims to answer. A study with low methodological appropriateness will also have low trustworthiness, regardless of how well the study was conducted. When critically appraising a study's trustworthiness, we therefore start by identifying its research design. The resultant methodological appropriateness is then expressed in a measure of trustworthiness (Table 7.5). Note that we don't judge the trustworthiness of a study as such, because studies are not intrinsically trustworthy or not. We can only judge the trustworthiness of a study's findings *given its research design* and the questions asked.

 Note

So where do these trustworthiness estimates come from?

As will be discussed in more detail in Chapter 12, we use probability estimates in evidence-based management to describe the trustworthiness of a claim, hypothesis or assumption given the available evidence (for example, findings from an empirical study). A trustworthiness estimate is quantified as a percentage between 0 and 100, where 100 per cent indicates absolute trustworthiness. Let's imagine that someone claims that companies committing themselves to an ethnically diverse workforce perform better financially. What is the trustworthiness of this claim? When there is no evidence against or in favour of a claim, trustworthiness is 50/50. It's the same as flipping a coin – the claim could be true, or not, we simply don't know because there is no evidence available. Now, imagine that there is a cross-sectional study that supports this claim. Given the fact that a cross-sectional study is not an appropriate design to demonstrate a cause-and-effect relationship, trustworthiness only increases slightly from 50 per cent to 60 per cent. This means that there is still a 40 per cent chance that a diverse workforce will not yield higher financial performance. However, when there is a randomized controlled trial that supports the claim, the trustworthiness would increase to 90 per cent. Of course, this estimation of trustworthiness also works the other way around. When there is a randomized controlled trial that does not support the claim, the trustworthiness would drop to 10 per cent, meaning that there is a 90 per cent chance that a diverse workforce will not lead to higher financial performance. Note that the highest level of trustworthiness is 90 per cent, as even the most rigorous and reliable study design is not perfect.

7.5 Critical appraisal: Methodological quality

Trustworthiness, however, is also affected by a study's methodological quality, that is, the way it was conducted. As a result, even a methodologically appropriate study can be untrustworthy. For example, the trustworthiness of a study with a high methodological appropriateness can drop dramatically when the study is not well conducted and contains several weaknesses. In fact, when a study contains too many flaws, we can reduce its trustworthiness score to 50 per cent, which means the study has the same predictive value as flipping a coin. Thus, a randomized controlled trial with several serious flaws can be less trustworthy than a well-conducted non-randomized controlled study that contains no weaknesses.

When we critically appraise a study's trustworthiness, we start with setting a baseline for its level of methodological appropriateness. Based on its number of weaknesses, we may downgrade the level of trustworthiness by one or more levels. To determine the final level of trustworthiness you can make use of the following rules of thumb:

- 1 weakness = no downgrade (we accept that nothing is perfect);
- 2 weaknesses = downgrade 1 level;
- 3 weaknesses = downgrade 2 levels;
- 4 weaknesses = downgrade 3 levels.

Table 7.4 Methodological appropriateness: Which design for which question?

Purpose	Example	RCT	CBA	BA	Contr	Cross	Qual
Effect, impact	Does A have an effect/impact on B? What are the critical success factors for A? What are the factors that affect B?	A	B	C	C	D	na
Prediction	Does A precede B? Does A predict B over time?	A	A	A	D	D	na
Association	Is A related to B? Does A often occur with B? Do A and B covary?	A	A	A	A	A	na
Difference	Is there a difference between A and B?	A	A	A	A	A	na
Frequency	How often does A occur? How many people prefer A?	na	na	na	na	A	na
Attitude, opinion	What are people's attitude towards A? Are people satisfied with A? Do people agree with A?	na	na	na	na	A	C
Experience, perceptions, feelings, needs	What are people's experience with A? What are people's feelings about A? What are people's perceptions about A? Why do people (think they) need to do/use A?	na	na	na	na	B	A
Exploration, theory building	Why does A occur? Why is A different from B? In what context does A occur?	na	na	na	na	B	A

Note RCT = Randomized controlled trial; CBA = Non-randomized controlled before–after study; BA = Before–after study; Contr = Controlled study; Cross = Cross-sectional study; Qual = Qualitative study; na = not appropriate

Table 7.5

Level	Methodological appropriateness	Estimated trustworthiness	Proper wording of the findings
A	High	90%	'It is shown that...'
B	Moderate	80%	'It is likely that...'
C	Limited	70%	'It could be that...'
D	Low	60%	'There are signs that...'

Critical appraisal questions to determine weaknesses in a meta-analysis or a systematic review

Meta-analyses and systematic reviews summarize studies on the same topic. They often use statistical analysis techniques to combine the results in order to achieve a more precise effect size. To determine their methodological appropriateness, we need to first identify the types of studies included. As Table 7.5 indicates, a meta-analysis or systematic review based on randomized controlled trials is a very appropriate design to measure an effect, impact or causal relation, thus the baseline trustworthiness is very high (95 per cent). When the studies included are cross-sectional (or when it is unclear what type of studies have been included), the baseline trustworthiness drops to 70 per cent. To determine the final level of trustworthiness, you can use the following critical appraisal questions:

Q: Is it likely that important, relevant studies were missed?

As explained in Chapter 6, the best place to start a comprehensive search for studies is with the major research databases (for example, ABI/INFORM, Business Source Premier and PsycINFO). However, a search should also include contact with active researchers, particularly to investigate whether there are any unpublished studies. You would typically find this information in the 'Method' section. If the above conditions are met, it is unlikely that key studies would have been missed, thus minimizing selection bias.

Q: Was the process to select studies clearly defined and reproducible?

To prevent selection bias, the choice of which studies to include should preferably be made by at least two reviewers, independently of each other, and using rigorously specified inclusion and exclusion criteria. Furthermore, this process should be clearly documented, for example in the form of a flow-chart that shows how many studies are excluded as a result of which criteria. You can find information about the selection process in the Method section.

Q: Was the process to extract data clearly defined and was the outcome presented in a table?

To prevent bias, the extraction of data (such as population, study design, sample size, variables measured, outcome and so on) should preferably be conducted by at least two reviewers, independently of each other. The outcome should be presented in a table showing clearly the data extracted for each included study. You can find information about the process of data extraction in the Method section, usually under 'Data extraction' or 'Coding procedure'.

Q: Was the methodological quality of each study assessed?

The quality of a systematic review or meta-analysis is determined by the methodological quality of the primary studies included (garbage in/garbage out). The quality of the studies included should therefore be appraised using predetermined criteria and validated checklists. This information would typically be provided in the Method section. However, keep in mind that a substantial number of systematic reviews or meta-analyses provide insufficient information as to whether or not the methodological quality of the studies included was critically appraised.

Critical appraisal questions to determine weaknesses in a randomized controlled trial

A randomized controlled trial is considered the gold standard to measure an effect, impact or causal relation. It is not appropriate for non-effect questions and therefore seldom used for such questions. A randomized controlled trial, however, can have multiple weaknesses that affect its internal validity.

Q: Was the control group similar to the intervention group at the start of the study?

If the randomization process worked (that is, achieved comparable groups) the groups should be similar. As a rule, the more similar the groups at the start, the better it is. The study should have a table of 'baseline character-istics', comparing the groups on variables that could affect the outcome. If not, there may be a description of group similarity in the first paragraphs of the Results section. In addition, there should be an indication of whether differences between groups are statistically significant. If the groups were not similar at the start, we cannot be sure that the outcome of the study is due to the intervention rather than any other (unknown) confounding factor(s).

Q: Did fewer than 20 per cent of the subjects drop out?

The percentage of dropouts or withdrawals after the first (baseline) measure should be minimal, preferably less than 20 per cent. In most studies, you can find this information in the Results section or the table with the results (for example, by comparing the number of subjects (n) at the start of the study with the number of measurements). If data are collected (or variables measured) from fewer than 80 per cent of the original subjects at the start of the study, the outcome may be less trustworthy.

Q: Were reliable and valid measurement methods used?

As explained earlier, the measurement of direct/objective variables (for example, production errors, staff turnover rate) is more likely to be valid and reliable than that of self-report/subjective variables (for example, self-reported accidents or performance). In addition, when a study makes use of a questionnaire, check whether it was developed for the present study ('self-made' or 'home-grown') or if it was also used in other studies. When a scale or questionnaire has been used in previous research, we may assume that it has some track record for validity and reliability, though such information should still be provided in the present study. In most studies, you can find this information in the Method section, usually under 'Measurements' or 'Tools'.

Critical appraisal questions to determine weaknesses in a non-randomized controlled before–after study

A non-randomized controlled study is an appropriate design to measure an effect, impact or causal relation. Like randomized controlled trials, the non-randomized controlled design is not appropriate for non-effect questions. To determine its methodological quality, we ask some of the same questions when critically appraising a randomized controlled trial. Additional questions are:

Q: Did the study start prior to the intervention/exposure?

A major drawback of retrospective studies is that they tend to be more susceptible to bias and confounding, therefore additional controls – such as blinding – should be applied.

Q: Was the intervention (or exposure to a variable) independent of other changes over time?

If the intervention or exposure did not occur independently of other changes (for example, a restructuring programme or the implementation of a new management model), or if the outcome was likely to have been influenced by historical events during the study period (for example, a merger), there may be a negative impact on a study's trustworthiness.

Critical appraisal questions to determine weaknesses in a non-randomized controlled study without a pretest

A non-randomized controlled study without a pretest (baseline measure) is not very appropriate for measuring an effect, impact or causal relationship. Nevertheless, this design is often used when higher quality methodologies are not possible for practical reasons. To determine its methodological quality, we ask the same questions as when critically appraising a randomized controlled trial.

Critical appraisal questions to determine weaknesses in a before–after study

Before–after studies without a control group are not a very appropriate design to measure an effect, impact or causal relation. For non-effect questions, before–after studies are inappropriate. To determine their methodological quality, we ask most of the same questions as when critically appraising a controlled study. An additional question is:

Q: Were the criteria used to select subjects clearly defined?

A clear description of the inclusion criteria increases the likelihood that subjects in the study (employees, teams, units, organizations and so on) were selected because they were representative of the target population, rather than for reasons of convenience (see selection bias in Chapter 3). In addition, the study should specify how the subjects were selected. Did they invite everyone in the population that met the criteria, or just a sample? You can usually find information about the selection criteria in the Method section.

Critical appraisal questions to determine weaknesses in an interrupted time series study

As explained in Chapter 5, an interrupted time series study measures subjects repeatedly on a particular outcome (dependent variable). Data are collected (or variables measured) at three or more points both before and after the intervention or exposure. These multiple measures serve as a form of control and for this reason, this is a moderately appropriate design to measure an effect, impact or causal relation. For non-effect questions, such studies are inappropriate. To determine their methodological quality, we ask most of the same questions as when critically appraising a before–after study.

Critical appraisal questions to determine weaknesses in a cross-sectional study

Cross-sectional studies such as surveys are appropriate for non-effect questions, especially when they relate to measuring frequencies, opinions or attitudes (see Table 7.4). Although they are very often used for studies that aim to measure an effect, impact or (causal) relation, they are in fact inappropriate for this purpose. We ask the following questions to appraise their methodological quality:

Q: Was the sample randomly selected?

When a sample is randomly selected, each member of the population has an equal chance of being chosen as a subject in the study. When other methods are used, the study is susceptible to selection bias (see also Chapter 3). The most reliable way to randomly select a sample is using computer software that generates numbers by chance (such as Excel or SPSS). You can typically find information about how the sample was selected in the Method section, usually under 'Sample' or 'Procedure'. A randomly selected sample is sometimes referred to as a 'probability sample', whereas a non-random sample is referred to as a 'convenience sample'.

Q: Was the sample size large enough?

Whether a cross-sectional study's sample size (n) is large enough depends on the population size (N), the margin of error (ME, usually 5 per cent) and the confidence interval (CI, usually 95 per cent). In general, you can use the following rules of thumb as a guideline (Table 7.6):

Table 7.6

Population (N)	Sample (n)
50	45
100	80
250	152
500	218
1,000	278
> 10,000	370

Q: Is it likely that data dredging has taken place?

Data dredging (also referred to as data fishing or data snooping) is an inappropriate practice in which a data set is exhaustively analysed and a large number of hypotheses or relationships tested to find combinations of variables that show a statistically significant correlation. Testing a large number (> 20) of correlations or exhaustively analysing the data, however, increases the chance of detecting a non-existing significant effect (a false effect). You can usually find information about the number of hypotheses or relations (correlations) tested in the Method section (typically under 'measurement' or 'independent/dependent variables'), or in the table(s) with the results.

Critical appraisal questions to determine weaknesses in a qualitative study

As explained, qualitative methods use data obtained from interviews, focus groups, documentary analysis, narrative analysis or participant observation. This type of method is very appropriate to gain an understanding of underlying reasons, opinions or motivations of study participants, or to generate hypotheses and/or theories that can be tested through subsequent quantitative methodologies. Qualitative methods are not appropriate for measuring an effect, impact or (causal) relation. To determine the quality of a qualitative methods, you can use the following questions:[13]

Q: Is the researcher's perspective clearly described and taken into account?

In qualitative studies the researcher is the primary tool for data collection and interpretation. This means that in assessing the methodological quality of qualitative studies, the core criterion to be evaluated is researcher bias. To minimize this, the researcher should therefore declare his or her assumptions and biases about the topic under study and make a clear statement of how this is likely to have influenced the results. Information about the researcher's assumption and biases can usually be found in the 'Research limitations' section, although it might also be found elsewhere. Bear in mind, however, that a substantial number of qualitative studies fail to provide this information.

Q: Are the methods for collecting data clearly described?

The researcher should provide adequate information about data-collection procedures. For instance, what method was used to collect the data (participant observation, interviews, document reviews, focus groups and so on)? And in what form did the data come (for example, audio recordings, video material, e-mails, notes and so on)? You can find information about how the data were collected in the Method section, usually under 'Data collection' or 'Procedure'.

Q: Are quality-control measures used?

Quality-control measures include:

- independently verifiable data formats (audio recordings, video);
- independent analysis of data by more than one researcher;
- verbatim quotes, sustained observation over time, peer debriefing (that is, involving impartial peer researchers to evaluate and make sense of findings);
- addressing negative or discrepant results.

You can find information about quality-control measures in the Method section, usually under 'Data analysis'.

7.6 Finally: The 'best available' evidence

Let's imagine that we want to know whether the introduction of virtual teams will improve our organization's performance. When we locate a single study in which a meaningful effect was found but a pre-measure was missing, we must, based on what we have learned in the previous paragraphs, conclude that this is not the 'best' evidence. It would have been better if the study had used a pre-measure, and it would have been great if a control group had also been used, but it would still not have been the 'best' evidence. Even a study in which a control group has been randomly assigned cannot be considered the 'best' evidence, as a single study is merely indicative. Now, as we just have learned, the 'best' study to answer our question would have been a systematic review or meta-analysis of multiple randomized controlled trials with no methodological weaknesses. You probably won't be surprised to hear that such studies are scarce. As a result the 'best' evidence is often not available. In fact, instead of a meta-analysis of randomized controlled trials, there are often only a handful of cross-sectional studies available.

Evidence-based management, however, is not about the *best* evidence, but rather about the *best available* evidence. In the situation described above, the handful of cross-sectional studies constitute the best available scientific evidence. But even this (perhaps disappointing) result could turn out to be important. It indicates that the evidence base on this topic is not (yet) well developed. And that *in itself* is important information. All managers and leaders have anxieties, and we all question whether what we are doing is right. So, when we find out that the scientific evidence is poor or even absent, it means that the answer to our question is (yet) unknown. And that can be a huge relief. We are agonizing whether doing X or Y is 'better' but now we know there is (as yet) no definitive answer to that.

At the same time, it is important to remember that evidence-based management is about the use of evidence from four sources, not just one. That means that regardless of whether the trustworthiness of the scientific evidence you have found is high or low, you should always consider the evidence from the multiple sources. No single source of evidence can be viewed as a universal or timeless truth or superior to any other – even a meta-analysis of randomized controlled trials comes with weaknesses and uncertainties. As we stated in the first chapter of this book, evidence-based practitioners make decisions not based on conclusive, solid, up-to-date information, but on probabilities, indications and tentative conclusions. Scientific evidence rarely tells you what to decide, but it always helps you to make a better-informed decision.

7.7 Overview of the appraisal process

Flowchart 7.1

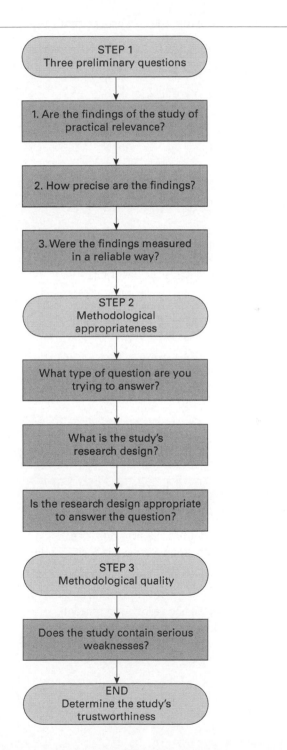

7.8 Checklists

- 1 weakness = no downgrade (we accept that nothing is perfect);
- 2 weaknesses = downgrade 1 level;
- 3 weaknesses = downgrade 2 levels;
- 4 weaknesses = downgrade 2 levels.

Table 7.7

Critical appraisal questions to determine weaknesses in a meta-analysis or a systematic review	Yes	No/ Unclear
Question 1: Is it unlikely that important, relevant studies were missed?		
Question 2: Was the process to select studies clearly defined and reproducible?		
Question 3: Was the process to extract data clearly defined and the outcome presented in a table?		
Question 4: Was the methodological quality of each study assessed?		

Table 7.8

Critical appraisal questions to determine weaknesses in a randomized controlled trial	Yes	No/ Unclear
Question 1: Was the control group similar to the intervention group at the start of the study?		
Question 2: Did fewer than 20 per cent of the subjects drop out?		
Question 3: Were reliable and valid measurement methods used?		

Table 7.9

Critical appraisal questions to determine weaknesses in a non-randomized controlled before–after study, or a non-randomized controlled study without a pretest	Yes	No/ Unclear
Question 1: Was the control group similar to the intervention group at the start of the study?		
Question 2: Did the study start prior to the intervention/ exposure?		
Question 3: Was the intervention (or exposure) independent of other changes over time?		
Question 4: Were reliable and valid measurement methods used?		

Table 7.10

Critical appraisal questions to determine weaknesses in a before–after study or an interrupted time series study	Yes	No/ Unclear
Question 1: Were the criteria used to select subjects clearly defined?		
Question 2: Did the study start prior to the intervention/ exposure?		
Question 3: Was the intervention (or exposure) independent of other changes over time?		
Question 4: Were reliable and valid measurement methods used?		

Table 7.11

Critical appraisal questions to determine weaknesses in a cross-sectional study	Yes	No/ Unclear
Question 1: Was the sample randomly selected?		
Question 2: Was the sample size large enough?		
Question 3: Is it unlikely that data dredging has taken place?		
Question 4: Were reliable and valid measurement methods used?		

Table 7.12

Critical appraisal questions to determine weaknesses in a qualitative study	Yes	No/ Unclear
Question 1: Is the researcher's perspective clearly described and taken into account?		
Question 2: Are the methods for collecting data clearly described?		
Question 3: Are quality-control measures used?		

Notes and references

1   Collins, JC (2001) *Good to Great: Why some companies make the leap… and others don't*, Random House, London

2   Field, A (2013) *Discovering Statistics Using IBM SPSS Statistics*, Sage Publications, London

3   Ellis, PD (2010) *The Essential Guide to Effect Sizes: Statistical power, meta-analysis, and the interpretation of research results*, Cambridge University Press, Cambridge

4   Cohen, J (1988) *Statistical Power Analysis for the Behavioral Sciences* (2nd edn), Lawrence Earlbaum Associates, Hillsdale, NJ

5   Cooper, HM and Lindsay, JLL (1998) *Research Synthesis and Meta-Analysis*, pp 271–85, Sage Publications, London

6   Note that direct or objective measures can also be unreliable, so it is important to examine how such measures were obtained and if they were checked for reliability and validity

7   Lazarsfeld, PF and Rosenberg, M (1955) *The Language of Social Research: A reader in the methodology of social research*, Free Press, New York

8   Salkind, NJ (2016) *Statistics for People Who (Think They) Hate Statistics*, Sage Publications, London

9   More hilarious examples of spurious correlations can be found at http://www.tylervigen.com/spurious-correlations

10   Technically, this is not completely accurate; there could be a so-called 'suppressor effect' due to a third (unknown) variable. For example, suppose that a researcher is interested in the relationship between workers' intelligence and the number of errors made on an assembly line task. It seems plausible that the more intelligent workers would make fewer errors, so we would expect a strong negative correlation. However, the more intelligent workers could also

exhibit higher levels of boredom, and boredom would be correlated with the number of errors. In that case, the effect of intelligence on errors would be negative, and the effect of boredom on errors would be positive. Combined, these two effects may cancel each other out, resulting in a total correlation of intelligence on errors equal to zero. This example is adapted from MacKinnon, DP, Krull, JL and Lockwood, CM (2000) Equivalence of the mediation, confounding and suppression effect, *Prevention Science*, **1** (4), pp 173–81

11 Luhmann, M, Hofmann, W, Eid, M and Lucas, RE (2012) Subjective well-being and adaptation to life events: A meta-analysis, *Journal of Personality and Social Psychology*, **102** (3), p 592

12 Again, technically, this is not completely accurate. When a study uses random assignment, all potential confounding variables that may affect the outcome are equally distributed among the groups. As a result they are similar at baseline, and thus a pretest is not strictly necessary. However, without a pretest we don't know whether the randomization was successful and thus we can't be certain that the groups were truly similar at baseline. For this reason, even in a randomized controlled trial a pretest is often used.

13 Tracy, SJ (2010) Qualitative quality: Eight 'big tent' criteria for excellent qualitative research, *Qualitative Inquiry*, **16** (10), pp 837–51

PART THREE
Evidence from the organization

ACQUIRE: Evidence from the organization

08

It is a capital mistake to theorize before one has data.

SHERLOCK HOLMES – SIR ARTHUR CONAN DOYLE

The modern organization continually generates data. From banks and hospitals to small retail stores, all organizations create data. Some data are created and recorded as part of regular operational activities, such as the appointment booking system at a hospital or cash register at the local bakery. Some data help managers make decisions or monitor the organization's performance. Some data aid compliance with laws, regulations and accounting standards. Whatever their type or reason for creation, organizational data represent one of the richest sources of evidence for managers. Not only can organizational evidence be richer in volume or detail than evidence from the scientific literature, but also it is specific to the organizational context. To use evidence from the organization, however, companies must have the skills to identify, combine and analyse data from multiple sources and possess the knowledge to build and apply analytical models to support decision-making. In this chapter, you will develop a better understanding of evidence from the organization and learn to acquire it in a valid and reliable way.

8.1 Why is evidence from the organization important?

As we have established, evidence-based management is about increasing the probability of making the right decision and understanding the degree of confidence you can place in that decision. In evidence-based management, managers and leaders make decisions within the context of a specific organization. Evidence from that organization is essential to:

- identify organizational problems or challenges;
- determine organizational consequences of a problem;
- recognize potential cause(s) of a problem;
- find plausible alternative solutions;
- monitor the effectiveness of management decisions or solutions.

Systematically evaluating organizational evidence can be an effective and reliable way to verify claims regarding organizational problems. In addition, you can use data-analytic techniques such as regression analysis or predictive modelling to identify effective solutions.[1] In fact, consulting organizational evidence is often the best way to assess the impact of a management decision. After all, you make a management decision, and you can most easily judge its impact using evidence based on your organization's own data. A general understanding of how evidence from the organization can be acquired and assessed is an essential skill for evidence-based managers.[2]

8.2 From data to information and evidence

In common usage, the terms *data*, *information* and *evidence* are used interchangeably. Data, however, refers to text, images, numbers or symbols that, if no context is provided, mean little or nothing to a human being. Bits of data are not meaningful without a context. Data can be regarded as raw material that can exist alone while information is data processed in a meaningful and useful way. Only when you process bits of data (organize, structure, analyse and interpret), putting them in context, do they provide meaningful information. Taking these distinctions one step further, evidence only exists in the context of a claim or an assumption. Simply put, evidence is always evidence for (or against) something.

Data: Numbers, words, figures, symbols, sounds, dates, images and so on, without context.

Information: Data relating to something or someone and considered meaningful or useful.

Evidence: Information supporting (or contradicting) a claim, assumption or hypothesis.

Information technology and computer science emphasize the distinction between data and information. Computer systems are inherently full of electronic representations of words, numbers, symbols and so on. Unprocessed or out of any specific context this form of data is meaningless. For example, a list of numbers stored on a computer becomes 'information' only when it is recognized as a list of the birthdates of employees. Put into context, the data becomes information when it answers such questions as 'What is the average age of an employee?' or 'How many people are likely to retire next year?' This means that if an IT professional refers to something as 'data', it is quite likely to require additional processing to make it meaningful or useful. In the context of this book, organizational evidence refers to data and the ways it has been transformed to make it more interpretable.

8.3 What questions to ask?

Chapter 2 explained that an evidence-based approach starts with asking questions. Setting out questions and framing diagnoses and problems correctly may be the most important steps in the evidence-based process. An evidence-based approach begins with the question 'What is the problem, and what is the evidence for this problem?' or 'What is the preferred solution, and what is the evidence that this solution will be effective?' Evidence from the organization can make the biggest difference in answering the latter part of these two questions. Acquiring evidence from the organization typically starts with a hypothesis or (assumed) causal mechanism. A hypothesis-led gathering and analysis of organizational data generates faster and more meaningful outcomes. It roots assumed problems (and preferred solutions) in 'real' data relationships rather than correlations that were statistically significant by chance.

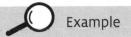 Example

A large international insurance firm experiences a decline in profitability. Based on the assumption that its biggest clients are also its most profitable, the firm acquires organizational data regarding the number of services each major client uses and its profitability. The outcome, however, is counterintuitive: its largest clients turn out to be among the least profitable. Moreover, clients in the middle percentile, which do not require substantial resources, tend to use more services and are therefore more profitable than the larger clients at the top. The company therefore concludes that the initial core assumption is wrong. When this surprising outcome is discussed with its top executives, a new hypothesis emerges: the use of the company's services is driven by client satisfaction and that usage determines a client's profitability. To see whether this assumed causal mechanism is correct, the company acquires organizational data regarding client satisfaction, service usage and net profitability, and determines that a client's satisfaction is indeed persistently and predictively linked to a client's profitability. The company must now work out which variables drive satisfaction.[3]

Some of the questions we identified as important in Chapter 2 have specific relevance to organizational evidence, including the following:

1 What is the problem[4] (what, who, when, where)?

2 Does organizational evidence confirm the problem?

3 Is there a trend (does the evidence suggest that the problem will worsen if nothing is done)?

4 What organizational consequences of the problem does the evidence indicate?

5 Does the evidence confirm the assumed causal mechanism? (Is there a correlation between the assumed cause, the problem and its organizational consequences?)

6 What is the preferred solution (what, who, when, where)?

7 Does organizational evidence confirm the assumed causal mechanism: is there an association between the preferred solution and the favoured organizational outcomes?

We note that organizational data may also be gathered in anticipation of future needs, as opposed to current problems. For example, as part of a project to build evidence-based management capabilities, an organization might build a **data warehouse**. Data warehouses are repositories that integrate data from multiple sources across the organization. Such data might be gathered as a basis for future hypothesis testing and learning as the organization's capacity to ask critical questions increases.

8.4 What types of organizational evidence are typically available?

Evidence from the organization comes in many forms. It can be derived from financial data such as cash flow or costs, from customers in the form of customer satisfaction or from employees through information about retention rates. Evidence from the organization can be 'hard' numbers, for example staff turnover rates, medical errors or productivity levels, but it can also include 'soft' elements such as perceptions of the organization's culture or attitudes towards senior management. There are many ways to classify organizational data and the evidence it produces, including the broad types below.

Finance and accounting

Historically, managers have paid considerable attention to financial and accounting data. Many events in the organization, such as the sale of a product or the delivery of a service, generate data relevant to the organization's financial position. The sale of a product will be represented by entries in one or more sets of records called ledgers. Organizations use data from ledgers to create key financial information, such as:

- statements of cash flow – a record of money received or given out;
- income statements – lists of an organization's profit or loss and income;
- statements of a firm's financial position (also known as a balance sheet) – lists of an organization's assets (money or things they own) and liabilities (money or things they owe).

Financial data use typically requires some understanding of financial and accounting concepts and thus may require specialized professional help with interpretation.

Human resources

Human resource evidence is fundamentally about people: who they are, their characteristics and their relationship to the organization. Examples are pay, grade, tenure, years of experience, attendance, job satisfaction, engagement and performance. They may also include staff surveys, policies and data regarding the activities an employee carries out.

Sales and marketing

Sales and marketing evidence includes facts about the number of products or services sold, market share, competitors, details of customer relationships, brand awareness and the impact of marketing campaigns.

Risk

Large companies typically have departments that manage and assess the multiple risks that can impact the organization. Perhaps the most developed risk functions are in banks and insurance companies, where organizational risk is managed and evaluated in terms of operational risk, market risk and credit risk. Evidence about risk may take the form of calculations about the potential risks to an organization based on its current state or strategy, but it may also entail a detailed analysis of what has gone wrong during standard operational procedures.

Production

Production evidence relates to the products or services that an organization creates, including measures of inputs, outputs and the overall quality level. Those outputs may be physical objects such as cars, personal services such as haircuts or intangible services like legal advice. Note that some organizations may use the term 'operations' instead of 'production'.

Quality and performance

Larger organizations often capture data to monitor, control and ensure the quality of their products or services. Especially high-reliability organizations in healthcare, aviation, petrochemical, food or the banking industries have complex quality management systems that closely monitor data such as accuracy, timeliness, failure frequency rate, safety and other Key Performance Indicators (KPIs, see later in this chapter).

Customer service

Specific customer service functions deal with client interactions that do not involve selling or production. For example, they produce data regarding the number and content of customer complaints.

8.5 Big data

'**Big data**', a particular kind of organizational data, is a hot topic in contemporary business. The concept, however, is still nascent and, as a result, many definitions exist. Most of these definitions have the following 'three Vs' in common:

Volume

Size is what first comes to mind when we think of big data. As a rule, big data comprises multiple terabytes or even petabytes of structured and unstructured data. To give you some idea of what this volume is, one terabyte stores as much data as 1,500 CDs or 220 DVDs, the equivalent of about 16 million Facebook photographs.[5] One petabyte equals 1,024 terabytes, which is enough to store the DNA of the entire population of Europe.

Variety

Big data come from a variety of sources. Organizational data are acquired from sources such as management information systems, personnel systems and physical records (spreadsheets, for example). These are referred to as 'structured' data. But nowadays data also come from e-mails, text messages, tweets, audio recordings, photographs, videos and so on – these kinds of data are unstructured data. Technological advances allow organizations to store, process and analyse these types of data, and thus use them for economic purposes.

Velocity

Velocity refers to the speed at which data are generated, leading to a growing need for real-time analytics. Nowadays even 'conventional' retailers generate data at a tremendously high rate. Walmart, for instance, processes more than 1 million transactions per hour.[6] Data also are pouring into organizations with increased speed due to 'firehose' data sources such as social media.[7]

These three characteristics of big data raise questions such as: How can I accurately analyse 100+ terabytes of heterogeneous data per day in real time? For this reason, new data analytics using artificial intelligence, machine learning and neural networks have emerged, suited to big data's complexity.

8.6 Where to find organizational evidence

Organizational evidence and the data that generate it can be found both inside and outside the organization. The types of organizational evidence data described above can be a good starting point to finding relevant data. For example, the finance department is the key custodian of the organizational and departmental budgets and is therefore often the most important source for acquiring financial data. Data may also be stored at locations outside the department that uses them. For example, human resources (HR) data are found in the HR department but also in the finance division and in local branches of the organization. It is therefore important to gain an understanding of how and where your organization captures and stores its data. Below is an overview of the most common places to find organizational data.

Databases and information systems

Databases usually are the core systems for capturing and processing many of the organization's daily activities. In general, a database consists of data structured into records of individual elements. For example, an address record may contain the house number, street name, city and postal code. Most databases link together different types of records using a common identifier – a case in point is employee salary records and employee addresses. These data may be kept in different records linked by a common identifier (such as staff ID or personnel number) stored in both. Identifiers also link data from different databases. Most information systems within an organization – such as management information systems, personnel systems or customer relationship management systems – consist of an underlying database you can query directly, with tools for searching, extracting and analysing its data. Sometimes the data in these separate information systems are uploaded into one large, integrated database, also referred to as a data warehouse.

Document and content management systems

A great many organizational data are stored in the form of documents or spreadsheets rather than as structured data in a database or data warehouse. There are a wide variety of systems for managing documents including document management systems and systems for managing intranet/internet content. These types of systems provide several functionalities for classifying and searching for documents.

Workflow systems

These are systems that manage the execution of a business process. **Workflow systems** are often hybrids between data and document-based systems: generating and storing both data and whole documents.

Physical records

Many organizations still use physical records, including documents in filing cabinets. This could be because of lack of funds to invest in new technology, legal requirements or simply habit. Physical records can present a challenge if they are a relevant source of organizational data. There are a variety of techniques for turning physical records into more easily analysed organizational data, from scanning/optical character recognition to physically reviewing and screening documents. Depending on the balance between the potential value of physical records and the additional costs of analysing, they may still be of great value. In fact, in some cases the explosion of digital data means that it is sometimes easier and quicker to find the relevant organizational evidence in physical rather than electronic format.

Staff

A great deal of organizational evidence exists at staff level. For example, relevant data may be kept by individual staff members on their own PCs, on shared drives or in the form of physical records (for example, physicians keeping patient records). As a result, senior management may be unaware how subordinates actually store and maintain data.

Industry bodies, professional associations and census bureaux

Industry bodies, professional associations and census bureaux often have relevant, high-quality information about an organization, its competitors and industry or sector. Often such organizations provide valid and reliable information about how a company's metrics and KPIs compare with the average in the sector.

Social media

Relatively novel, but increasingly important, sources of organizational evidence are social media sites such as Facebook and Twitter. Not only do social media generate data regarding customer satisfaction, brand awareness, brand identity or perceived quality, but they also provide information about the organization's relationship with society.

External stakeholders

External stakeholders such as customers, regulators, shareholders, suppliers and even the society at large may be an important source of evidence about a specific organization. These external stakeholders are a rich source of opinions about the output, results, interactions and behaviour of an organization.

8.7 Techniques and tools for acquiring data

There is a range of techniques and (software) tools available for acquiring the organizational data that can become evidence for managerial decisions. Below is a brief overview of the most common.

Management information and business intelligence systems

There are many specialized tools available to extract data from both core processing systems and specifically designed reporting systems. These are commonly referred to as management information or **business intelligence systems**. The purpose of these systems is to support the decision-making process by organizing, processing and analysing the data and turning them into useful information. Such systems often comprise multiple components, such as an ETL function (extract, transform, load – the process of extracting data from source systems and bringing them into the company's data warehouse), and a separate database along with reporting and analysis software. In addition, they often include advanced dashboards and visualization tools that present data in graphs, charts and accessible visualizations.

Querying existing databases and systems using Structured Query Language

Most information systems store data in an underlying database (ie data warehouse). It is possible to 'query' the database, extracting data from the database in a readable format according to the user's request, by using what is known as **Structured Query Language** (SQL). Writing basic queries in SQL, however, is a technical skill that requires the support of the organization's IT department.

Analysing organizational data using statistical software

Choosing statistical software and/or a data analytics tool is a trade-off between costs, benefits and ease of usage. Popular packages are SPSS, SAS, R, Python and Excel. SPSS is a user-friendly package offering a range of data analytical functions. The downside is it is costly. SAS is a good choice for a person who analyses complex data sets daily. However, if you use a statistics program only once or twice a month, it may not be worth spending hundreds of hours learning SAS language. The same counts for R and Python, two popular programs in the data science world. Both have a command-line interface, requiring code or scripts, making them labour intensive to master. R is open source and downloadable for free. Finally, Microsoft's Excel too provides a wide range of statistical functions. Excel is easy to learn and straightforward to use, and it produces attractive graphs and storytelling charts.

Review of documents and reports

A review of documents can be a quick and easy method of uncovering useful organizational data. It can be done with or without the assistance of specialist software such as a program for content analysis or text mining.

Surveys

A common form of acquiring organizational data is the survey. As explained in Chapter 3, effective survey design requires training to avoid bias. Probably the most popular survey program is SurveyMonkey, a free online tool you can use to construct a questionnaire (based on a customizable template), collect responses and analyse results.

8.8 Organizational data turned into information

Besides categorizing organizational evidence based on the function or physical location of its original data, organizational evidence can be thought about in terms of the value it adds to the organization's decision-making. In Figure 8.1[8] the vertical axis represents the level of added value, a composite index of the degree of interpretability and uncertainty reduction forms of organizational evidence provide. Typically, raw data add the least value because without some degree of processing they are difficult to interpret. In contrast, predictive models can indicate the importance of current evidence for future outcomes, for example the effect of employee turnover rates on important organizational outcomes like safety or service quality. The horizontal axis indicates the nature of the analyses performed on the organizational data. Descriptive evidence is used to monitor current organizational evidence relative to past facts (last year's sales) or current environmental conditions or standards (benchmarks). Inferential evidence transforms descriptive evidence

Figure 8.1

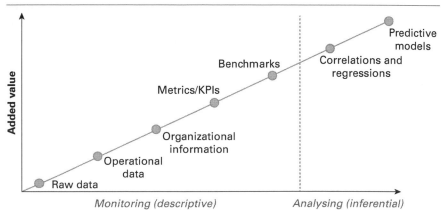

through analytic techniques into indicators of association (for example, the correlation of employee demographics with turnover) or predictive models (for example, regression modelling used to forecast future turnover from present employee demographics and other evidence). As you can see, we expect greater added value from inferential analyses of organizational evidence than from descriptive evidence used for monitoring.

Operational data

Organizations create large amounts of operational data during their everyday activities – even if it is not always easy to extract, aggregate or interpret those data. Operational data are collected automatically within systems related to production, sales, services delivered, personnel, customer service and many other routine functions. Operational data are descriptive in nature: they describe what is going on in an organization. Sometimes operational data are 'real time', providing a snapshot of the present situation, but more often they are retrospective, providing a picture of how things were in the past. Collecting operational data enables an organization to identify general trends, typically expressed as frequencies, averages (means, medians, modes), proportions or ratios.

Organizational information

Although operational data can provide managers with useful information, the added value is often low. For example, an individual sales transaction may not give a manager much help in making decisions. However, combining all the sales for a month into a sales report can make it possible to make judgements and identify trends. Aggregated operational data presented within a functional context (for example, sales, finance or HR) is referred to as 'organizational information'. Within most companies some form of organizational information is available about:

- staff;
- physical assets (eg building, equipment, inventory);
- clients/customers;
- financial assets (eg bank balances) and liabilities (eg debts);
- business processes;
- operations, marketing and sales;
- quality.

Although you can find certain organizational information in readily identifiable systems, much of it is likely to be dispersed across the organization, especially in large and complex firms. Organizational information is, like operational data, descriptive in nature. It is, however, beneficial for developing a general understanding of how the company currently performs and identifying changes in the organization's performance over time.

Metrics and key performance indicators (KPIs)

A metric is a measure. An organization's performance metrics can be a single measure or derived from a combination of two or more measures. Examples are financial ratios (for example, leverage, profitability, total revenue over time), daily occupancy rate, number of medical errors per 1,000 patients or average handling time per phone call. When we tie a metric to a target, goal or norm critical to the organization's success, we often refer to it as **Key Performance Indicator (KPI)**. Although many metrics are presented as numbers, KPIs may take the form of ratings on a scale such as the RAG status (for red, amber, green), with red meaning that there is a severe problem and corrective action is required, amber indicating a potential problem, with the situation needing to be monitored closely, and green signifying that the performance is on target and no action is needed.

KPIs tend to add more value than operational data and organizational information because they are applied relative to targets or guidelines, that is, their use is contextualized. Typically KPIs are measured in the context of performance goals for individuals or units, and provide information regarding both past performance and goal progress. KPIs can also function as performance guidelines specifying minimums and maximums. They can operate in settings with minimum guidelines, as in the case of the number of patients a physician needs to see a week in order to cover practice expenses. Or they may be maximums such as capacity limits as in the case of the number of clients an account manager can effectively serve. KPIs are used to determine whether the organization's performance has changed over time, and, if so, at what rate and in which direction. In addition, KPIs are a convenient shortcut to identify problems, or to determine the impact of management decisions. However, as we will discuss in the next chapter, the existence of a colourfully presented and precise KPI does not necessarily mean that the underlying measures are relevant or based on good-quality data. In fact, not all KPIs are based on hard numbers, but may simply be a subjective judgement.

Benchmarks

These are metrics that are tied to standards or best practices within the industry. Thus, 'benchmarking' is a method of systematically improving a company's performance by measuring and comparing its performance against an organization that is considered to be the 'best in class'. For example in healthcare, there are industry data indicating 'door to needle time' for treating stroke victims. A hospital manager would want to acquire information on door to needle time in the hospital's emergency department in order to learn whether it should be improved. In general, benchmarking does not just involve the collection and comparison of benchmarks, but also further data analytics to identify the underlying cause of underperformance and actions for improvement. Benchmarks can be rich sources of information that can help managers determine how the organization measures up to others in the sector. In fields such as healthcare, benchmarking has been encouraged by setting national standards and by the publication of hospital performance metrics.

A caveat regarding benchmarks is warranted. You need to critically evaluate whether the benchmarked organization is truly 'best' on some criterion. Don't confuse hype or publication relations with actual evidence of success. Copying what others do only makes sense if you know that what was done was effective and is likely to be appropriate in your context. The expression 'best practices' implies that these practices are best for most organizations and that there is good evidence to support this claim: both claims are unlikely.

Correlations and regressions

Two metrics are correlated when a change in the value of one metric leads to a change in the value of the other – a matter we detail in Chapter 9. For example, temperature and ice-cream sales are correlated: when the temperature increases, ice-cream sales go up as well. **Regression** concerns the prediction of an outcome metric from one predictor metric (simple regression) or several predictor metrics (multiple regression). For example, for every one-degree rise in temperature, about 1,200 more ice creams are sold on average.

Correlations and regressions are inferential measures. Whereas descriptive measures such as operational data and KPIs provide rather basic information about the organization's performance, inferential measures are produced by statistical calculations that allow us to infer trends, identify cause-and-effect relationships and make predictions about organizational outcomes. However, as we will see in the next chapter, inferential measures can be misleading, and therefore require the highest degree of scrutiny.

Predictive models

A **predictive model** is a statistical model we use to make a prediction. The term, however, is subject to debate. Some use it in a generic sense to refer to any statistical model that is used to make predictions (such as correlations and regressions), whereas in the realm of 'big data' it often refers to a model that uses complex algorithms derived from advanced data analytic techniques based on artificial intelligence or machine learning. Predictive models are powerful tools in the decision-making process: they can identify drivers and predictors for outcomes relevant to the organization. Although the possibilities of predictive models such as artificial intelligence and neural networks are exciting, all the usual principles of evidence-based management apply: a predictive model is just another tool in your toolkit, and its use requires a critical mindset and attention to the quality of the evidence used to construct and populate the model.

 Note

The data-analytics myth

Articles on data analytics often refer to analytics in terms of machine learning, neural networking and artificial intelligence. These tools are useful but the real value in data analytics comes from simple statistical techniques that can be deployed by most managers. If you have access to Excel, you can work out correlations and regressions, and if you don't know how to, there are some helpful short tutorials on YouTube. The analytical tools are important, but so is the mindset of evidence-based management – the attitude of 'Hey, we don't know the answer. Let's get some data and find out!'[9]

8.9 Other considerations when acquiring data

The hype of the current era regarding data analytics and big data could give the impression that organizational data are always readily and cheaply available. This, however, is often not the case. In fact, many organizations struggle to manage and fully utilize their data. In addition, many data-analytics projects in organizations have started with high expectations but failed to deliver on their promises, because fundamental issues in data usage were not considered. Some of these issues might include:

Data protection/information security

There are many laws and regulations aimed at keeping employees' sensitive information safe and the privacy of customers secure. These include the Data Protection Act (1998) in the United Kingdom, the General Data Protection Regulation (2016) in the European Union, and the Federal Information Security Management Act (2002) in the United States. We need to consider the impact of these laws when using organizational data. Multinational firms in particular may be impacted by different, sometimes conflicting, regulations. In some cases, this makes it difficult to use data from multiple locations. In other cases, we need to obscure some of the data (for example, names and addresses of customers replaced with codes). Working with organizational data means negotiating the data protection rules. This means that as managers we need to think carefully about the type of organizational data we require (need to have) and what data we can exclude (nice to have) without reducing the value of the evidence we have in hand.

Costs and benefits

Acquiring and analysing organizational data may come at a considerable price, so a thorough assessment of the expected costs and benefits is important. Several large companies have invested millions of dollars in building data warehouses or implementing big data projects where the quality of the data fed into the systems was so weak the cost expended was unwarranted.

Accessibility

While some organizational data may be captured and stored in an easily accessible central database, much is likely to be dispersed across the organization, especially in large and complex companies. Acquiring data from multiple systems and locations may require a lot of time and effort. In addition, when we lack a common identifier, it will be very hard to link together data from different systems. For this reason, we often require assistance from an internal IT department or an external data analytics expert.

Politics

Finally, internal politics sometimes stand in the way of successful use of organizational evidence. Even when we capture and store data in an accessible database and have sufficient knowledge of data analytics we still may face challenges in using organizational evidence to support decision-making. In fact, lack of executive sponsorship is consistently cited as the main reason data analytics projects fail. One of the reasons is that evidence-based management sometimes challenges authority. It brings in evidence that may contradict the intuition and judgement of business leaders. For example, when the board has decided to move the company's customer service operation overseas, and you want to test the hypothesis that profitability has dropped due to a decrease in customer satisfaction, you should not be surprised if some managers object to gathering relevant evidence. As a data analyst once stated: 'At day's end, we depend on data and technology, but we live and die by politics.'[10] Chapter 15 details ways of overcoming resistance to use of evidence.

Notes and references

1 Note that organizational data are also valuable sources of evidence for scientific inquiry in management. Researchers need to be able to work with organizational data too.

2 Barton, D and Court, D (2012) Making advanced analytics work for you, *Harvard Business Review*, 90 (10), pp 78–83

3 This example is partly adapted from Mauboussin, MJ (2012) The true measures of success, *Harvard Business Review*, 90 (10), pp 46–56

4 Of course, evidence-based management is not only about assumed problems but also about opportunities. In the case of an (assumed/perceived) opportunity the questions above can be rephrased accordingly.

5 Gandomi, A and Haider, M (2015) Beyond the hype: Big data concepts, methods, and analytics, *International Journal of Information Management*, 35 (2), pp 137–44

6 Cukier, K (2010) Data, data everywhere: A special report on managing information, *The Economist*, 25 February [Online] http://www.economist.com/node/15557443

7 Dykes, B (2017) Big Data: Forget volume and variety, focus on velocity, *Forbes*, 28 June [Online] https://www.forbes.com/sites/brentdykes/2017/06/28/big-data-forget-volume-and-variety-focus-on-velocity/

8 Cascio, W and Boudreau, J (2010) *Investing in People: Financial impact of human resource initiatives*, FT Press

9 This example is partly adapted from Creelman, D (2016) McKinsey is (largely) wrong about people analytics, LinkedIn blog, published 24 July

10 Vaughan, R (2015) Politics over analytics: BI and Data Science findings need a pitch [LinkedIn] 28 January [Online] https://www.linkedin.com/pulse/politics-over-analytics-bi-data-science-findings-need-vaughan-robison/

APPRAISE: Evidence from the organization

09

If you torture the data long enough, it will confess.

RONALD COASE

Scientists are well aware of the need to be sceptical. They acknowledge that research findings can be misleading, due both to methodological shortcomings and problems with the underlying data. As a result, even well-respected, peer-reviewed journals sometimes publish flawed findings. In the realm of organizational evidence, the same fundamental problems arise, but practitioners are often less sceptical, unaware of the need to critically appraise their organizational evidence.

The decision-making process in many organizations resembles a form of competitive storytelling, where organizational evidence plays a small supporting role in the face of arguments practitioners use to persuade each other. Uncritical use of organizational evidence can lead to unnecessary, and unconscious, organizational risks.

A key point of this chapter is that managers need to ask not only 'What do the data say?' but also to get in the habit of asking critical follow-up questions such as 'Where do the data come from?', 'What kind of analyses were conducted?' and 'How confident should we be in the findings?'[1] Hence, a fundamental step to improve the quality of decision-making in organizations is to learn how to gather relevant organizational evidence and critically appraise its quality.

Before you start reading this chapter...

This chapter provides an overview of the most common barriers to overcome when using organizational evidence: data, facts and figures gathered from and about the organization. Gathering and analysing organizational evidence is similar to gathering and analysing scientific evidence. In fact, we argue that there is no fundamental difference between conducting scientific research and examining data gathered from your own organization. We must base both on the principles of the scientific method to ensure trustworthiness. Most of what is written in Chapter 7 on the critical appraisal of scientific research also applies to the critical appraisal of organizational evidence. As a result, issues of bias, statistical significance, practical relevance, effect size, confounders, reversed causation, moderators, mediators and the like should also be taken into account when evaluating the quality of organizational evidence. For this reason, we recommend reading Chapter 7 first before you read this chapter.

9.1 Barrier 1: Absence of a logic model

Chapter 8 explained that using organizational evidence in the decision-making process is not just about collecting and analysing data to identify interesting patterns. An evidence-based approach starts by asking questions like 'What is the problem to be solved and what is the evidence for this problem?' or 'What is the preferred solution, and what is the evidence that this solution will be effective?' Organizational data and information are important to answering the second part of these two questions – 'what is the evidence for either the problem or the solution?' To acquire evidence from the organization, we need to start by formulating a logic model.

A logic model (also referred to as a causal model or theory of change) spells out the process by which we expect underlying cause(s) to lead to a problem and produce certain organizational consequences. It is a graphic representation of the logical connections between inputs (resources, antecedents), activities and processes (what is done to inputs), outputs and outcomes (immediate results and longer-term consequences). Think of a logic model as a short narrative explaining why or when a problem occurs and how this leads to a particular outcome. Logic models provide a way of conceptualizing problems and processes that allows more information and data points to be factored in to our thinking than is possible in unaided human judgement. Just as a day planner or agenda helps you keep in mind all the things to do in a day, a logic model helps you stay on top of the array of issues related to a particular problem, project or situation.

In Chapter 2 (ASK) we provided an example in which Marissa Mayer, former CEO of Yahoo, decided to eliminate all work-from-home arrangements. This decision was based on her assumption that 'speed and quality are often sacrificed when we work from home'. In this example, the logic model can be depicted as in Figure 9.1.

Such a logic model helps us determine which organizational data and information to collect and analyse. In this case, organizational evidence should be obtained to answer the following questions:

- How many employees at Yahoo frequently work from home?

- How does this number compare to the total number of employees at Yahoo? Is this substantial?

- What is the average performance of employees who frequently work from home?

- What is the average performance of comparable employees who don't work from home?

- Is there a difference in performance between these two groups?

- If so, is the difference practically relevant?

- If so, what is the impact of this difference on the total performance of Yahoo?

Figure 9.1

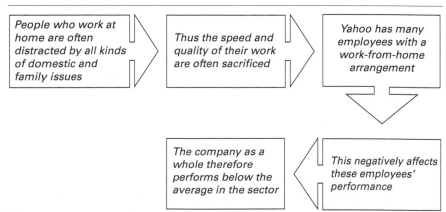

Formulating a logic model prevents a 'fishing expedition' in which a voluminous amount of data is captured and exhaustively analysed – an inappropriate practice that increases the chance of detecting non-existing relationships between the variables. A logic model helps to tie assumptions about problems (or preferred solutions) to 'real' tangible relationships linked by evidence.[2]

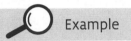
Example

Military intelligence analyst Tyler Vigen demonstrates various kinds of spurious, non-existing correlations.[3] On his site, you can find examples of bizarre, non-existent correlations, such as between the divorce rate in Maine and the per capita consumption of margarine ($r = 0.99$), and between the marriage rate in Kentucky and the number of people who drowned after falling out of a fishing boat ($r = 0.95$). Similar strong but spurious correlations are found when large sets of organizational data are exhaustively analysed, such as the nonsensical relationship between sales representatives' shoe size and number of sales, or the relationship between a firm's financial performance and its CEO's handicap with the United States Golf Association. Without a logic model to guide our assessments and analysis, we are likely to identify other such meaningless relationships.

9.2 Barrier 2: Irrelevant data

In the previous chapter, we explained that organizational data are often presented as a metric – an indicator of the organization's performance derived from a combination of two or more measures. Examples include financial ratios, daily occupancy rates, or average time per phone call. Metrics are an important input to management decisions, if what they measure is meaningful (for example, the turnover rate in a department's staff or the production volume of a manufacturing company). Unfortunately, it is all too easy with modern technology to create an array of colourful metrics, giving a false impression of understanding. For example, the number of sightings of unicorns by members of the staff at a food-processing company may provide insight into their mental health, but it is likely to be irrelevant to the company's financial performance. Metrics are likely to be more relevant when you assess outcomes rather than activities. For example, evaluating what sales agents do in terms of type of activity and time spent can provide a valuable source of data for investigating productivity, but an even more useful metric is the number of actual sales per agent per week. Unfortunately, organizations are often tempted to create metrics from easily available data rather than make the effort to gather more relevant data that add real value to management decisions. Keep in mind that more metrics do not always equate with better understanding. Organizations can be better off with a small number of relevant and accurate metrics rather than a large number of fancy but irrelevant ones. Don't collect organizational data just because it is easy to do so: distinguish between what is easily measured and what is relevant to measure.[4] An important indicator of relevance is whether the data have a key place in your logic model.

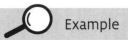 Example

In an effort to drive sales, an automobile manufacturer launched a marketing campaign to draw more customers to its showrooms and thus increase car sales. The campaign encouraging free test rides seemed a big success, substantially increasing customer visits. Indeed, the metric indicating the number of visits per day went up by 20 per cent. The number of sales, however, did not increase. Dealers offered the company an important explanation: 'A lot more people are visiting the showroom, but most are 17- or 18-year-old boys, and they aren't going to be buying.' This example illustrates how you may get a good result on a misleading metric unrelated to the desired outcome.

Other misleading or irrelevant metrics are those that are not actionable. For example, revenue is an important indicator of how a company is doing, but just knowing that revenue increased without knowing its possible cause is not very helpful – unless the metric indicates a significant change before and after a specific event or intervention, you lack essential information on how to sustain or amplify the result.

9.3 Barrier 3: Inaccurate data

Decades after the expression 'garbage in, garbage out' (GIGO) was coined, many companies still struggle with data accuracy. It is important to remember that data aren't the same as facts. The metrics and KPIs presented in a management information system or business dashboard are numbers collected and recorded by *people*. These data may represent facts, but all kinds of biases and distortions can slip into them. By the time metrics and KPIs are reported to senior management they can take the form of authoritative-looking numeric data. However, even subjective opinions can be transformed into numbers, and as a result organizational data sometimes look more objective than they really are. An important question to ask is 'How were the data collected, processed and reported?' In most companies, organizational data will typically have gone through one or more of the following steps before being presented as metrics or KPIs.

Collection

Organizational data first need to be collected – also referred to as 'data capture'. Ideally, a person or an automated system collects data routinely. As a rule, the collection of direct/objective data (for example, production errors, staff turnover rate) is more likely to be accurate than that of indirect/subjective data based on personal reports (for example, self-reported accidents or perceived performance). In addition, the accuracy of self-reported data can be seriously harmed if data are collected after the actual activity being described. People lack 100 per cent recall, even after a short time delay.

Extraction

Ideally, data are extracted from the original source. The more steps the original source is from the final data capture system, the greater the risk of bias or inaccuracy. In addition, some methods of data extraction are more flawed than others. Copying data from an Excel spreadsheet into another application by hand will, for example, be less accurate than automatically extracting data directly into a database.

Aggregation

Organizational data may be captured and combined from multiple sources. Avoid combining organizational data of different types on the (invalid) assumption they are comparable (like comparing apples with oranges). For example, when a hospital collects data on patient treatments, it would make little sense to add together the treatments of a department that deals with minor injuries with one that performs open-heart surgery. The data of these departments are too different in terms of impact, cost, time taken and skills required.

Conversion and (re)formatting

When data are captured from different sources, they must be converted into a standard format. The conversion process may involve splitting data apart in some fields, while combining data in other areas. Each stage of reformatting, however, introduces the risk of error and distortion of the original data.

Interpretation

Creation of metrics from raw data generally requires some form of interpretation. For example, KPIs often take the form of ratings on a scale. This requires defining a norm or threshold; for example, what data should be scored as low or high or as 1 or 2 or 3? Interpretation is typically carried out by people. If their analyses are not based on clear rules and guidelines, then KPIs are prone to bias and may be inaccurate.

Summarization

Large amounts of organizational data can be difficult to manage let alone interpret, so it makes sense that metrics and KPIs are often a summary of the data. However, summarization typically requires some degree of subjective interpretation (see above) and may involve losing valuable information.

While the steps described above are necessary to provide managers with an understandable set of metrics, the more steps the data go through the more likely they will be inaccurate. As a rule, inaccuracy increases wherever people are involved in any of these steps – due to human error, incentives to manipulate the data, or even a simple lack of understanding of the data.

9.4 Barrier 4: Missing contextual information

Organizational data can be misleading without context. Consider the following statement made by a manager at a large bank: 'My team is carrying out 25 activities that other teams should be doing instead!' The number 25 was repeated meeting after meeting, until a project team was formed to migrate the activities. After one year's effort, there had been little progress, because the activities were generally too complex and expensive to move. An additional question was then asked about the 25 activities: 'How long do those activities take to complete in a typical month?' To everybody's surprise it turned out that most of the activities did not take place very often and on average only a few hours per month were spent on all of them.

Metrics and KPIs empty of important contextual information are surprisingly common. In the example above, looking only at the number of activities without considering total time spent leads to a considerable amount of money being spent on a project of little value. The same applies to organizations that use 'headcount reduction' as a metric for cost savings. For example, a cardiologist's average base salary in the United States is US $550,000,[5] whereas the annual salary of a nursing aide is only US $25,000[6] so a headcount reduction of 10 per cent is a meaningless metric when information about the functions involved is missing. Other contextual information often missing is the average in the sector, setting or industry. A staff turnover rate of 200 per cent annually sounds pretty terrible, until we learn that the organization comprises fast food restaurants and the industry average is over 300 per cent. Widely used metrics such as absenteeism, staff turnover, job satisfaction, failure frequency, customer complaints and so on, are meaningless when we can't compare them to the average in the sector.

Finally, another contextual factor that is often overlooked is size. Whenever organizational data in the form of a metric are presented, always ask yourself, 'Is that a big number?'[7]

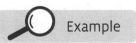 Example

The annual records of a large multinational corporation show that over the past five years the company has spent US $2 million to provide subsidized childcare for 20,000 employees. Is US $2 million a big number? When you spread out this amount over five years and divide it by the number of employees, it equals only $20 per employee. Spread this amount across 52 weeks of the year and it leaves 38 cents per week. Would you be able to find childcare for 38 cents a week?

The organizational data of a back office of a health insurance company indicates that every year more than 1,500 errors are being made, accounting for an annual loss of US $1.5 million. Is that a big number? Not when the total number of transactions is about 4.8 million per year, representing a total sum of US $46.5 billion. And certainly not when the average error rate in the sector is about 0.5 per cent.

9.5 Barrier 5: Measurement error

Most organizational data are measurements, that is, estimations of quantities such as an amount, volume or frequency of something. A measurement is typically expressed as a number of standard units, such as products sold, errors made or employees hired. Unfortunately, whenever something is measured, its score is likely to deviate somewhat from its true value. This deviation is referred to as **measurement error**.

Of course, we can measure some things more precisely than others. For example, the measurement of a company's total revenue may be more precise than the measurement of its corporate reputation or employee morale. In addition, if we measure outcomes using different measurement methods, we will probably get different results. But even if we measure something perfectly, there always will be a measurement error. This is not necessarily a problem, especially when the measurement error is negligible. However, small measurement errors tend to be larger when the metric is a 'difference score': a score that is derived by subtracting one variable from another. A widely used difference score is profit: sales minus costs. As a rule, difference scores have a larger measurement error (and thus a lower reliability) when the two variables composing it are correlated. In other words, two variables (for example, sales and costs) measured with very little error can yield a difference score (for example, profit) with more measurement error.

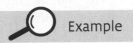

Example

The organizational data of a global entertainment company show that the annual profit over 2015 was US $986 million. This number was calculated by subtracting the annual costs from the total sales. Both sales and costs were measured quite reliably. Sales and costs, however, are highly correlated. Thus, although little measurement error exists in the sales and costs data, there may be a large measurement error in the profit metric. As a result, the reported profit could be substantially lower (or higher) than the actual profit.[8]

You should always be aware of measurement error in using organizational evidence. Error can seriously distort metrics and KPIs. Sound methods exist to adjust for measurement error, getting you closer to the true value.

9.6 Barrier 6: The small number problem

A notorious problem with organizational evidence is the **small numbers problem**. This problem stems from what is known in probability theory as the **Law of the Large Numbers**. This law states that the larger the sample size, the more accurate its predictions regarding characteristics of the whole population, and thus the less the sample value deviates on average from the population value. As a general principle, the average (mean) of a large sample of organizational data will be closer to the 'true' average of the total data than an average drawn from a small sample. Thus, when we use a small sample of organizational data, the metrics and KPIs based on that sample are most likely to deviate from the 'true' value. The small number problem often arises in three situations:

1 **When organizations compare units (for example, teams, departments or divisions) unequal in size.** Smaller units are more likely to report data that deviate from the true value than larger units. For example, when the monthly average absentee rate of the total number of employees is 2.5 per cent, a small unit is more likely to yield an average with a greater deviation from this 2.5 per cent than a large unit. This deviation has nothing to do with the employees' health status or the quality of its management,

but results solely from the small number problem. The same is true, of course, for metrics such as daily occupancy rate, number of defects per 1,000 products or average handle time per phone call. Metrics from smaller units will deviate more than those from larger units.

2 **When organizations collect data from a sample rather than from the whole organization.** This makes sense, as collecting data from the whole organization is often time-consuming and expensive. However, the smaller the sample, the greater the chance that the values measured deviate from the true value. For example, if only a small sample of employees participates in a survey, the data derived from this sample will most likely deviate from the data derived from the total population.

3 **When organizations have access only to a small sample of the total market population.** For example, insights into customer behaviour based on the data drawn from an organization with a small market share are less likely to be representative of the whole market population than insights based on the data of customers of a global brand such as Nike, L'Oréal or Heinz.

A key approach for dealing with the small number problem is simply to be aware of it. In addition, the following four remedies also help:

1 Sample from the whole population.

2 Aggregate internal data to achieve larger sample sizes.

3 Pool data from several firms (this occurs in many industries) to develop a larger data set.

4 Clearly state the sample size and report confidence intervals (see Barrier 10).

9.7 Barrier 7: Confusing percentages and averages

Percentages

We use percentages to express a proportion out of a total; for example, '67 per cent of all employees are male', or 'the failure rate of a newly designed product is 0.5 per cent'. We also use percentages to express differences or degree of change – the absentee rate in a company has gone up by 5 per cent, for example. Change and differences, however, can be relative or absolute. An absolute change (increase or decrease) expresses the difference between two comparable values, such as differences in products sold, total revenue or employees hired at two points in time. For example, when last year's revenue was $5 million and this year's revenue is $4 million, then this is an absolute difference of $1 million. Absolute change or differences are useful when the amount of change itself is relevant, regardless of the base value. For example, an increase of $1 million in revenue may be relevant regardless of whether that increase came from a large company with an annual financial turnover of $100 million or a small company making only $5 million a year. Relative change, on the other hand, expresses difference as a percentage of the base value. In the example above, for the $5 million company an increase of $1 million is 20 per cent, whereas for the $100 million company this is an increase of only 1 per cent. Although the absolute change is the same for both companies ($1 million), the relative change is very different (1 per cent versus 20 per cent).

For this reason, it is often assumed that relative change expressed as a percentage of the base value is a more accurate metric. As we demonstrate in the example below, however, this is not always the case.

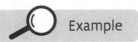

Example

A pharmaceutical company has tested a new, experimental drug for Parkinson's disease. Compared with drugs currently prescribed, the new drug decreases symptoms such as tremors, limb stiffness, impaired balance and slow movement by 30 per cent. However, compared with the existing drugs, the mortality rate of patients taking the new drug (those dying because of serious side effects) has increased by 200 per cent. Would you decide to bring this new drug to the market?

Most people will be inclined to say no, because a 200 per cent mortality rate increase sounds pretty dramatic. However, this depends on the base value. If the mortality rate of the existing drugs is only 1 in 350,000 patients (0.000003 per cent), a relative increase of 200 per cent means an absolute increase of only 2 in 350,000 patients (0.000006 per cent). In all, the new drug sounds like it has better outcomes, especially as a patient's improvement in health would be substantial.

Whenever changes or differences are presented as percentages, we must make clear whether these differences are relative or absolute. Ideally, both types – including the number of standardized units they represent – should be reported.

Finally, make sure whether the data concern 'per cents' or 'percentage points'. If the unemployment rate last year was 4.8 per cent and this year it is 6.0 per cent, is that an increase of 25 per cent? (6.0 – 4.8 = 1.2 and 1.2/4.8 = 0.25, which equals 25 per cent). Or is it just an increase of 6.0 – 4.8 = 1.2 per cent? We can use either, but to avoid confusion, the latter is referred to as a percentage point. In this case, the government would probably use 1.2 per cent, whereas the opposition would prefer 25 per cent. There is no rule here, so always ask about the underlying data.[9]

Averages

Much of the organizational information used by companies is expressed as averages. Like percentages, averages look simple, but that simplicity is deceptive. In fact, there are three ways to calculate an average and each yields a different number. For this reason, we avoid the term average and use instead the more precise terms mean, median and mode. In some cases they are identical, but often not. In addition, when the word 'average' is used, this usually refers to the mean, but unfortunately not always.

 Example

Five people are sitting in a bar, each earning about $100,000 per year. Here are their earnings:

   Person 1: $96,000

   Person 2: $96,000

   Person 3: $99,000

   Person 4: $104,000

   Person 5: $105,000

The mean is calculated by simply adding all observations (for example, reports, metrics) and then dividing the outcome by the number of observations. Here the mean is exactly $100,000. The median is the middle number in a set of numbers. In this case, the median is $99,000. The mode is the most frequent number in a set. Here the mode is $96,000.

In this example the mean, median and mode are more or less of the same value. This, however, is not always the case. For example, let's assume Bill Gates walks into the bar (and his annual earnings are assumed to be US $1 billion). The mean in our bar example has increased from $100,000 to more than $166 million. But the point of an average is to represent a whole pile of data with a single number. In the first example the mean is a good representation of these five people's annual incomes, but in the second example, when Bill Gates shows up, it is not, then we should use the mode or the median instead.

An average is by definition an inaccurate metric: it combines a large amount of data and represents it with one single number. As a result, averages tend to obscure the natural variance. Thus, whenever a metric represents an average, you should look for an indication of what the variance is, that is, how the numbers are spread out around the average.

Standard deviation

To determine whether an average is a good metric to represent the data, statisticians have come up with the **standard deviation**, a measure that tells us how much the data deviates from the average. For example, when the mean age of all employees is 40 and the 'standard deviation' is 10, this tells us that the typical deviation from the mean is around 10 years. Now, here is a very useful rule of thumb: about 95 per cent of the data will be covered by two standard deviations plus or minus the average. Thus, in the example above, a standard deviation of 10 tells us that 95 per cent of the employees are between 20 years (40 minus two times 10) and 60 years old (40 plus two times 10). Likewise, when the mean age of all employees is 50 years and the standard deviation is 5, then 95 per cent are between 40 and 60 years old, indicating that the company's workforce is rather senior.

The standard deviation (often abbreviated SD) is also helpful in determining the size of a change or difference. If you take the percentage of change and divide it by the standard deviation, you get a good impression of its magnitude. In the social sciences, a change of 0.2 is usually considered a small difference, while 0.5 is considered a moderate difference, and 0.8 is a large difference.[10]

Example

In the past four years, an Italian shoe factory has experienced multiple restructurings and downsizings, reducing its workforce from 800 to fewer than 500 factory workers. The HR Director believes that this has been very stressful for the workers, causing a dramatic productivity decline. He decides to introduce a stress-reduction programme, including on-site chair massage therapy, a technique successfully used at AT&T, Apple and Google. A few months after the programme is introduced, organizational data indicate productivity has gone up: the workers' average (mean) productivity has increased by 5 per cent from 200 shoes to 210 shoes per day, with a standard deviation of 7. A 5 per cent change equals $5/7 = 0.7$ standard deviation, so this suggests that the programme may have had a large impact.

9.8 Barrier 8: Misleading graphs

As explained in Chapter 8, there are many specialized tools available to present organizational data, such as 'management information' or 'business intelligence' systems. Most include advanced dashboards and visualization tools that present data in graphs, charts and appealing visualizations. When used appropriately, graphs such as pie charts, bar graphs and scatterplots help us to intuitively grasp complex data. Graphs, however, can be misleading. Below we provide some well-known examples.

Omitting the baseline

From the graph on the left in Figure 9.2, it looks as if the number of car sales has tripled in one year. This graph, however, is misleading because the baseline is missing: the vertical axis does not start at 0. The right-hand graph presents the same data, but here the vertical axis correctly starts at 0. This graph indicates that the increase in sales was rather small.

Figure 9.2

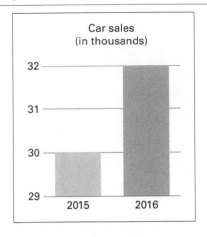
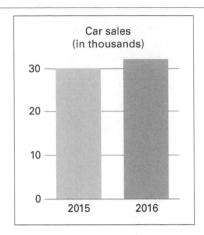

Manipulated axis

Although the vertical scale in the left-hand graph of Figure 9.3 correctly starts at the baseline (0), it does not go up in equal steps. This distorts the graph (as you can see in the right-hand graph using equal steps) and makes it look as if the highest turnover was in Q1 and Q2, rather than Q3 and Q4. In addition, it is not clear what the numbers on the vertical scale (0 to 16) mean.

Figure 9.3

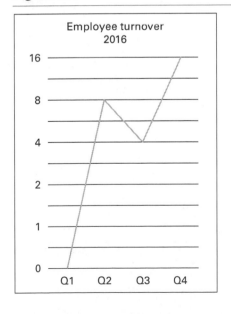
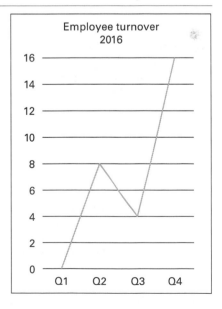

Figure 9.4

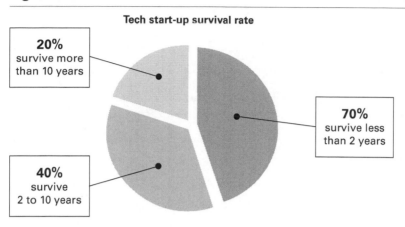

The numbers don't add up

The pie chart in Figure 9.4 measures the survival rate of technology start-ups. Note its categories are mutually exclusive and its percentages should add up to 100 per cent, not 130 per cent.

Cherry-picking

The graph on the left in Figure 9.5 shows that between 2000 and 2008 the average housing prices have been steadily growing from 200k to 300k. As you can see in the graph on the right, this increase can be visualized

Figure 9.5

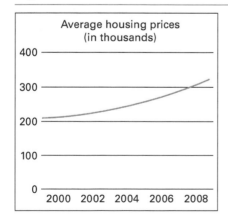
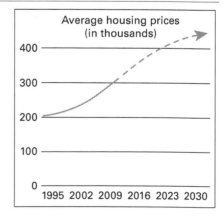

more dramatically by extending the x-axis into those years where no data are available. As a result, the slope of the curve increases, suggesting that the prices have gone up faster than they really have. In addition, a dotted trend line is added, suggesting that prices will keep growing for the coming decades. Note that the dotted line starts at 2008, the year that the housing market collapsed.

Cumulative versus interval data

Instead of plotting data for separate time intervals, sometimes cumulative data are presented. For example, the number of sales can be visualized for each month, quarter or year separately, but it is also possible to present them as cumulative sales per month, quarter or year – that is, total sales to date. When the cumulative sales are presented in a graph, each single sale makes the graph's line go up. This is particularly convenient when the total number of sales is decreasing. This is exactly what Apple's CEO Tim Cook did during a presentation on iPhone sales in 2013.[11] In Figure 9.6 you can see that the graph suggests that the iPhone sales are still increasing. However, by plotting cumulative sales instead of quarterly sales, Apple hid

Figure 9.6

the fact that iPhone sales were actually declining.[12] If you look carefully at the graph, you can see that after 2013 the line is going up less steeply, indicating a decrease in sales.

9.9 Barrier 9: Correlations and regressions – overfitting the data

In Chapter 7 we explained that two metrics are correlated when a change in the value of one metric leads to a change in the value of the other. For example, temperature and ice-cream sales are correlated; when the temperature increases, ice-cream sales go up as well. Regression involves the prediction of an outcome metric from one predictor metric (simple regression) or several predictor metrics (multiple regression). For example, for every one-degree rise in temperature, about 1,200 more ice creams are sold on average.

Correlations and regressions are *inferential* measures. Whereas descriptive measures such as operational data and KPIs provide basic information, correlations and regressions allow us to infer trends, identify relationships and make predictions about organizational outcomes. However, correlations and regressions can be misleading, and therefore require the same scrutiny as percentages and averages.

Correlation coefficients

A correlation coefficient is a numerical index that reflects the strength of the relationship between two variables. There are different types of correlation coefficient, depending on the type of variables we are measuring, but they all have a value that ranges between -1 and +1. A correlation of $r = 0.10$ is considered a weak relationship, whereas a correlation of $r = 0.60$ is regarded as a strong one. A correlation coefficient can be influenced by several factors, including outliers, that is, the normal range of values in a dataset. In the example used in the section on averages, Bill Gates' annual earnings of US $1 billion are an outlier, as the other five people earn much less than this, about $100,000. We always recommend checking the 'scatter plot' (Figure 9.7), a graph that shows the relationship between two metrics and helps identify outliers.

Figure 9.7

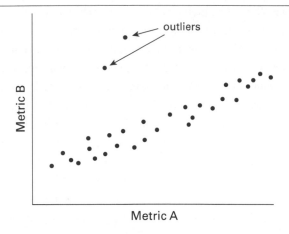

Metric B

outliers

Metric A

r-squared: Variance explained

To get a better idea of how strongly two metrics are correlated, we can take a look at the r^2 (pronounced '**r-squared**'). The r^2 indicates the extent variation or differences in one metric can be explained by a variation or differences in a second metric. The r^2 is expressed as a percentage and can easily be calculated by squaring the correlation coefficient. For example, if the organizational data show that the correlation between customer satisfaction and sales performance is $r = 0.5$, then the r^2 is 0.25, indicating that 25 per cent of the variation in sales (increase or decrease) might be explained by differences in customer satisfaction.

Range restriction

Another aspect to consider when judging correlations is **range restriction**. Range restriction occurs when a metric in a dataset has a more limited range (minimum and/or maximum value) than it has in the whole population. As a result, the correlation between that metric and another metric can be constrained.

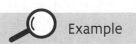 Example

A Midwestern branch of a US trading company analysed its organizational data to see whether some factors strongly correlated with the performance of sales agents. It gathered the data of the top 20 per cent of sales agents based on their monthly sales performance. The assumption was that both age and years of experience were important factors. When they analysed the data, however, they found only small correlations. After some months, however, it became clear that the company's Northeastern branch had conducted the same analysis, but found that the correlation with sales performance was 0.36 for age and 0.55 for years of experience. When the data analysts of the two branches examined this remarkable difference, they discovered that the Northeastern branch had included the data of all sales agents rather than only the top 20 per cent. It was therefore concluded that the low correlations of the Midwestern branch were due to range restriction. This means that the Midwestern branch used only one part of the sales data (the high end of the distribution), reducing the possibility of observing a relationship between sales agent characteristics and their performance.

Range restriction can occur because the dataset comprises a subset of the total data (as in the example above), but also because the organization itself is a subset. For example, in the general population the correlation between General Mental Ability (otherwise known as 'IQ') and performance is about 0.6.[13] In a prestigious law firm that recruits only lawyers with a degree from Stanford, however, this correlation will likely be closer to zero. This is because their lawyers' IQ is probably on the high side, perhaps between 125 and 140, whereas the IQ of the general population ranges from 70 to 130.

Regression coefficients

A regression coefficient tells you how much the outcome metric is expected to increase (if the coefficient is positive) or decrease (if the coefficient is negative) when the predictor metric increases by one unit. There are two types of regression coefficient: unstandardized and standardized. An unstandardized coefficient concerns predictor and outcome metrics that represent 'real' units (for example, sales per month, points on a job satisfaction scale or numbers of errors). In that case, the coefficient is noted as 'b'. For example, when a predictor metric temperature is regressed on the number of ice creams sold, a regression coefficient of $b = 8.3$ means that for every one-degree rise in temperature, 8.3 more ice creams are sold on average.

A standardized coefficient involves predictor and outcome metrics expressed in standard deviations. In that case, the coefficient is noted as β (pronounced as beta). Betas provide information about the effect of the predictor metric on the outcome metric. As explained in Chapter 7, in the case of a simple regression a β of 0.10 is considered a small effect, whereas a β of 0.60 is considered a large effect. In the case of a multiple regression the thresholds are slightly higher ($\beta = 0.20$ is considered small, $\beta = 0.80$ is considered large). Both b and β provide important information: the b tells us how much exactly the predictor metric is expected to change, whereas the beta (which expresses that change in standard units) informs us whether that change is considered small, moderate or large. For this reason, both unstandardized (b) and standardized (β) **regression coefficients** should be reported.

Multiple regression tells you how the outcome metric is expected to increase (or decrease) when several predictors are considered at the same time. The logic used to determine the factors that contribute to a particular outcome metric can provide insight into which predictors to use. For example, a logic model specifying how new car sales are driven by a) advertising to appropriate market segments (for example, drivers who are not teenage boys), b) sales agent skills, and c) other predictors (for example, discounts, special offers), can be used to run a multiple regression analysis to test whether its predictions are supported.

Multiple R-squared: goodness of fit

There are a lot of factors that should be examined when critically appraising a regression, such as variable types, multicollinearity, distribution and linearity. Unfortunately, it is not possible to address all these aspects in this book.[14] In addition, it is always recommended to check the '**residual plot**', a graph that shows if (and how) the observed (true) values in a dataset differ from the values as predicted by the regression. This is also referred to as '**goodness of fit**'. Figures 9.8 and 9.9 are two examples of a residual plot. The dots represent the observed values, and the line represents the values as predicted by the regression equation. As you can see the observed values in the Figure 9.8 plot are closer to the regression line than those in the Figure 9.9 plot, indicating a better goodness of fit.

Unfortunately, a residual plot is often not available. In that case, we can use the multiple R-squared instead. (Note that this indicator is different from the r-squared above, which involves squaring a correlation coefficient to find out how much covariation exists between two metrics. That is why we use

Figure 9.8

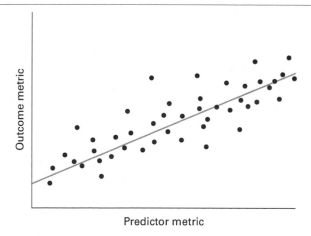

Figure 9.9

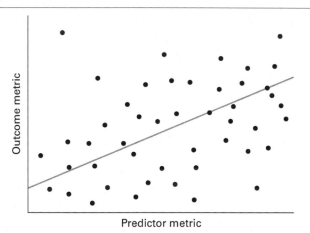

a lower-case r for the variance explained and a capital R for the goodness of fit). In a regression analysis, the R^2 tells us how close the observed data are to the regression line. Put differently, it is the percentage of the outcome metric that, based on the regression coefficient, is predicted by the predictor metric. For example, when the unstandardized regression coefficient b for customer satisfaction and the number of sales is 30.2, this indicates that for one point of improvement in the level of customer satisfaction, on average 30.2 more products are sold. However, when the R^2 is only 0.18, this means that the level of customer satisfaction can predict only 18 per cent of the number of sales.

9.10 Barrier 10: Wide confidence intervals

In Chapter 7 we explained that effect sizes such as correlation and regression coefficients differ across samples, meaning that they are only an estimate of the 'true' effect size. The same is true of estimates such as percentages, averages and the R-squared. This means that whenever a sample or subgroup of the total population (or whole dataset) is used, we need to know how precise the estimate is. We can determine the precision of a percentage, mean, b, β, R^2 or any other estimate by looking at its confidence interval. A confidence interval provides the upper and lower boundaries between which we expect – usually with 95 per cent confidence – the true value to fall. A confidence interval is stated as '95% CI'. If the 95% CI is fairly narrow, then the estimated value is a precise reflection of the 'true' value. A 95% CI is considered too wide if the decision you would make based on the value of the lower boundary of the interval would be different from the decision you would make based on the value of the upper one.

 Example

A British car insurance company routinely measures the satisfaction of its clients. In the last annual quarter, the level of customer satisfaction dropped from 7.5 to 7.0 on a 10-point scale. Because customer satisfaction has been shown to be a good predictor for the number of sales ($R^2 = 0.62$), the sales director feels that action should be taken. The HR director, however, points out that the customer satisfaction metric is based only on a sample of the company's total number of clients, so he asks the company's data analyst to calculate a confidence interval. This 95% CI turns out to be between 6.2 and 7.8, meaning that there is 95 per cent confidence that the true level of customer satisfaction falls somewhere between these two values. Both the sales director and the HR director consider this confidence interval to be too wide, and therefore decide to take no further action at this point. In effect, it is possible that customer satisfaction remains at least as high as last quarter.

As the example above illustrates, it is important that whenever a percentage, average, coefficient or any point estimate is provided, you always check (or ask for) the confidence interval.

9.11 Artificial intelligence, machine learning and artificial neural networks

As explained in the previous chapter, big data refers to extensive, diverse and rapidly changing datasets. Walmart, for instance, processes more than a million transactions per hour.[15] Such data are on a scale quite different from what most analysts are used to. For this reason, new data analytics techniques have emerged, using machine learning and artificial neural networks. Most of these techniques are based on the principle of artificial intelligence (AI). There are many definitions of AI, but in general it means a program using data to build a model of some aspect of the world. This model is then used to make informed decisions and predictions about future events.[16] Machine learning is an application of AI that enables computer systems to automatically learn, adapt and improve from experience (predict, test and revise) and pattern recognition – without being explicitly programmed by a human being. The underlying principle of artificial neural networks is similar, but in this case learning occurs from web-like connections among a large number of small processor units. These techniques mimic the way humans learn, by refining the algorithms used to autonomously observe and analyse data.

Most organizations, however, do not have big data – they don't need to analyse 100+ terabytes of heterogeneous data per day in real-time, and thus 'conventional' statistical techniques suffice. In addition, big data and AI technology raise serious social, ethical and political concerns. For example, the output of big data and AI techniques is based on extremely complex mathematical algorithms, often protected by copyright, and thus function as a black box. Moreover, in some cases, even the developers themselves don't know exactly how their techniques work. As a result, algorithms can have hidden biases, inadvertently introducing gender or racial biases into the decision-making process. At the same time, big data and AI can be very helpful. Yet, there is the danger of being blinded by the glamour of these new fields, failing to recognize their limitations. Critical appraisal and attention to data quality are as important to both big data and small.

9.12 Organizational evidence: Quality versus purpose

A last word on organizational evidence, the raw data that comprise it and the issue of quality: the applications of organizational data and the people who apply them are very diverse. For example, data can be gathered by the government to assess regulatory compliance; by senior executives to make strategic decisions; by supervisors to make operational decisions; or they can be used to identify problems that require immediate attention (for example, equipment breakdown, security breach). The quality of data in terms of reliability and validity will vary depending on their use and the people who use them. Regulatory use, for example, is subject to the highest quality standards because such data are used to evaluate compliance with legal requirements. Data alerting us to a possible problem, however, require a different standard – such data first and foremost need to be timely, so we accept that they are biased towards false positives – finding a relationship between data when none really exists. For example, a hypersensitive smoke detector – triggering sometimes a false alarm – is preferable to one that requires a huge fire before sounding. In the middle of the quality spectrum are data used for strategic and tactical decisions. The people who use such data may differ as to how valid and reliable they think the data should be. When critically appraising organizational data, we must keep in mind that they are used by different kinds of people for different kinds of decisions requiring different kinds of quality. Consulting additional evidence sources (for example, subject matter experts, relevant stakeholders) helps you to determine what level of data quality you need, and thus the extent to which you need to scrutinize the data. As explained in Chapter 1, evidence-based management is about critically appraised evidence from multiple sources. Thus, organizational data, big or small, should not be the sole sources of evidence in any decision-making process.

9.13 Checklist

Table 9.1

	Yes	No	Unclear
1. Is the collection of organizational data based on a logic model?			
2. Are the data relevant to the organization's decision-making processes?			
3. Are the data accurate? Consider: – How were the data captured? – How were the data processed? – Were the interpretation and summary of the data based on clear rules and guidelines? – How often were people involved in these steps?			
4. Are the data's context taken into account?			
5. How reliable are the data – could there be a measurement error? Consider: – Are the data based on direct/objective outcome measures or indirect/subjective measures? – Are the reported measures a difference score?			
6. Is the data set sufficiently large enough to prevent the small number problem from occurring?			
7. When a change or difference in the form of a percentage is presented, is it clear whether this involves a relative change or an absolute change?			
8. When an average (mean, median, mode) is presented, is it clear what the variance is – is the standard deviation reported?			
9. When a graph is presented, could it be misleading? Consider: – Is there a baseline? – Do the units on the axes represent equal steps? – Do the numbers add up? – Does the graph present missing data? – Does the graph present cumulative or interval data?			
10. When a correlation or regression coefficient is presented, is it accurate? Consider: outliers, R^2, range restriction.			

Table 9.1 (*Continued*)

	Yes	No	Unclear
11. When a regression coefficient is presented, does the regression model fit the data? Consider: R^2.			
12. When estimates are presented (frequencies, ratios, proportions, averages, percentages, difference scores, correlation or regression coefficients, etc), are confidence intervals provided? If so, are they sufficiently small?			

Notes and references

1 McAfee, A, Brynjolfsson, E and Davenport, TH (2012) Big data: The management revolution, *Harvard Business Review*, **90** (10), pp 60–8

2 Calude, CS and Longo, G (2017) The deluge of spurious correlations in big data, *Foundations of Science*, **22** (3), pp 595–612

3 See www.tylervigen.com/spurious-correlations

4 Herrmann, DS (2007) *Complete Guide to Security and Privacy Metrics: Measuring regulatory compliance, operational resilience, and ROI*, Auerbach Publishers

5 Merritt Hawkins & Associates (2012) Review of Physician Recruiting Incentives

6 Bureau of Labor Statistics (2012) National Compensation Survey

7 Blastland, M and Dilnot, AW (2008) *The Tiger That Isn't: Seeing through a world of numbers*, Profile Books, London

8 This example is adapted from Donaldson, L (2012) Evidence-based management (EBMgt) using organizational facts, in *The Oxford Handbook of Evidence-Based Management*, ed DM Rousseau, Oxford University Press, Oxford

9 This latter example is adopted from Hans van Maanen, a Dutch science journalist who is the author of the chapter 'Understanding statistics' for the WFSJ Online Course in Science Journalism (www.wfsj.org/course/en/)

10 As explained in Chapter 7, according to Cohen's rule of thumb a 'small' effect is one that is only visible through careful examination. A 'medium' effect, however, is one that is 'visible to the naked eye of the careful observer'. Finally, a 'large' effect is one that anybody can easily see because it is substantial

11   Levitin, D (2016) *A Field Guide to Lies and Statistics: A neuroscientist on how to make sense of a complex world*, Penguin, UK

12   Blodget, H (2013) These Two Charts Show Why Apple's Stock Price Is Collapsing, *Business Insider*, 24 April [Online] http://www.businessinsider.com/two-charts-show-why-apple-stock-dropped-2013-4

13   Schmidt, FL and Hunter, JE (1998) The validity and utility of selection methods in personnel psychology: Practical and theoretical implications of 85 years of research findings, *Psychological Bulletin*, **124** (2), pp 262–74

14   For a detailed discussion of aspects that determine the validity and reliability of a regression analysis we recommend Andy Field's book *Discovering Statistics Using IBM SPSS* (Sage, 2013)

15   Marr, B (2017) Really Big Data At Walmart: Real-time insights from their 40+ petabyte data cloud, *Forbes*, 23 January [Online] https://www.forbes.com/sites/bernardmarr/2017/01/23/really-big-data-at-walmart-real-time-insights-from-their-40-petabyte-data-cloud/#509055a56c10

16   Sample, I (2017) It's Able to Create Knowledge Itself: Google unveils AI that learns on its own, *The Guardian*, 18 October [Online] https://www.theguardian.com/science/2017/oct/18/its-able-to-create-knowledge-itself-google-unveils-ai-learns-all-on-its-own

PART FOUR
Evidence from stakeholders

ACQUIRE: Evidence from stakeholders

10

> Ethical decisions ensure that everyone's best interests are protected.
> When in doubt, don't.
>
> HARVEY MACKAY

Consider these two real-life examples:

In October 2016, KLM – a Dutch airline company – decided to assign one fewer flight attendant in economy class on 40 per cent of its long-haul flights. According to KLM's management, the change would produce a productivity gain of 4 per cent while having minimum impact on customers. KLM's flight attendants, however, strongly felt that reducing the number of crew members would increase their workload considerably, creating problems with customer service. KLM's crew members announced a 24-hour strike, which would cost the company more than US $10 million. After flight attendants and the airline reached an agreement, the strike was called off. KLM's management granted flight attendants a 3.5 per cent salary increase, and cancelled the reduction in staff on long-haul flights.[1]

In September 2017, Uber – a global taxi company from the United States – was stripped of its London licence, dealing a serious blow to one of Silicon Valley's fastest rising companies. Uber's licence was rejected on the basis that the firm lacked corporate responsibility. Especially in London, Uber faced serious criticism from unions, lawmakers and cab drivers over its working conditions. London mayor, Sadiq Khan, backed the decision, saying '… all companies in London must play by the rules and adhere to the high standards we expect'. Uber's chief executive, Dara Khosrowshahi, said that he disagreed with the decision because it was based on past behaviour.[2]

We define stakeholders as people (individuals or groups) whose interests affect or are affected by an organization's decision and its outcomes. Stakeholders can be inside the organization as in the case of employees facing downsizing and restructuring or IT staff responsible for implementing a new online purchasing system. Stakeholders also can come from outside the organization as in the case of equipment suppliers subject to a firm's new requirements on energy use, or the neighbours of a manufacturing plant that cuts back on the frequency of garbage pickup. Given their potential connection to a decision's consequences, stakeholder interests, values and concerns are essential considerations when making organizational decisions, making them an important source of evidence.

In the context of organizational or managerial decisions, evidence from stakeholders pertains to both practical and ethical considerations. Practical considerations arise from the effect, appropriateness or fairness of a decision *in the eyes of its stakeholders*. The impact a decision has on stakeholders, whether objective or perceived, can affect their willingness to accept (or support) that decision. In the example of KLM, the cabin crew – an important and powerful group of stakeholders – perceived the company's decision to reduce the number of flight attendants as considerably increasing their workload, and as harmful to passengers. As a result, the company's decision wasn't implemented. Evidence from stakeholders, however, can also address ethical considerations, particularly in terms of the *distribution* of harms a decision generates relative to its potential benefits. In the example of Uber, many people perceived the company's business strategy and market practices as disproportionately harmful to competitors. As a result, policymakers and regulators – powerful external stakeholders – regarded the company's practices as unethical, demonstrating a lack of corporate responsibility.

In this chapter, we will explain how to identify a company's most relevant stakeholders. We also discuss methods for exploring stakeholder interests and concerns, and describe how paying attention to both practical and ethical aspects of the decision process can improve the quality of your decisions. Before we start, however, we must dedicate a few words to the difference between stakeholder evidence and other sources of evidence.

10.1 Not all evidence from stakeholders is stakeholder evidence

Not all evidence from stakeholders is stakeholder evidence. Sometimes evidence from stakeholders actually represents organizational data or practitioner judgement. Consider, for example, the case where the distribution centre of a large food retailer experiences high error rates. Senior management suggests that introducing Lean Management practices would optimize the centre's operational processes and thus reduce errors. Consultation with the centre's staff, however, suggests this change wouldn't have the intended effect: staff perceive the problem as the result of recently hired low-skilled employees rather than inefficient processes. They point to the increase in error rates over the past year, coinciding with a cost-cutting programme prohibiting the hiring of more skilled (ie more expensive) employees. In this example, the various kinds of information staff might provide represent different kinds of evidence. First, the staff can provide stakeholder evidence (that is, how their interests might be affected by senior management's decision), which might be that their preferred way of working may change if Lean Management is introduced. Second, staff can provide organizational evidence in the form of information regarding objectifiable facts related to the assumed problem (high error rates due to low-skilled employees) and the likely effectiveness of the proposed solution (Lean Management practices). Now consider the evidence from the stakeholders in the KLM example. In this case, the stakeholders strongly felt that the decision would have a negative effect on their perceived workload. The same counts for the policymakers and regulators in the Uber example: they perceived Uber's practices as conflicting with the city's ethics and values. In all these cases, the evidence from stakeholders concerns subjective feelings and perceptions that cannot be considered as objectifiable facts regarding an assumed problem or proposed solution.[3] Such information is, however, relevant to the decision and constitutes stakeholder evidence.

Why is this distinction important?

With practitioner, organizational and scientific evidence, the key issue in critical appraisal is whether we can trust the evidence. As explained throughout the book, we should always critically appraise the evidence. We ask questions about how the organizational data were collected or the outcome measured, whether practitioners consulted had sufficient experience and the quality of the feedback they received, if the scientific evidence came from a study using a control group and had a large enough sample and so on. In contrast, stakeholder evidence involves subjective feelings and perceptions – so reliability and validity is not the major issue. Critical appraisal instead focuses on whether stakeholder evidence accurately represents the feelings and perceptions of all stakeholders in that group. A key idea is that the type of evidence determines how the evidence is critically appraised. As we will see in Chapter 11, when we are dealing with stakeholder evidence, representativeness is a major indicator of its quality.

10.2 Types of stakeholders

Stakeholders take a variety of forms. As a result, there are many ways of classifying stakeholders. The most common distinction is probably between internal stakeholders (for example, employees, managers and board members), connected stakeholders (for example, customers, suppliers, distributors, financiers and shareholders) and external stakeholders (for example, regulators, government, professional bodies, local communities and the society at large). Another relevant distinction is that between direct versus indirect stakeholders, reflecting whether a decision has a direct impact on the stakeholder's interests or an indirect impact through the actions of other stakeholder groups. For example, a call centre agent working for a retail company that decides to open up all stores one hour later on workdays is not directly affected by this decision, but he or she may be confronted by customers who are. This makes the agent an indirect internal stakeholder and the customer a direct external stakeholder. Another distinction is that between primary and secondary stakeholders, which is based on the company's responsibility towards the stakeholder. For example, current employees, customers and suppliers are primary stakeholders, whereas future employees, regulators and the local community are secondary stakeholders.

Mapping stakeholders related to a decision or problem

A **stakeholder map** is a useful tool to overcome the decision maker's biased consideration of a decision's implications for other people. This map illustrates the potential array of stakeholders related to a specific decision. Because decision makers often differ in their views of whom these stakeholders might be, it helps to make stakeholder mapping a public process and seek advice from experienced practitioners in doing so. Figure 10.1 is a map to identify stakeholder groups affected by a decision. Note that a stakeholder's position on the map (for example, direct versus indirect) depends on the decision being made. When a decision changes, so may the position of the stakeholder(s).[4]

Figure 10.1

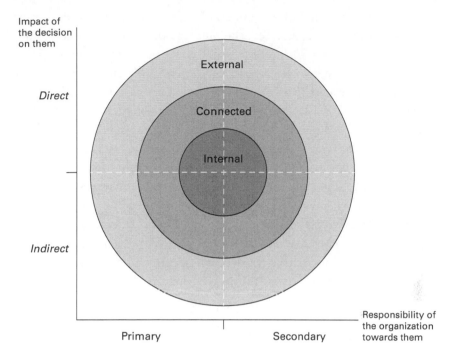

Organizational decisions often have lots of stakeholders, both inside and outside the organization. In some situations, this may lead to 'information avoidance' – the tendency for decision makers to avoid paying attention to stakeholder groups for whom less information is available. In addition, some stakeholders may be 'out of sight' and not come to mind initially, particularly when a decision has indirect or long-term effects. Awareness and concern for possible effects on stakeholders (or lack thereof) is a focus of much debate regarding corporate social responsibility.[5]

10.3 Who are the most relevant stakeholders?

After mapping all stakeholders for a decision, the next step is to determine the most relevant. A stakeholder's relevance is determined by two variables: the extent to which the stakeholder's interests are affected by the decision (harms and benefits), and the extent to which the stakeholder can affect the decision (power to influence).

Harms and benefits

Harms and benefits can differ considerably across stakeholders. For example, some managers, employees and shareholders may benefit from a decision to close a line of business while certain customers and suppliers may be harmed. The key idea is that some stakeholder groups may experience gains and benefits from an organizational decision while others bear more costs and harms. In general, the more a stakeholder group stands to benefit or lose by a decision, the stronger their interest in the decision tends to be. When identifying stakeholders' interests, keep in mind that the focus is on their *perception* of harms and benefits, not whether these harms and benefits will actually occur. Finally, the more costs and harms stakeholders perceive, the more likely they may seek to influence the decision-making process. Nonetheless, stakeholders whose interests are affected by a decision may be unaware of it or otherwise unable to exert influence over it. Some stakeholders may only surface relative to a decision after it has been made. Nonetheless, the ultimate quality of the decision may be affected by how all stakeholders are affected by it.

Power to influence

Whether stakeholders can exert influence over a decision depends on the power they can exercise. This power can derive either from the stakeholders' authority and position within the organization or their ability to entice/convince/persuade others with power to influence the decision-making process. In either case, the more power stakeholders have, the better they will be able to positively or negatively affect the decision.

In general, stakeholders with a high level of interest and power can be considered particularly *relevant* stakeholders. As illustrated in Figure 10.2, you can assess stakeholders' relevance by mapping their level of power and interest.

Ethical considerations

As we explained in the introduction of this chapter, evidence from stakeholders can address both practical and ethical considerations in organizational or managerial decisions. Practical considerations arise from stakeholders' level of power and interest, indicative of the effect they may have on the

Figure 10.2

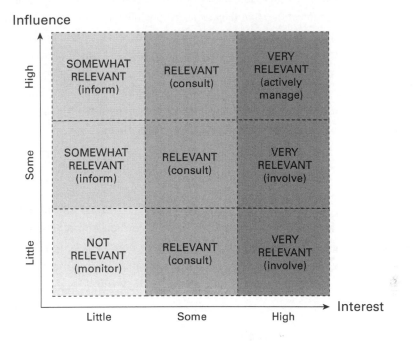

Influence

decision process itself. Ethical considerations arise from the distribution of a decision's potential harms relative to its benefits. In Figure 10.2, stakeholders with high interests but little influence are often considered by decision makers to be less relevant to those with high influence. From an ethical perspective, however, this is problematic.

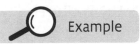 Example

Between 2005 and 2007, Goldman Sachs, one of the most prestigious financial firms in the world, sold its clients so-called mortgage-backed securities (MBSes), a type of investment that is secured by a mortgage – allowing its clients to benefit from the booming housing market, without having to buy an actual house. In 2006 however, home prices began to slide and an increasing number of homeowners struggled to pay their monthly mortgage. As a result, the value of MBSes declined, and the bank's clients were likely to lose their investment. However, despite these worrying signs, Goldman Sachs did not alert the 200,000 clients who had bought MBSes; instead they secretly made a bet that the clients would lose their money.[6, 7] As a result, the bank made a profit of billions of dollars. Although the bank stated that they were simply following normal business practices and did nothing illegal, their decision to put corporate profit before stakeholder interest was considered by many as unethical. As a result, Goldman Sachs had to pay up to US $5 billion to settle claims of wrongdoing. Associate Attorney General Delery said that the settlement 'makes clear that no institution may inflict this type of harm on investors and the American public without serious consequences'.[8]

As a rule, regardless of whether they have the power to influence the decision-making process, its implementation or outcome, when stakeholders' interests are affected by a decision, we consider them relevant. In Chapter 13, we will discuss how you can account for ethical aspects when incorporating stakeholder evidence into the decision-making process.

10.4 Whom to ask?

We have explained how to identify stakeholder groups pertaining to a decision and how to determine the most relevant stakeholders – using the stakeholder map (Figure 10.1) and the power/interest diagram (Figure 10.2). However, to fill out the map and diagram, we need to answer these questions first:

- Who could *affect* this decision, its implementation or its outcome?
  - What are their interests and concerns?
  - What are their feelings and perceptions of this decision?
  - How much influence do they have?
  - Do they have legal rights to participate in this decision?
  - How could they affect the decision?
  - Do they have the power to block the decision or impede its implementation?
- Who could be *affected* by this decision?
  - What are their interests and concerns?
  - What are their feelings and perceptions of this decision?

- Who may experience *harm* from this decision?
  - What are their interests and concerns?
  - What are their feelings and perceptions of this decision?
  - How well are their interests balanced with those who may benefit?
- Who may stand to *benefit* from this decision?
  - What are their interests and concerns?
  - What are their feelings and perceptions of this decision?
  - How well are their interests balanced with those who may be harmed?

Using the answers to these questions, you should be able to fill out the stakeholder map and the power/interest diagram, and determine who are – given the decision at hand – the most relevant stakeholders. In general, these are the stakeholders to consult in the decision process. However, sometimes it is not feasible (or desirable) to obtain evidence from all relevant stakeholders; for example, when the number is simply too large or some stakeholders are inaccessible (geographic distance and so on). In those cases, one could rely on 'key' stakeholders – opinion leaders who represent the interests of a stakeholder group – or experts knowledgeable regarding stakeholders' interests, values and concerns. For reasons of representativeness and legitimacy, however, we strongly recommend you to acquire evidence from a larger representative sample rather than a small group of individuals. In addition, you should consider consulting secondary data, like scientific evidence regarding employee or customer perceptions, as other evidence sources may enhance your understanding of the perception and feelings of the employees and customers in your own organization. Remember that the critical issue of stakeholder evidence is its representativeness for the broader set of members in that group.

10.5 What to ask?

Asking questions of relevant stakeholders can help you to broaden the problem definition and avoid the decision frame becoming too narrow.[9] In addition, consulting evidence from stakeholders mapped to a particular problem or solution can clarify what needs to be improved, what results are wanted and what support is needed. However, as explained in Chapter 2, gathering evidence is not a fishing expedition – it starts with an assumed problem and/or a proposed solution. Before consulting stakeholders, it is important that you first clearly describe the problem to be solved or the opportunity to be addressed. As discussed in Chapter 2, a good problem definition entails at least four elements:

1 The problem itself, stated clearly and concisely. (What? Who? Where? When?)

2 Its (potential) organizational consequences.

3 Its assumed major cause(s).

4 The PICOC (Population, Intervention, Comparison, Outcome, Context).

Evidence from stakeholders inside and outside the organization is an essential component to determine whether the assumed problem is indeed a serious problem and in identifying possible causes. Important questions you can ask are:

1 Do you agree with the description of the problem?

2 Do you see plausible alternative causes of the problem?

3 Do you agree that the problem is serious and urgent?

Gathering evidence from stakeholders is also an essential component in determining how likely a proposed solution is to work. But here, too, having a clear description of that solution is a prerequisite. Again, a good description entails at least four elements:

1 The solution itself, stated clearly and concisely. (What? Who? Where? When?)

2 Its (potential) effect on the problem and underlying cause/s.

3 Its costs and benefits.

4 The PICOC (see Chapter 2).

Even the best solution can fail upon implementation if important stakeholders see serious downsides or when they feel an alternative solution may work better. Asking questions about these possible downsides or alternative solutions therefore provides relevant information. In addition, stakeholders are often in a good position to judge the preferred solution in terms of implementation costs and other feasibility/risk issues. Important questions you can ask are:

1 Do you agree on which solution is the 'best' and/or 'most feasible'?

2 Do you see downsides to or unintended negative consequences of the preferred solution?

3 Do you see alternative solutions to the problem that may work better?

10.6 How to ask?

You can acquire evidence from stakeholders in many ways. Numerous books and websites are informative about how to gather evidence in a valid and reliable way. They cover important aspects such as sampling procedures, methodology and questionnaire development. In addition, the tools and techniques of marketing research are also useful in gathering evidence from stakeholders, particularly in the case of external stakeholders such as clients, consumer groups or the general public. Negative sentiments spread like wildfire through social media, so for some companies it may be useful to monitor platforms such as Facebook, Twitter and LinkedIn, and to follow key stakeholders active on social media. For most organizations, however, traditional quantitative and qualitative methods will suffice.

Quantitative methods

Quantitative methods are used to gather data (evidence) that can be quantified, that is, measured and written down with numbers. We usually obtain these data from surveys, **structured interviews**, tests or voting systems. Quantitative methods are widely used to acquire evidence from practitioners. In Chapter 3 an overview of the most common methods is provided. When acquiring evidence from stakeholders, you can use quantitative methods to *quantify* their perceptions and feelings (*how many* stakeholders feel/perceive…). However, when it comes to exploring or *identifying* these feelings and perceptions (*how* do stakeholders feel/perceive…), qualitative methods are often more appropriate.

Qualitative methods

Qualitative methods are used to gather data that cannot be scored or written down with numbers. We typically obtain these data from interviews, focus groups or text analysis. Qualitative methods are often exploratory in nature: they are used to gain a better understanding of underlying feelings, opinions or motivations. Thus, qualitative methods are particularly useful in obtaining stakeholder perspectives in their own words.

Focus groups

One of the most widely used methods to gather evidence from stakeholders are focus groups. A focus group is a set of 6 to 10 people who are asked about their perceptions, feelings, opinions or attitudes towards a product, service, idea or – in case of an evidence-based approach – about an assumed problem or proposed solution. The questions are asked by a skilled moderator in an interactive group setting where participants exchange points of view with other group members. The group needs to be large enough to generate rich discussion but not so large that some participants are left out. Focus groups are a qualitative methodology where the researcher/moderator takes notes or makes recordings of the most important points obtained from the group. Decision makers can review the resultant transcripts or summary. Focus groups typically yield data and insights less accessible without interaction between the group members. Members of the focus group should be selected carefully in order to obtain representative responses. In addition, measures should be taken to prevent groupthink and other biases that may distort the outcome, as discussed in Chapters 3 and 4. A related method is a so-called 'public review process' where stakeholder perspectives are obtained, discussed and vetted in a public session.

Qualitative interviews

Interviews often are used to gather information from an individual stakeholder or group. Interviews can be structured, semi-structured or unstructured. Structured interviews use a fixed format in which all questions are prepared beforehand and are asked in the same order. To ensure that answers can be reliably aggregated and comparisons made, all stakeholders are asked the same questions. Most qualitative interviews, however, are unstructured or semi-structured. **Unstructured interviews** don't use a predetermined questionnaire and may simply start with an opening question such as 'Can you tell me how you feel about X?' and then advance depending on the stakeholder's response.[10] Unstructured interviews are often difficult to conduct, as the lack of predetermined questions provides the interviewer little guidance on what to ask. For this reason, **semi-structured interviews** are perhaps the most widely used. This type of interview consists of a limited number of key questions that define the topic or issue to be explored while allowing the interviewer to explore relevant information not thought of beforehand.

When interviewing stakeholders, it is important to inform them in advance about why you need their input. You also need to set clear expectations regarding anonymity, confidentiality and how stakeholder information will be used, as this increases the likelihood of honesty.[11] Many books and

Flowchart 10.1

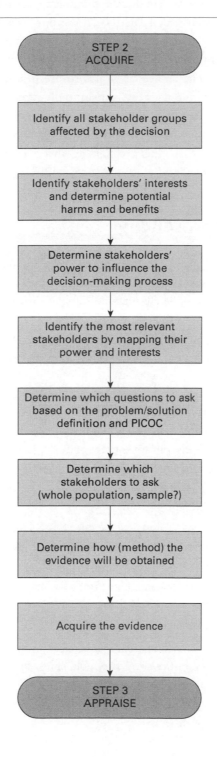

guidelines describe how to conduct a qualitative interview. Generally, we recommend using open-ended (that is, questions that require more than a yes/no answer), neutral (non-value-laden or leading) and understandable questions. Formulating questions, however, is a process that requires particular attention. The choice of words to use in a question is critical – even small wording differences can substantially affect the answers people give. Chapter 3 provides tips to reduce comprehension error as a result of the question's wording. Finally, we recommend you to record all interviews and focus group sessions, as this prevents against bias and provides a verifiable record of what was (and what was not) said.[12]

Notes and references

1   This example is adapted from Pieters, J (2017) KLM Cabin Crew Announce 24 Hour Strike at Schiphol Next Month, *NL Times*, 12 April [Online] nltimes. nl/2017/12/04/klm-cabin-crew-announce-24-hour-strike-schiphol-next-month

2   This example is adapted from Butler, S and Topham, G (2017) Uber Stripped of London Licence Due to Lack of Corporate Responsibility, *The Guardian*, 23 September [Online] www.theguardian.com/technology/2017/sep/22/ uber-licence-transport-for-london-tfl

3   Obviously, KLM's executive management could have easily tested the cabin crews' claim that their workload would substantially increase and that passenger service would suffer, for example by pilot-testing the measure (see Chapter 14). Apparently, this was not feasible.

4   Magness, V (2008) Who are the stakeholders now? An empirical examination of the Mitchell, Agle, and Wood theory of stakeholder salience, *Journal of Business Ethics*, 83 (2), pp 177–92

5   Reynolds, SJ, Schultz, FC and Hekman, DR (2006) Stakeholder theory and managerial decision-making: Constraints and implications of balancing stakeholder interests, *Journal of Business Ethics*, 64 (3), pp 285–301

6   Popper, N (2016) In Settlement's Fine Print, Goldman May Save $1 Billion, *The New York Times, Business & Policy*, 11 April

7   This practice is also known as short-selling.

8   Press release by The United States Department of Justice, 11 April 2016 [Online] https://www.justice.gov/opa/pr/goldman-sachs-agrees-pay-more-5-billion-connection-its-sale-residential-mortgage-backed

9   Nutt, PC (2002) *Why Decisions Fail,* Barrett-Kohler Publishers, San Francisco, CA

10 Gill, P, Stewart, K, Treasure, E and Chadwick, B (2008) Methods of data collection in qualitative research: Interviews and focus groups, *British Dental Journal*, **204** (6), p 291

11 Britten N (1999) Qualitative interviews in healthcare, in *Qualitative Research in Health Care,* 2nd edn, ed C Pope and N Mays, pp 11–19, BMJ Books, London

12 Oltmann, S (2016) Qualitative interviews: A methodological discussion of the interviewer and respondent contexts, *Forum: Qualitative Social Research*, **17** (2)

APPRAISE: Evidence from stakeholders

11

It is not important whether or not the interpretation is correct.
If men define situations as real, they are real in their consequences.

WI THOMAS

Stakeholders are people whose interests affect or are affected by an organization's decision or its outcomes. As explained in the previous chapter, not all evidence from stakeholders is stakeholder evidence. Sometimes evidence from stakeholders actually represents organizational data or practitioner judgement, for instance when the evidence they provide concerns objectifiable facts regarding the assumed problem or the appropriateness of a preferred solution. Stakeholders can also provide evidence of their *subjective feelings* and *perceptions*, for example whether (and to what extent) a problem or solution might affect their interests.

In the previous chapter, we explained why it is important to distinguish the types of evidence stakeholders can provide. With practitioner, organizational and scientific evidence, we critically appraise their reliability and validity. In contrast, with stakeholder evidence – feelings and perceptions – reliability and validity are not the major issue, but rather whether the evidence accurately represents the feelings and perceptions of all stakeholders. This means that we appraise evidence from stakeholders that concerns objectifiable facts differently, that is, as organizational evidence or professional judgement, according to the criteria discussed in Chapters 4 and 9. In these chapters, we addressed important notions such as bias, confounding, measurement, moderators and reliability. The present chapter on the other hand focuses on the critical appraisal of *stakeholders' perceptions and feelings*, core elements of stakeholder evidence. Where stakeholder evidence is concerned, impact and representativeness are the major focus of critical appraisal.

11.1 The importance of subjective feelings and perceptions

You may wonder why stakeholders' perceptions and feelings – evidence that is highly subjective and sometimes even irrational – have a place in evidence-based decision-making. The answer is in the opening quote of this chapter. It reflects what is known as the Thomas Theorem – it basically means that what people feel and perceive to be true constitutes a social fact that has an actual effect on them – whether these feelings and perceptions are true or not.[1] How stakeholders perceive a decision is a social fact too, regardless of whether their perception is based on subjective feelings, irrational beliefs or personal values. As illustrated by the KLM and Uber examples in the previous chapter, sometimes stakeholders have the power to block a decision or impede its implementation. Taking into account stakeholder evidence can therefore substantially increase the likelihood of a favourable outcome of that decision. It helps decision makers identify ways to reduce avoidable harms or obtain the informed consent of those stakeholders who incur the risks of a negative outcome from that decision. In addition, attention to stakeholders contributes to the ethical nature of decisions. Ethical deliberation can improve decision quality, by prompting decision makers to consider options with better outcomes for all parties involved. Because of the broader information considered, using evidence regarding stakeholder perspectives and feelings tends to improve decision quality as well as the short- and long-term outcomes of your decision.[2]

11.2 What is the impact of the decision?

In Chapter 7 it is explained that when critically appraising evidence from the scientific literature, we first need to determine whether the findings are of practical relevance. To determine this, we have to look at the impact of the findings. Before we critically appraise the trustworthiness of stakeholder evidence, that is, its representativeness, here too we must first determine the practical relevance of the evidence by looking at the impact. In the previous chapter, we have explained that we can distinguish two types of impact: 1) the extent of influence a stakeholder has on a decision, and 2) the extent of harm a decision brings on a stakeholder.

Practical relevance

The first type of impact concerns practical relevance: evidence indicating that a powerful and influential group of stakeholders perceive a decision as unfavourable, which may have serious practical implications for the decision-making process, particularly when these stakeholders have the power to block a decision or impede its implementation. In Chapter 10, it is explained how you can use a power/interest diagram to determine a stakeholder's impact.

Ethical relevance

The second type of impact concerns ethical relevance: evidence indicating that a specific group of stakeholders may be harmed in some fashion by a decision's outcome. Potential harms have serious ethical implications for the decision-making process, particularly when they are perceived as unfair. A restructuring programme in which only employees of 50 years of age and older are laid off is likely to be perceived as unethical by many people. Ethical concerns, however, not only arise from unevenly distributed harms, but also from unevenly distributed benefits. Imagine a company that has developed a self-driving car that decreases the number of fatal accidents involving pedestrians by 90 per cent. Now imagine that the remaining 10 per cent tend to be children. Although this self-driving car saves lives, the fact that it tends to save the lives of only adults is a serious ethical concern.

Note

In general, when the evidence suggests that the impact on stakeholders has limited (practical or ethical) relevance, it is not useful to consider it, and thus we may omit the appraisal of its trustworthiness.

11.3 Representativeness

Critical appraisal is the process of carefully and systematically assessing the evidence in order to judge its trustworthiness. Critical appraisal of scientific evidence, for example, looks at a study's methodological appropriateness and examines factors such as internal validity. Critical appraisal of practitioner evidence, on the other hand, evaluates the extent to which a practitioner's judgement could be affected by cognitive biases. Stakeholder evidence, however, concerns *subjective feelings* and *perceptions* that we don't necessarily consider as objectifiable facts. For this reason, *representativeness* is a major indicator of stakeholder evidence quality. Representativeness means how well the data obtained regarding stakeholder perspectives accurately represents all stakeholders in a particular group or category. The more representative the sample, the more confident we can be that we can generalize the evidence to the whole population. For example, a focus group of six employees might be used to get a sense of how employees in general might react to a planned change. But if the change potentially affects hundreds of employees, this sample may be insufficiently representative. In that case we could improve representativeness by corroborating the focus group's results with a follow-up survey of a larger sample of employees. In the previous chapter, several methods are described for gathering stakeholder evidence. The trustworthiness of the evidence that results from these methods depends on: 1) the opportunity stakeholders had to freely express their views and feelings regarding the problem or decision, and 2) the representativeness of the sample. The first aspect is largely determined by the skills of the moderator (in case of focus groups) or the interviewer (in case of interviews), and the way questions are worded. The second aspect – sample representativeness – is determined by the way that sample was obtained.

11.4 How representative is my sample?

In the previous chapter, a power/interest diagram was provided to determine who – given the decision at hand – the most relevant stakeholders are. Obviously, the most representative sample would not be a sample at all, but includes all relevant stakeholders. In most cases, however, for practical reasons, you need to get the evidence from a smaller portion (sample) of the whole population of stakeholders. Then the challenge is to obtain a representative sample. Although it sounds straightforward, obtaining a truly representative sample can be a challenge. For example, contrary to what is often assumed, the size of the sample has no direct relationship with representativeness; even a large random sample can be insufficiently representative. In fact, no sample is 100 per cent representative.

As we discussed in Chapter 3, our main concern here is selection bias. Selection bias, also referred to as sampling bias, occurs when your selection of stakeholders leads to an outcome that is different from what you would have had if you had obtained evidence from the entire group of stakeholders. You can minimize selection bias by taking a random sample of the population. When a sample is randomly selected, each member of the population has an equal chance of being chosen. Thus, variation between the characteristics of the stakeholders in the sample and those of the entire group is just a matter of chance. Unfortunately, even a random sample might, by chance, turn out to be anything but representative. For this reason, you should always (especially when a non-random sample is used) check whether your sample matches the characteristics of the entire group. You can do this by generating relevant base statistics for the entire population, and then comparing them with those of your sample. Examples of such base statistics are listed in Table 11.1.

Table 11.1

Age	Occupation
Gender	Function
Ethnicity	Position
Level of education	Tenure
Income	Full-time/part-time

When the characteristics of your sample are comparable to those of the entire population, you may safely assume that you have obtained a representative sample, and that you can generalize the evidence to the whole group of stakeholders.

11.5 Checklist

Table 11.2

		Yes	No	Unclear
1.	Is the decision's impact on the stakeholders practically relevant?			
2.	Is the decision's impact on the stakeholders ethically relevant?			
3.	Did the method in which the evidence was obtained allow the stakeholders to freely express their views and feelings regarding the problem or decision?			
4.	Were the questions asked worded adequately?			
5.	Was a sample used?			
6.	Was the sample randomly selected?			
7.	Could there be selection bias?			
8.	Are the base statistics of the sample comparable to those of the entire population?			

Notes and references

1 Thomas, WI and Thomas, DS (1928) *The Child in America: Behavior Problems and Programs,* Knopf; Merton, R K (1995) The Thomas theorem and the Matthew effect, *Social Forces,* **74** (2), pp 379–422

2 Hagafors, R and Brehmer, B (1983) Does having to justify one's judgments change the nature of the judgment process? *Organizational Behavior and Human Performance,* **31** (2), pp 223–32; Nutt, PC (2002) *Why Decisions Fail,* Barrett-Kohler, San Francisco, CA

AGGREGATE: Weighing and pulling together the evidence

12

> There is no such thing as the truth,
> we can only deliver the best available evidence and calculate a probability
>
> BLAISE PASCAL

Imagine the following situation: at a board meeting of a large financial service organization the poor performance of the company is discussed – for the fourth year in a row the company performs below the average for its sector and none of the interventions to improve this situation has worked. The HR director of the firm points out to his colleagues – all white, 50 to 60-year-old men with MBAs – that companies with a more diverse workforce tend to perform better. To substantiate his claim, he refers to a report by McKinsey & Company – the United States' largest and most prestigious consulting firm – entitled *Why Diversity Matters*.[1] This report examines the data of 366 public companies across a range of industries in Canada, Latin America, the United Kingdom and the United States. The findings of the report are clear: companies in the top quartile for ethnic diversity are 30 per cent more likely to have above-average financial returns for their respective industries.

Taking an evidence-based approach, the board asks 10 experienced professionals within the company whether they support the claim that investing in an ethnically diverse workforce will lead to substantially better financial performance, with an increase of at least 10 per cent. Most professionals state that, based on their experience at work, they strongly believe that this claim is likely to be true.

Next, the scientific literature is consulted. A comprehensive search of the scientific literature yields five meta-analyses that all demonstrate very small (and sometimes even negative) correlations between ethnic diversity and financial performance. The organizational evidence shows a similar picture. There seems to be no difference in financial performance between the teams and departments with ethnically diverse workforces and those that have a more homogeneous makeup.

However, a sample of eight of the most important stakeholders, including regulators and institutional clients, indicates that they too believe increased ethnic diversity will have a substantial impact on the company's financial performance. In addition, they point out that the McKinsey report was based on the data of 366 companies, and that this evidence should count heavily in the board's decision.

The company's CEO now sees himself faced with a difficult problem. He and his colleagues have taken an evidence-based approach, but now the evidence seems to be far from equivocal and even contradictory in some ways. So, what should he decide? Should he assign more weight to the evidence from the practitioners and stakeholders? They all seem to be very confident, but, on the other hand, human judgement, even from experienced professionals, is often flawed. And what about the five meta-analyses? They are all based on cross-sectional studies (not longitudinal or controlled research), although findings all point in the same direction. The same goes for the evidence from the organization where higher performing units do not tend to have a more diverse workforce. And, finally, what about the report by McKinsey? Surely the United States' largest and most prestigious consulting firm can't be wrong – can they?

The CEO in the example above is faced with several challenges. First, he must weigh the different sources of evidence. As explained in Chapter 1, not all evidence is created equal, thus some may count more than others.[2] But how should the CEO balance the evidence from different sources, especially when they contradict each other? Second, how can he combine the evidence into one overall probability score? And, finally, how can he make a decision based on this probability score?

In this chapter, we will demonstrate how you can conduct the fourth step of evidence-based management: aggregate – weighing and combining evidence from different sources. Aggregating evidence, however, requires some understanding of probabilistic thinking and what is referred to as **Bayes' Rule**. Although this may sound somewhat daunting, you probably already apply Bayes' Rule when making daily decisions without realizing it. The first step to probabilistic thinking and Bayesian inference, however, is to understand the difference between a probability estimate and the truth.

12.1 Evidence-based management is about probabilities

Truth and proof

You may think that the purpose of an evidence-based approach is to find out whether a claim, assumption or hypothesis is true or false. This is not the case. First, evidence is not the same as data. Where data can be numbers or figures that can exist on their own, evidence only exists in the context of a claim or an assumption. Simply put, evidence is always evidence for (or against) something. Hence, data only become evidence when they stand in a 'testing' relationship with a claim or a hypothesis.

Second, in evidence-based management, the term *evidence* is used deliberately instead of proof. This emphasizes that evidence is not the same as proof, and that evidence can be so weak that it is hardly convincing or so strong that no one doubts its correctness. In fact, 'proof' is a concept that is useful only in the realm of mathematics: you can create 'proof' that a mathematical statement or equation is true, but in many other domains, such as the social sciences, you can't create 'proof' of anything. This has to do with our third point, which is the concept of *truth*. Just as evidence is not proof, the outcome of an evidence-based process is not the *truth*, but rather *an estimate of a probability*.

Truth – like proof – is a concept from a different domain. In mathematics, you can *prove* that an equation is *true*, but you cannot do this for a claim or hypothesis in the domain of management. In fact, you could argue that in management – as in the social sciences in general – there is no such thing as *the* truth. After all, findings from empirical studies are often influenced by multiple variables, and thus you can never definitely prove causality. Instead, as the French scientist and philosopher Blaise Pascal in the 17th century noted, we can only deliver *the best available evidence* and calculate a *probability*. And this is exactly what evidence-based management is about: making decisions under conditions of uncertainty through the use of the best available evidence from multiple sources to increase the probability of a favourable outcome. This means that the question for the CEO in the example above is not whether an ethnically diverse workforce will lead to a higher financial performance but rather what the *probability* is, *given the available evidence*, that an ethnically diverse workforce will lead to a higher financial performance.

Figure 12.1 Probability

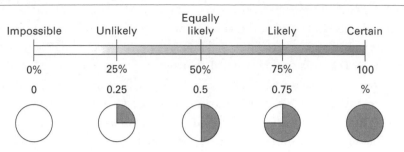

Probability versus chance

In evidence-based management we refrain from using the words *proof or truth*, but instead use terms such as *probable*, *likely*, *chance* and *odds*. All these terms are related to the concept of probability, which is the extent to which something is likely to happen or to be the case. In daily life, probability is the same as chance, but in the realm of science (and evidence-based management) it is a calculation of the chance of an event taking place in percentage terms. Thus, probability is a *measure* of the chance that an event (or outcome) will occur. Probability, indicated with the symbol P, is quantified as a number between 0 and 1, so $P = 0$ indicates impossibility (a chance of 0 per cent that an event will happen) and $P = 1$ indicates moral certainty (a chance of 100 per cent that an event will happen). The higher the probability of an event (or outcome), the more certain that the event will occur (Figure 12.1). In the example above, if the probability of the HR director's claim is high, then it is more certain that investing in an ethnically diverse workforce will indeed result in higher financial performance. When this probability is 0.8, this means that this certainty is 80 per cent. When this probability is 0.4, this means that this certainty is only 40 per cent, meaning that there is a 60 per cent chance that a diverse workforce will **not** lead to a higher financial performance, or that it may even result in a lower financial performance. When the probability is 0.5 the certainty is 50/50, like flipping a coin, meaning that both a positive and a negative effect on financial performance are equally likely.

Why probability is always conditional

Imagine that someone asks you what the probability is that it will rain tomorrow.[3] Your answer to this question would depend on several factors, such as the country you are in, the time of the year and how the weather is today.

Your estimate of the probability of rain tomorrow is therefore *conditional* on the information (evidence) you have available. If you know that you are in the Netherlands during the autumn and that today it is raining heavily, your estimate of the probability will be different from the situation in which you know that it is summer, that the current weather is beautiful, and that the forecast says that tomorrow it will be sunny. This also means that when the available evidence changes, the probability of it raining may do so too. It follows that to deal with probability in the realm of evidence-based management, it is necessary to recognize that the probability of a claim, assumption or hypothesis being true is always *conditional* on the available evidence.

Notation

At this point it is necessary to introduce some notation. We already know that probability is denoted by the letter P. For the claim or hypothesis of concern we will use the letter H. Thus, we denote the probability of the hypothesis being true as $P(H_{true})$. As explained above, the probability P of the hypothesis H is conditional on the available evidence, so we will use the letter E for evidence. This leaves us with the notation of 'conditional on', which is denoted as a vertical line. Thus, the notation $P(H_{true}|E)$ means: the probability of the hypothesis being true *given* the available evidence.

12.2 Bayes' Rule

As explained above, the purpose of the fourth step of evidence-based management – aggregate – is to answer the question: 'What is the probability of the hypothesis (claim, assumption) being true given all the available evidence?' We can write this as $P(H_{true}|E) =$. To find an answer, we need the help of Reverend Thomas Bayes, an English minister and amateur mathematician who lived between 1701 and 1761. Very little is known about Bayes' life, even though he lent his name to a whole new branch of statistics and to a hugely influential theorem. At some point during the 1740s Bayes came up with his rule: the probability of a hypothesis being true given the evidence depends on both prior knowledge and the likelihood of the evidence. Then, in 1774 the mathematician Pierre-Simon Laplace (independently of Bayes' work) formulated the same rule in its current form – that of a mathematical equation. After more than two centuries of controversy, Bayes' Rule is now widely applied in fields such as genetics, image processing, epidemiology, forensic science and medical diagnostics. The strength of Bayes' Rule is that it can deal with all kinds of evidence, making it applicable to all kinds of questions that involve probability. For example, during the Second World War Bayes' Rule was used to crack the Enigma code, while during the Cold War, it helped to find a missing H-bomb and to hunt down Russian submarines; it has also been used to investigate the safety of nuclear power plants, predict the tragedy of the Space Shuttle Challenger, demonstrate that smoking causes lung cancer, build Google's search engine, and much, much more.[4] On the face of it, the rule is a simple one-line theorem: *posterior probability equals prior probability times likelihood*. Mathematically it can be written as follows:

$$P(H|E) = \frac{P(H)\ P(E|H)}{P(E)}$$

If you are put off by this equation, don't worry: we have developed a downloadable app for your smartphone that will do the calculation for you.[5] In addition, you can use the online calculator on the CEBMa website.[6] Bayes' Rule can be written mathematically in many different forms.[7] Although each form is somewhat different, all contain the same three elements: the **prior probability,** the likelihood of the evidence and the posterior probability.

The prior probability:

$P(H_{true})$ = The initial estimate of how probable it is that the hypothesis (claim, assumption) is true to start with.

The likelihood of the evidence:

$P(E|H_{true})$ = The likelihood of the evidence being available/showing up if the hypothesis would be true.

$P(E|H_{false})$ = The likelihood of the evidence being available/showing up if the hypothesis would be false.

The posterior probability:

$P(H_{true}|E)$ = The revised estimate of the probability of the hypothesis being true given the available evidence.

In the following sections, we will discuss each element in more detail and demonstrate how you can use Bayes' Rule to combine evidence from different sources and calculate an overall probability.

12.3 The prior probability

The prior probability (known simply as 'the prior') is the initial estimate of how probable it is that the claim or hypothesis is true to start with, that is, without the benefit of the available evidence. In most cases, we should set this prior probability at 0.5, which means we do not have any reason to assume the hypothesis is either false or true. This is the case when we know nothing about the hypothesis or have no prior relevant experience that may help us to determine its probability. We may have a strong opinion, but, in general, merely having an opinion is not sufficient to set a reliable prior. This may change, however, when so-called 'baseline information' is available. Consider the following example: *Marie-Claire is 23 years old, her favourite writer is Marcel Proust and her preferred holiday destination is France. In her leisure time, she loves to read French poetry. Which of the following is more likely?*

A *Marie-Claire is a law student.*

B *Marie-Claire studies French literature.*

Although you may be inclined to answer B, the right answer is actually A. There are many more law students than French literature students – so many more, in fact, that a student who reads French poetry and likes spending her holiday in France is more likely to be a law student. Sometimes a *prior* probability can be very strong and have a large impact on the overall probability. This is not to suggest that prior probabilities always dominate the available evidence and thus the outcome of Bayes' Rule. In fact, in the realm of management the opposite is often true – in most cases there is no reliable prior available other than your professional judgement. So, unless we have a reliable prior estimate available – such as the average in the sector, incidence/prevalence numbers, general statistics or census data – we set the prior at $P = 0.5$ (meaning 50/50, like flipping a coin).

12.4 The likelihood of the evidence

In evidence-based management, the phrase 'the likelihood of the evidence' is often used. This is shorthand *for the likelihood of the evidence being available/showing up given the hypothesis (claim, assumption).* The notion of likelihood takes into account two different aspects that can be considered to be two sides of the same coin. First, it estimates the likelihood of the evidence being available/showing up if the hypothesis would be true. It then estimates the likelihood of the evidence being available/showing up if the hypothesis would be false.

Note

Probability versus likelihood

You will notice that we use the term probability when referring to the hypothesis and likelihood when referring to the evidence. In daily life these terms are synonyms, but in statistics and probability theory there is a distinction between them (see also the 'prosecutor's fallacy', below). The exact, technical explanation of this difference, however, falls beyond the scope of this book.

To get a good understanding of the concept of likelihood, consider this example: *Julia comes home from a short business trip. When her husband unpacks her suitcase, he finds another man's underwear. What is the probability that Julia has cheated on her husband given the evidence: men's underwear in her suitcase?*[8] As mentioned, the likelihood of the evidence is determined by two elements:

- $P(E|H_{true})$, *the likelihood of the evidence showing up if the hypothesis were true.* In this case, this is the likelihood of the underwear showing up in the suitcase if Julia is cheating on her husband. If so, it is easy to imagine how the underwear got there. Then again, even (and perhaps especially) if she was cheating on her husband, you might expect her to be extremely careful, especially when she knew her husband might unpack her suitcase. So, we could argue that the probability of the underwear appearing in Julia's suitcase, if she was cheating on her husband, would be rather low – say 30 per cent.

- $P(E|H_{false})$, the likelihood of the evidence showing up if the hypothesis were false. In this case, this is the likelihood of the underwear showing up in the suitcase if Julia had NOT cheated on her husband. Could there be other plausible explanations for the garment being in Julia's suitcase? With some imagination, you can easily come up with several alternative explanations: maybe Julia's colleagues played a prank on her, or the contents of Julia's suitcase got mixed up during a security check at the airport, or the underwear might be a gift to her husband that she forgot to wrap. In fact, they could even be hers! Taking all these less or more plausible alternative explanations into account we would set this likelihood at 20 per cent.

As you can see, the difference between $P(E|H_{true})$ and $P(E|H_{false})$ is rather small (0.3 versus 0.2), which indicates that the evidence is not very convincing. This means that in this example the likelihood of the evidence is rather low. Now let's assume that the prior probability of Julia cheating on her husband was very low to begin with – for instance, because Julia is a very faithful, honest person – so we set the prior at 10 per cent. If you use the app or the online Bayes calculator to work out $P(H_{true}|E)$, you will find a probability of only 0.14, meaning that the available evidence has increased the posterior probability by only 4 per cent (Table 12.1). The reason for this slight increase is the low likelihood of the evidence: $P(E|H_{true})$ is only slightly higher than $P(E|H_{false})$. The ratio between these two estimates is also known as the Likelihood Ratio.[9]

In some cases, however, the likelihood of the evidence is so powerful that it strongly updates the prior probability. Consider this example: your colleague claims that disabled employees tend to achieve higher performance ratings at work. Since there is no reliable prior probability available, other than your personal judgement, you set the prior at 50 per cent. A search in ABI/INFORM (see Chapter 6), however, yields a well-conducted meta-analysis based on 13 RCTs (randomized controlled trials) demonstrating

Table 12.1

Prior probability		
The initial probability of how likely it is that Julia would cheat on her husband	$P(H_{true})$	0.10
Likelihood of the evidence		
The likelihood of men's underwear being in Julia's suitcase if she was cheating on her husband	$P(E|H_{true})$	0.30
The likelihood of men's underwear being in Julia's suitcase if she wasn't cheating on her husband	$P(E|H_{false})$	0.20
Posterior probability		
The revised probability of Julia cheating on her husband given the men's underwear in her suitcase	$P(H_{true}|E)$	0.14

a large positive effect. So, what is the probability of your colleague's claim being true, given the likelihood of the evidence?

- $P(E|H_{true})$, the likelihood that a meta-analysis based on 13 RCTs would demonstrate a large positive effect if your colleague's claim were true. We would argue that if the claim that disabled employees tend to achieve higher performance ratings at work were indeed true, a meta-analysis of 13 randomized controlled studies would be very likely to demonstrate a positive effect, so we would set this likelihood at 90 per cent.[10]

- $P(E|H_{false})$, the likelihood that a meta-analysis based on 13 RCTs would demonstrate a large positive effect if your colleague's claim were false. We would argue that if your claim were not true, it would be very unlikely that the meta-analysis would demonstrate a positive effect, so we would set this likelihood very low, at only 5 per cent.

As you can see in Table 12.2, when you apply Bayes' Rule to calculate $P(H_{true}|E)$ you will find a posterior probability of 0.94, meaning that due to the high likelihood of the evidence the initial probability has increased from 50/50 (like flipping a coin) to 94 per cent (an almost certainty).

Table 12.2

Prior probability		
The initial estimate of how probable it is that disabled employees achieve higher performance ratings	$P(H_{true})$	0.50
Likelihood of the evidence		
The likelihood of 13 RCTs demonstrating a large positive effect if disabled employees achieve higher performance ratings	$P(E|H_{true})$	0.90
The likelihood of 13 RCTs demonstrating a large positive effect if disabled employees do NOT achieve higher performance ratings	$P(E|H_{false})$	0.05
Posterior probability		
The revised probability that disabled employees achieve higher performance ratings given 13 RCTs demonstrating a large effect	$P(H_{true}|E)$	0.94

Note

The prosecutor's fallacy

Many people assume that the likelihood of the evidence given the hypothesis – $P(E|H)$ – is the same as the probability of the hypothesis given the evidence – $P(H|E)$. This is incorrect. Imagine, for example, a US court of law, where the forensic expert has demonstrated that there is a partial DNA match between the perpetrator and the defendant, and that only 1 in 100,000 persons have that same partial match. Based on this information the prosecutor wrongly concludes that the probability of the defendant being innocent given this evidence is 1 in 100,000, thus the probability of the defendant being guilty is 99,999 per cent. This error is known as the 'prosecutor's fallacy'. After all, there are about 325 million people in the United States, meaning that 1 in 100,000 would still account for 3,250 partial matches, which would make the probability that the defendant would be guilty 1 in 3,250, which is 0.03 per cent, not 99.999 per cent. Still confused? Think of it this way: some popes are Italian, but not all Italians are popes. Therefore, the probability of a person being Italian given that he is a pope is not the same as the probability that a person is a pope given that he is Italian.

12.5 Updating the posterior probability when new evidence becomes available

In the sections above we have seen how we can use Bayes' Rule to calculate the probability of a claim or hypothesis being true given the available evidence. The strength of Bayes' Rule, however, is that it allows you to update this probability when new evidence comes available. Sometimes this new evidence is so strong that it can update a hypothesis's near-zero probability to an almost certainty. Consider this example from Nate Silver's *The Signal and the Noise*. Before the September 11 attacks, we would have assigned a near-zero probability to the possibility of terrorists crashing planes into a skyscraper in Manhattan – let's say 1 in 20,000 or 0.005 per cent. However, we would also have assigned a very low probability to a plane hitting a skyscraper by accident. In fact, this probability can be estimated empirically: 1 in 12,500 or

0.008 per cent.[11] When we use Bayes' Rule to calculate the posterior probability, we find that after the first plane hit the World Trade Center the prior probability increased from 0.005 per cent to 38 per cent (Table 12.3).

As mentioned above, the strength of Bayes' Rule is that it allows you to update the posterior probability when new evidence becomes available. In the example of the September 11 attacks this means that we can update the posterior probability of a terror attack happening after the first plane hit the WTC to 38 per cent by using this as our prior probability when the second plane hit

Table 12.3

Prior probability		
The initial probability of a terror attack on Manhattan skyscrapers	$P(H_{true})$	0.00005
Likelihood of the evidence		
The likelihood of a plane hitting the WTC if terrorists are attacking Manhattan skyscrapers	$P(E\|H_{true})$	0.99
The likelihood of a plane hitting the WTC if terrorists are NOT attacking Manhattan skyscrapers (ie an accident)	$P(E\|H_{false})$	0.00008
Posterior probability		
The revised probability of a terror attack on Manhattan skyscrapers, given a plane hitting the WTC	$P(H_{true}\|E)$	0.38

Table 12.4

Prior probability		
The initial probability of a terror attack on Manhattan skyscrapers	$P(H_{true})$	0.38
Likelihood of the evidence		
The likelihood of a plane hitting the WTC if terrorists are attacking Manhattan skyscrapers	$P(E\|H_{true})$	0.99
The likelihood of a plane hitting the WTC if terrorists are NOT attacking Manhattan skyscrapers (ie an accident)	$P(E\|H_{false})$	0.00008
Posterior probability		
The revised probability of a terror attack on Manhattan skyscrapers, given a second plane having hit the WTC	$P(H_{true}\|E)$	0.9999

the WTC. If you calculate the new posterior probability you can see that, based on the new evidence (a second plane having hit the WTC), the posterior probability of a terror attack becomes a near-certainty: 99.99 per cent (Table 12.4).

The examples above demonstrate that we can apply Bayes' Rule to all types of evidence: medical tests, unfaithfulness, terror attacks and findings from social science. This means that we can use Bayes' Rule to combine evidence from different sources and estimate an overall probability.

12.6 Using Bayes' Rule to aggregate evidence from different sources

We started this chapter with an example of how evidence from multiple sources is sometimes contradictory. Even when the evidence is equivocal, however, the question is how to combine it into one overall probability score. We can do this by applying Bayes' Rule. Bayes Rule, however, works best with a claim or hypothesis that concerns a specific (for example, numerical or dichotomous) outcome.[12] Claims such as 'X will substantially increase Y' are rather vague and are therefore hard to test against the evidence. In the case cited right at the start of this chapter, the claim contains a very precise outcome, that is, a 10 per cent increase in the company's financial performance. This means that the question to answer is:

What is the probability that the claim that an ethnically diverse workforce leads to an improvement in the company's financial performance by at least 10 per cent is true, given:

- *the judgement of 10 experienced professionals;*
- *the five meta-analyses;*
- *the organizational data;*
- *the opinion of eight of the most important stakeholders?*

According to Bayes' Rule, we first need to determine a prior probability. In this case, we could use McKinsey's report. So, what is the trustworthiness of this report? As you may recall from Chapter 7, findings from a survey conducted by a commercial company such as McKinsey published in a non-academic journal – for example, a report or a white paper – cannot be considered to be highly trustworthy.[13] In addition, a cross-sectional survey is not an appropriate research design for measuring the effect of ethnic diversity on financial performance. We therefore assign a low trustworthiness score to the report (55 per cent) and thus a correspondingly low prior probability of $P = 0.55$. A table with trustworthiness scores for scientific evidence is provided in Chapter 7.

▌░░░ Professional expertise

Next the board obtained evidence from practitioners. But what is the likelihood of this evidence? To be more precise, what is the likelihood that experienced professionals will agree that an ethnically diverse workforce will improve the company's performance by at least 10 per cent if this hypothesis were true? We would argue that this likelihood is quite high. For this reason, we set $P(E|H_{true})$ at 90 per cent. According to Bayes' Rule, however, we must also consider $P(E|H_{false})$: what is the likelihood that experienced professionals would agree if the hypothesis were NOT true (for example, if the effect on performance were much lower than 10 per cent, or even negative)? We would argue that this likelihood is substantial – after all, as you learned in Chapter 4, human judgement, even from experienced professionals, is often flawed, especially in a situation where the work environment is rather unpredictable and direct, objective feedback is lacking. We therefore estimate this likelihood at 50 per cent. When we calculate the revised (posterior) probability, we get the following outcome (Table 12.5).

As you can see, the evidence from practitioners has increased the prior probability from 55 to 68 per cent.

Table 12.5

Prior probability		
The initial probability of the hypothesis – that an ethnically diverse workforce would increase the company's performance by at least 10 per cent – being true	$P(H_{true})$	0.55
Likelihood of the evidence		
The likelihood that experienced professionals would confirm the hypothesis if this hypothesis were true	$P(E|H_{true})$	0.90
The likelihood that experienced professionals would confirm the hypothesis if this hypothesis were false	$P(E|H_{false})$	0.50
Posterior probability		
The revised probability of the hypothesis being true given the available evidence	$P(H_{true}|E)$	0.68

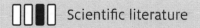 Scientific literature

Next, the board consulted the scientific literature and found five meta-analyses that all demonstrated very small and sometimes even negative correlations. What is the likelihood of this new evidence being available/showing up given the hypothesis? Again, we must consider both $P(E|H_{true})$ and $P(E|H_{false})$. What is the likelihood that all five meta-analyses would demonstrate only small or negative correlations if the hypothesis – that an ethnically diverse workforce has a large, positive effect on performance – were true? We would argue that this would be very unlikely, so we therefore set $P(E|H_{true})$ at 10 per cent. We can apply the same logic to $P(E|H_{false})$: if an ethnically diverse workforce does NOT increase performance, then it would be very likely that five meta-analyses show only small or negative correlations, so we set this likelihood at 90 per cent.[14] We can now use Bayes' Rule to calculate the new posterior probability by using the first posterior as a prior (Table 12.6).

As you can see, the evidence from the scientific literature has dramatically decreased the posterior probability from 68 to 19 per cent.

Table 12.6

Prior probability		
The probability of the hypothesis – that an ethnically diverse workforce would increase the company's performance by at least 10 per cent – being true, given the evidence from practitioners	$P(H_{true})$	0.68
Likelihood of the evidence		
The likelihood that five meta-analyses would demonstrate only small or negative correlations if the hypothesis were true	$P(E|H_{true})$	0.10
The likelihood that five meta-analyses would demonstrate only small or negative correlations if the hypothesis were false	$P(E|H_{false})$	0.90
Posterior probability		
The revised probability of the hypothesis being true, given the available evidence	$P(H_{true}|E)$	0.19

Stakeholders' view

The board, however, also consulted eight important stakeholders, who all stated that they too consider the hypothesis likely to be true. So again, what is the likelihood of this evidence? We would argue that $P(E|H_{true})$ and $P(E|H_{false})$ are similar to those of the experienced professionals, as the stakeholders' judgement too is prone to cognitive biases.[15] Again, we can use Bayes' Rule to calculate the new posterior probability by using the previous posterior as a prior (Table 12.7).

As you can see, the evidence from stakeholders has now slightly increased the posterior probability from 19 to 29 per cent.

Table 12.7

Prior probability		
The probability of the hypothesis – that an ethnically diverse workforce would increase the company's performance by at least 10 per cent – being true, given the evidence from practitioners and the scientific literature	$P(H_{true})$	0.19
Likelihood of the evidence		
The likelihood that stakeholders would confirm the hypothesis if this hypothesis were true	$P(E|H_{true})$	0.90
The likelihood that stakeholders would confirm the hypothesis if this hypothesis were false	$P(E|H_{false})$	0.50
Posterior probability		
The revised probability of the hypothesis being true given the available evidence	$P(H_{true}|E)$	0.29

 Organizational data

Finally, the board also consulted organizational evidence, which showed no significant difference in performance between the teams and departments with an ethnically diverse workforce and those with a more homogeneous makeup. Again, what is the likelihood of this evidence showing up given the hypothesis? We would argue that the likelihood of the organizational data NOT demonstrating any difference if the hypothesis were true would be very low. Again, the opposite is true for $P(E|H_{false})$: if the hypothesis were false, we would expect the organizational data to show no difference. We therefore estimate $P(E|H_{true})$ and $P(E|H_{false})$ at 20 per cent and 80 per cent respectively. Again, we use Bayes' Rule to calculate the new posterior probability by using the previous posterior as a prior (Table 12.8).

As you can see, the evidence from the organization has decreased the posterior probability from 29 to 9 per cent.

Table 12.8

Prior probability		
The probability of the hypothesis – that an ethnically diverse workforce would increase the company's performance by at least 10 per cent – being true, given the evidence from practitioners, the scientific literature and the stakeholders	$P(H_{true})$	0.29
Likelihood of the evidence		
The likelihood that the organizational data would show no significant difference in performance if the hypothesis were true	$P(E|H_{true})$	0.20
The likelihood that the organizational data would show no significant difference in performance if the hypothesis were false	$P(E|H_{false})$	0.80
Posterior probability		
The revised probability of the hypothesis being true given the available evidence	$P(H_{true}|E)$	0.09

This means that we can now answer our question:

What is the probability that the hypothesis that an ethnically diverse workforce leads to an improvement in the company's performance by at least 10 per cent is true, given the evidence from ten professionals, five meta-analyses, organizational data and eight of the most important stakeholders?

The answer to this question is 9 per cent. This means there is a 91 per cent chance that an ethnically diverse workforce will NOT lead to a performance improvement of 10 per cent (that is, substantially lower or even a decrease).

The CEO in our example was initially faced with contradicting evidence: the professional and stakeholder evidence supported the HR director's claim that diversity will improve performance whereas the scientific and organizational evidence did not. However, by using Bayes' Rule the CEO was able to weigh the evidence and calculate an overall probability score (ie 9 per cent). Based on this score the CEO should conclude that investing in an ethnically diverse workforce is NOT the best way to increase the company's performance. Of course, there may be several reasons why a company should invest in a diverse workforce (such as for ethical or social reasons), but in this particular example performance is not one of them.

12.7 Bayesian thinking

The strength of Bayes' Rule is that it allows us to aggregate different types of evidence – medical diagnoses, terror attacks, suspected cheating – and revise our initial estimate when new evidence becomes available. Note that Bayes' Rule is not some kind of magic formula or merely a rule of thumb, but a *theorem*, which means it has been mathematically *proven* to be true. (Note that this is the only place in the book where we claim something is proven to be true.) But Bayes' Rule is more than a mathematical equation. It's a way of thinking that you can apply to all aspects of daily life. It can help make better decisions in a world we can never fully understand. In addition, it makes us aware that claims, assumptions and beliefs about how the world works are never black and white – true or false – but greyscale.[16] As pointed out earlier, most people already apply Bayes' Rule without knowing: when we go through the world and encounter new ideas and insights, the level of confidence in our beliefs changes accordingly, especially when we face evidence that we cannot reconcile with our prior beliefs. Since our beliefs are never 100 per cent certain, our confidence in them changes when we encounter new evidence.

Bayes' Rule also explains why some people are so hard to convince in spite of the evidence: if your prior assumption is close to zero, only an overwhelming amount of evidence can increase your prior belief. In fact, closed-minded people with a prior of zero will never learn anything from any evidence, because anything multiplied by zero is still zero.[17] In the same way, Bayes' Rule explains why Carl Sagan's dictum that 'extraordinary claims require extraordinary evidence' is correct: the prior probability of an extraordinary claim is extraordinarily low (otherwise it wouldn't be deemed 'extraordinary'), so we need an extraordinarily high $P(E|H_{true})$ – and thus an extraordinarily low $P(E|H_{false})$ – to move the needle. This means that any manager, leader, consultant, professor or policymaker who makes an outlandish claim needs to provide more compelling, trustworthy evidence than those who make a more modest claim.

In this chapter, you have learned how you can use Bayes' Rule to weigh and aggregate evidence from multiple sources. It is a formalization of how to revise the initial probability of a claim or assumption being true when new or better evidence becomes available. Although it helps to understand the mathematics behind Bayes' Rule, you don't need to learn the formula by heart – we have developed a smartphone app and online calculator to do that for you. What is more important is to internalize the general idea behind it and learn to intuitively apply its basic principles: whenever a claim is being made, automatically consider the prior probability, estimate the likelihood of the evidence if the hypothesis or assumption is true – $P(E|H_{true})$, estimate the likelihood of that same evidence if the hypothesis or assumption is false – $P(E|H_{false})$, and adjust your posterior probability when new, compelling evidence becomes available.

Flowchart 12.1

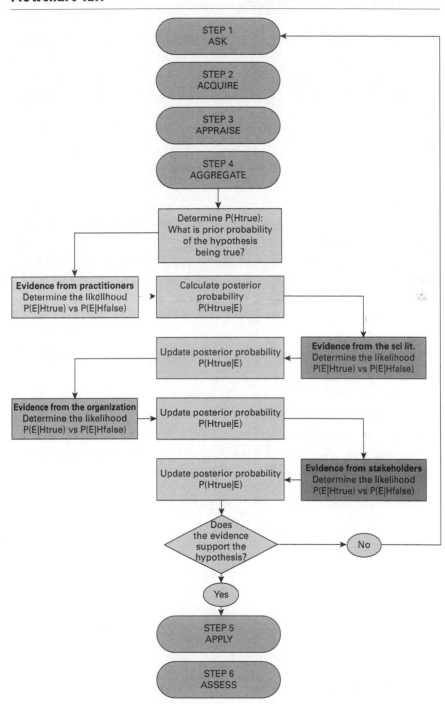

Notes and references

1   Hunt, V, Layton, D and Prince, S (2015) *Why Diversity Matters*, McKinsey & Company, London

2   For example, evidence about an assumed cause and effect from a cross-sectional study should weigh less than evidence from a controlled, longitudinal study. The same is true for evidence from practitioners. Valid and reliable professional expertise results from prolonged practice in a sufficiently stable and predictable environment, combined with frequent and direct, objective feedback. Thus, evidence from professionals that stems from a situation in which these conditions are not met should be considered less trustworthy.

3   This example and some of the explanations are adapted from Evett, IW (1998) Towards a uniform framework for reporting opinions in forensic science casework, *Science & Justice*, **38** (3), pp 198–202

4   A great overview of the history and application of Bayes' Rule is provided in McGrayne, SB (2011) *The Theory That Would Not Die: How Bayes' Rule cracked the Enigma code, hunted down Russian submarines, and emerged triumphant from two centuries of controversy*, Yale University Press, Cambridge, MA

5   The app is named 'Bayes Manager' and is available through the Apple store and Google Play.

6   https://www.cebma.org/resources-and-tools/bayes/

7   Bayes' Rule can mathematically be written in many different forms, such as the simple form, the odds form, the relative odds form, the general form and the sigma form. In evidence-based management we often use the 'extended' form, which can be written as follows:

$$P(H_{true}|E) = \frac{P(H_{true})\, P(E|H_{true})}{P(H_{true})\, P(E|_{Htrue}) + P(H_{false})\, P(E|_{Hfalse})}$$

8   This example and some of the explanations are adapted from Silver, N (2012) *The Signal and the Noise: Why so many predictions fail – but some don't*, Penguin.

9   When the likelihood ratio is larger than 1, the evidence is said to support the hypothesis. As a matter of convention, when the likelihood ratio is larger than 10 the support is strong.

10   Note that the estimate for the probability of research findings being true can also be derived from the study's level of trustworthiness (see Tables 7.4 and 7.5) or by using the CAT Manager app. The CAT Manager helps you to critically appraise the trustworthiness of scientific studies published in academic journals. The app is available for iPhone and Android and can be downloaded from Apple's App Store or Google Play.

11 See Silver, N (2012) *The Signal and the Noise: Why so many predictions fail – but some don't*, Penguin, p 247. 'In the previous 25,000 days of aviation over Manhattan prior to September 11, there had been two such accidents: one involving the Empire State Building in 1945 and another at 40 Wall Street in 1946. That would make the possibility of such an accident about 1 chance in 12,500 on any given day.'

12 'Without numbers, there are no odds and no probabilities; without odds and probabilities, the only way to deal with risk is to appeal to the gods and the fates. Without numbers, risk is wholly a matter of gut.' Bernstein, PL (1996) *Against the Gods: The remarkable story of risk*, John Wiley & Sons, New York.

13 The findings would be more trustworthy if they came from surveys conducted by scholarly researchers, who strive to be objective; and if it were published in a journal maintaining a high standard of quality, accuracy and academic integrity. Research conducted by organizations and published in press releases, newspapers or magazines could be more biased or influenced by the desire to obtain certain findings.

14 You may be confused by the fact that we estimate the probability (and thus the trustworthiness) of the findings of a meta-analysis based on cross-sectional studies at such a high percentage. After all, a cross-sectional study is not an appropriate design to examine a causal relation. This is correct. As you have seen in Chapter 7, a cross-sectional study lacks both a control group and a before-and-after measurement, meaning that even when a meaningful, relevant correlation is found, only one out of three criteria for causality is met. However, when little or no correlation is found (evidence of no effect), none of the three criteria for causality is met, which is a strong and more trustworthy indication that no causal relation exists. Think of it this way – when it snows there may be enough snow for skiing tomorrow (possibility), but when it doesn't snow there will certainly not be enough snow for skiing tomorrow (high certainty).

15 For example, there could be authority bias – their judgement may be influenced by the findings of the McKinsey report.

16 Galef, J (2013) Think rationally via Bayes' Rule, *Big Think*, [YouTube] 8 October

17 Butterworth, J (2014) Belief, bias and Bayes, *The Guardian*, 28 September

APPLY: 13
Incorporating the evidence into the decision-making process

> Knowing is not enough; we must apply.
> Willing is not enough; we must do.

JOHANN WOLFGANG VON GOETHE

Consider the example of a board of directors in a large Canadian hospital. The board considers introducing a performance appraisal system that evaluates physicians' medical performance and that provides them with feedback to help them learn, grow and develop. After consulting the scientific literature, the board finds a large body of evidence suggesting that performance appraisal can indeed have positive effects on a person's professional development. These effects are, however, contingent upon a wide range of moderating factors, including the purpose of the appraisal, rating reliability, perceived fairness, ratee and rater personality variables and so on.[1] The research literature also suggests that evaluations based on objective outcome measures tend to be more reliable than those based on a rater's personal judgements. In addition, the hospital's physicians report that they are more likely to accept feedback from other physicians (rather than non-physicians), preferring feedback from respected colleagues. Overall, the board estimates that the probability that performance appraisal will enhance the physician's professional development is about 70 per cent. Given this evidence, should the board introduce the performance appraisal system? In most cases, the answer as to whether to implement a management practice is not a simple yes or no. Rather, 'It depends'. It depends on whether the evidence applies to the particular organizational context and goals, whether the anticipated benefits outweigh the risks and whether the evidence is 'actionable'. In this chapter, we will discuss the factors that you need to take into account when applying evidence in the decision-making process.

13.1 Does the evidence apply?

After we have acquired, appraised and aggregated the evidence in support of an identified problem or preferred solution, we must ask ourselves: does the evidence apply? Is the evidence generalizable to our organizational context?[2] This question is especially important when the evidence comes from people outside the organization, or from external sources such as the research literature. The evidence may be valid and reliable, but it might come from a different industry such as medicine, aviation or the military. The circumstances in those industries may or may not be relevant to our organizational context. It is important to determine whether your context is different from the context in which the evidence was acquired. Contextual factors can influence the outcome of your decision or necessitate adaptations in the ways in which you apply the evidence. To determine whether the evidence applies to your organizational context you can use the mnemonic we discussed in Chapter 2: PICOC (Table 13.1).

Table 13.1

Population	Who?	Type of employee, people who may be affected by the outcome
Intervention	What or how?	Management technique/ method, factor, independent variable
Comparison	Compared to what?	Alternative intervention, factor, variable
Outcome	What are you trying to accomplish/improve/change?	Objective, purpose, goal, dependent variable
Context	Organizational setting or circumstances	Type of organization, sector, relevant contextual factors

In the example above, the PICOC could be formulated as follows:

P =   Physicians

I =   Performance appraisal

C =   Status quo

O =   Professional development

C =   A large Canadian healthcare organization

The underlying notion is that all five PICOC elements can pertain to whether performance appraisal will have a positive effect on a person's professional development. Thus, the answer to the question of 'Does X work?' is less relevant than the response to the question 'For whom does X work, for what purpose and in which context?' Unfortunately, assessing whether the evidence is sufficiently generalizable to the organizational context is often rather subjective. No one-size-fits-all guidelines exist for this. Some research findings are generalizable to all human beings, but sometimes what works in one setting might not work in another. For example, there is strong evidence that a person's reaction to feedback determines the extent to which his or her performance will improve. How someone reacts to feedback, however, is partly determined by a person's 'openness to feedback'. Some people argue that medical specialists – especially surgeons – are less open to feedback than other professionals, so for them performance feedback may be less effective. However, this could also be a stereotype for which the evidence is limited.[3] The same is true for stereotypes about the organization. As discussed in Chapter 1, managers and leaders often assume that their organization is unique, making the applicability of external evidence limited. However, it is commonplace for organizations to have myths and stories about their own uniqueness. In general, they tend to be neither exactly alike nor unique, but somewhere in between.

13.2 What is the expected value?

In the previous chapter, we demonstrated how you can estimate the probability of a claim or hypothesis being true regarding an assumed problem or preferred solution by weighing and aggregating the available evidence. By using Bayes' Rule, we can combine evidence from different sources and calculate an overall (posterior) probability to help us make an evidence-based decision. When there is only a 0.09 (9 per cent) probability that a claim/hypothesis regarding a preferred solution is true, the conclusion is obvious: the available evidence suggests very strongly that the solution will not solve the problem. In this case, the decision is clear: go back to the drawing board and come up with a better (more evidence-based) solution. But what if the probability score is somewhere between 0.3 and 0.6? In that case, what would be the best decision? The answer is that it depends on the **expected value**.

The decision as to whether or not to implement a solution depends on the notion of 'expected value': the (sometimes monetary) outcome expected from the decision.[4] To calculate the expected value, you need to know four things:

1 The cost-benefit of the solution if the claim is true (outcome 1).

2 The probability that the claim is true given the evidence (P1).

3 The cost-benefit of the solution if the claim is false (outcome 2).

4 The probability that the claim is false given the evidence (P2).

You can now calculate the expected value as follows:

$$\textit{Expected value} = (P1)(\textit{outcome 1}) + (P2)(\textit{outcome 2})$$

For example, imagine that it is claimed that solution A will lead to a productivity increase of 1.5 million dollars (outcome 1). Now let's assume the probability that this claim is correct, given the available evidence, is 60 per cent (P1). This means there is a 40 per cent probability that this claim is incorrect (P2). Let's also assume that if the claim is false, the productivity may decrease by 150,000 dollars. In that case the expected value is 900,000 (0.6 × 1,500,000) minus 60,000 (0.4 × 150,000) = 840,000 dollars. With this expected value you will most likely decide to implement solution A.

Now consider the following example. Imagine that it is claimed that solution B will lead to a productivity increase of 300,000 dollars, and that the probability that this claim is correct, given the evidence, is again 60 per cent. Now, also assume that if the claim is incorrect, the productivity will decrease by 800,000 dollars. In this example, the expected value is 180,000 (0.6 × 300,000) minus 320,000 (0.4 × 800,000) = a 140,000 dollar loss. With this expected value, you will most likely decide not to implement solution B. This demonstrates that your decision should not only depend on the probability a solution will work, but also on its anticipated costs and benefits.

13.3 Is it the biggest bang for your buck?

You may notice that the PICOC element 'Comparison' is seldom defined, as in most organizations no 'comparison' is considered. For a meaningful calculation of a decision's expected value, however, you need a point of comparison. After all, in evidence-based management the question is not so much 'Does X have an effect on Y?' but rather 'Does X have a larger effect on Y than Z does?' For example, in medicine the question is not whether a new medicine has a positive effect on a certain disorder, but rather if this new medicine works better than existing medicines. For example, when a traditional sleeping pill increases a person's amount of sleep by 60 minutes, the added value of a new pill that extends this time by only 5 minutes is limited, especially when this new pill has side effects. The same is true of new management methods and 'cutting-edge' techniques. As explained in Chapter 5, due to placebo effects, many methods and techniques have a positive effect on organizational outcomes anyway. The question is whether these new methods and techniques work better than do existing ones. For example, many companies invested lots of time and money in the now popular notion of 'employee engagement', as it has been widely believed that engaged workers are likely to perform better than their disengaged peers. And indeed, there are empirical studies suggesting engagement has a positive correlation with performance. However, this correlation is similar to that of 'employee satisfaction', a rather traditional but more valid and reliable construct.[5] In addition, other existing constructs such as social cohesion, information sharing and goal clarity tend to have a substantially higher correlation with performance than does engagement,[6] thus giving you more 'bang for your buck'. Other things you can consider regarding new methods and techniques are the ease of implementation, speed and feasibility. Option A may have a slightly bigger impact on the desired outcome than option B, but when option A requires a two-week training of the company's workforce, option B, which does not, may be the better choice.

13.4 Is the level of risk acceptable?

Calculating – or estimating – the expected value helps you to make better decisions. It helps you to decide whether the probability of a certain outcome makes taking a risk worthwhile. The probability that a negative outcome will occur represents risks. **Risk acceptance** – also referred to as risk appetite – is the level of risk a manager or organization is willing to accept. Individual people and organizations, however, don't value probabilities in the same way, and thus have different risk appetites. Entrepreneurial people, for instance, may place high value on the small probability of a huge gain and low value on the larger probability of a substantial loss. In contrast, an administrator of a public organization funded with taxpayers' money may place little value on the probability of gain because his or her strategic goal may be to preserve the organization's capital. This difference stems from the difference in risk acceptance/risk appetite. Many managers, leaders and policymakers determine in advance the level of risk they consider acceptable. A manager's level of risk acceptance, however, is affected by many factors, such as (perceived) accountability, timing, context and individual perception. All these factors affect the extent to which a manager perceives a risk as 'acceptable'. As a result, CEOs, executive boards, steering groups and individual managers can sometimes reach very different decisions based on the same evidence.

 Note

A few (more) words on probabilities

In Chapter 12 we explained that evidence-based management is all about probabilities: the extent to which something is likely to happen or to be the case – given the evidence – expressed as a percentage. The higher the probability of an outcome, the more certain that the outcome will occur. For example, if we find that the probability of a claim (for example, 'engaged workers perform better than their disengaged peers') given the available evidence (such as a meta-analysis) is 20 per cent, this means there is an 80 per cent probability that this claim is incorrect. The problem with probabilities, however, is that they are hard to grasp. This is especially true of what is referred to as a single event or outcome. Most people understand that when they throw a die 100 times, they will score some 6s. But when they see the probability of a single event or outcome happening – which is the case with many claims, assumptions or hypotheses in the realm of management – they tend to think: Is this true/is this going to happen – or not? In an attempt to make sense of probabilities, most people will round them to either 0 or 100 per cent.[7] That's what many people in the United States did when they heard that Donald Trump had a probability of 10 to 20 per cent of winning the 2016 presidential election.[8] When he won, many people complained that the probabilities were wrong. They were not. Just because a probability is low, it does not mean it won't happen. In daily life, we experience improbable events all the time: we unexpectedly meet friends in unlikely places, we win a prize in the lottery, and our new car breaks down just when we have that important job interview. As an evidence-based manager, you should resist saying that a claim, assumption or hypothesis is 'right' or 'true' if its probability is above 50 per cent and 'wrong' or 'untrue' if it is below 50 per cent. A thorough understanding of probabilities and being able to calculate a decision's expected value and level of risk is a prerequisite for evidence-based decision-making.

13.5 Are there ethical issues to consider?

As discussed in Chapter 10, the possibility that a decision may harm a particular group of stakeholders – a department whose already stressful workload increases, the environmental impact of a product packaging change that increases waste and pollutants, or the neighbourhood facing greater noise or traffic from a facility expansion – raises issues of a decision's ethicality when we consider its full ramifications. A key issue is not that a decision may have negative outcomes. Organizational changes often have winners and losers and even successful decisions can involve considerable effort and difficulty for the people involved. Rather ethical concerns arise when a decision's benefits and harms aren't evenly distributed across stakeholders. Cutting jobs and employee pay while increasing the compensation to senior executives may raise issues regarding perceived justice (a key issue in ethics) as well as possible harms to the organization in terms of reputation and other market-related effects. When considering a decision's ethicality there are three ethical principles that may help managers reflect on the implications of the decisions they make.

Beneficence

Beneficence deals with the welfare of stakeholders, particularly whether the benefits from a decision exceed the harms that it might bring. Certain organizational decisions involve legitimate harms, such as putting a competitor out of business, raising prices or closing a line of business. We often regard such outcomes as the price of doing business. However, when the organization's mission or corporate values have committed it to quality relationships with its suppliers and customers, such legitimate harms may be perceived as violating the principle of beneficence, especially when they are deemed avoidable. Decisions by drug companies to raise prices without a compelling economic need to do so can fall into this category. On the other hand, where the ecological impact of a decision is concerned, Greenpeace might be expected to make decisions different from Shell, as a result of their distinct corporate values, mission and stakeholders' interests.

Respect

Respect for persons is the ethical principle promoting the exercise of autonomy in managing one's life and making personal decisions. It involves avoiding imposing undue demands or risks that undermine an individual's well-being and providing appropriate information to help people make choices that reflect their goals and interests. For example, managers who fail to inform stakeholders about the potential consequences of working with hazardous substances like asbestos or toxins would violate the principle of respect.

Justice

Justice is the ethical principle to treat people equitably and distribute benefits and burdens fairly. One of the major concerns in organizational decisions is when decision makers ignore adverse effects on parties 'not in the room' or stakeholders with little power and voice. Disproportionately benefiting one set of stakeholders while another is harmed raises issues of injustice. For example, Uber – a global taxi company from the United States – was stripped of its London licence, because the organization disregarded the values and concerns of important stakeholders (employees, competitors, local community) and by ignoring laws and regulations protecting the interests of conventional taxi companies.[9]

13.6 Is the evidence actionable?

Imagine you are an executive at a large Italian hotel chain. You are thinking about reducing the number of middle managers and granting local teams more autonomy. Before you implement this change, you want to make sure that collaboration within the company's teams is at its best. So you ask the question: Which factors positively affect team collaboration? When consulting the scientific literature, you find that one of the most important antecedents of team collaboration is trust among team members.[10] The company's experienced managers and team members confirm this finding and assert that interpersonal trust is indeed a prerequisite for a well-functioning team. Since the scientific evidence stems from two meta-analyses representing 80 samples from various industries, you judge the evidence to be applicable to your organizational context. To measure the teams' level of interpersonal trust, you apply a short questionnaire that researchers widely use. The outcome indicates that some teams score below average. You therefore decide to try to improve this situation. However, you now face a new question: How can you increase trust among team members? The scientific evidence only explains what team trust is and how you can measure it. It fails to explain *how* team trust can be *increased*.

In this example, the evidence you have in hand is actionable only for the diagnostic stage of the decision-making process; that is, do we have a problem with trust within our teams and how can we measure this? For the solution stage – how can we increase trust among team members – its applicability is rather limited. You can't act on it. As a result, you will have to consult the scientific literature for a second time and search for studies on factors that increase intra-team trust. The problem of non-actionable evidence often occurs when only cross-sectional studies are available, in which only a correlation between two variables is measured. In contrast, controlled longitudinal studies in which the independent variable (for example, trust) is manipulated by the researchers often provide more actionable information. The same is true of case studies describing organizational interventions and practices. Although the internal validity of this type of study is rather low (see Chapter 7), case studies often provide practical examples of how findings might be applied.

 Note

Implications for practice

When dealing with evidence from research, make sure you consult the section in research articles labelled 'Implications for Practice'.

Most research articles include it, and in general such sections are informative for management practice. However, be critical if general terms such as 'focus', 'align' or 'enhance' are used. These terms suggest actionability, but the recommendation 'Our findings suggest that in order to increase cooperation within a team, managers should focus on enhancing intra-team trust' is correct from an academic point of view but useless from a practical perspective. Assess critically whether the constructs referred to in the Results section or Implications for Practice are actionable and represent interventions or methods that you can use in practice.

When the evidence from the scientific literature is not actionable, evidence from practitioners and stakeholders can help. Always ask employees and managers for their professional judgement and experience. Experienced practitioners often have a wealth of practical knowledge, and although this knowledge may be based merely on personal experience, it may provide indispensable insights when it comes to practical application of research findings. Relevant questions to ask are:

- How can we apply this?
- What should we take into account?
- What do you need to apply this?

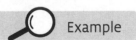 Example

An international IT firm wants to improve the performance and timeliness of its software development teams. When consulting the scientific literature, they find that one of the most important antecedents of team performance is information sharing.[11] Several studies indicate that, especially if complex problems have to be addressed, information sharing is indispensable in that it allows team members to pool their knowledge and past experiences by exchanging ideas, which is particularly important for the generation of new ideas. The firm's managers and software developers confirm that information sharing between team members is indeed important, and acknowledge that within some of the company's teams this may be an issue. To check this assertion, the teams' level of information sharing is measured with a short questionnaire that researchers often use. The outcome confirms that several teams indeed score poorly. It is therefore decided that action should be taken to improve this situation. The available evidence, however, fails to provide guidance for possible actions. For this reason, the firm's senior managers are consulted by means of a Delphi procedure (see Chapter 3). The outcome indicates that there are a variety of methods available to enhance information sharing, such as 'show and tell' sessions or informal gatherings where members can share their expertise. Another relatively new but promising method is a daily 'scrum': a short stand-up meeting at the beginning of the day during which team members share information and speak up about any problems that might prevent project completion. Based on this information the company decides to inform all teams about the value of information sharing and the various ways in which this can be increased and to ask them to choose for themselves a method that they consider the most effective and feasible.

13.7 Are there moderators that you need to take into account?

Another important aspect that you need to take into account when applying evidence is the effect of moderators. As explained in Chapter 5, a moderator is a variable that affects the direction and/or strength of the relation between a predictor (such as information sharing) and an outcome (such as performance). Put differently, moderators indicate when or under what conditions we can expect a particular effect. For instance, in the example above the evidence suggests that information sharing has a larger (positive) impact on performance when discussions within the team are structured and focused.[12] Thus, the positive effect of information sharing on performance is moderated by the factor 'discussion structure' (Figure 13.1).

Often there are several moderators that affect an outcome. As a result, moderators are important success factors for the application of the evidence when addressing a problem or implementing a solution. You need to take into account moderators from the organizational context such as industry sector, team size and task type, as they may weaken or strengthen the effect of an intervention or practice. For example, a healthcare organization facing

Figure 13.1

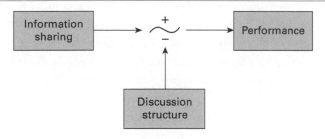

an issue of low productivity may find evidence that financial incentives increase motivation and productivity. However, when most of the organization's staff works in groups, the evidence needs careful examination, as the effect may be moderated by whether the incentive is based on individual or team performance.[13]

13.8 How and in what form can you apply the evidence?

Managers and leaders make a wide variety of decisions. Some decisions are rather mundane, such as sending an e-mail, booking a room or drawing up an agenda. Other decisions may have a huge impact on the organization, such as the decision to initiate a hostile takeover of a large competitor. As a rule, the type of decision determines how you can effectively apply the evidence to the decision-making process. There are many ways of classifying management decisions – the most widely used is probably the distinction among strategic, tactical and operational decisions. The classification below is not completely clear-cut, but it provides you with a guide to effectively applying evidence in decision-making.

Routine decisions

Often operational, routine decisions are made using an organization's existing set of rules and procedures. They may not have a major impact on resource allocation and are typically taken by middle or first-line managers: How much of a given product to stock in a shop? Who to hire to fill an existing role? How to deal with a customer complaint? Routine decisions are 'routine' because we make them repeatedly. They concern the typical problems every manager faces on a daily or weekly basis and often involve issues such as performance feedback, goal setting, conflict management, motivating employees, recruitment and selection, sales performance, absenteeism and so on – all issues for which much research evidence is available. Important reasons for taking an evidence-based approach to making routine decisions are to get good results more consistently, to find ways of improving results and to free up time to make other decisions better.

We typically apply evidence for routine decisions by using a 'push' approach: actively distributing information to the organization's relevant stakeholders. Such evidence may take the form of procedures of known effectiveness, where repeated practice demonstrates what works and what does not. This evidence can be provided in easily accessible and user-friendly forms such as a protocol, checklist, flowchart, decision tree or standard operating procedure (SOP). Checklists and protocols are widely used in high-risk industries, such as aviation and healthcare. For example, to reduce the number of medical errors in surgery the WHO 'Safe Surgery Checklist' was introduced in 2008. This checklist comprises a simple time-out procedure before the start of the surgery, where the surgical team checks the patient's name, the intended medical procedure and the patient's site (for example, left or right kidney). In 2009, the WHO concluded that the use of the checklist is associated with a significant decrease in postoperative complications (30 per cent) and mortality rates (50 per cent).[14]

 Note

Avoid over-simplification and over-standardization

When applying evidence in the form of a checklist, protocol or SOP, it is important to avoid over-simplification and over-standardization.[15] Although technical rationality may be needed in a cockpit or operating room, it can be too rigid for informing managers about how to give performance feedback to employees or how to select candidates in an unbiased way. Keep in mind that all checklists, protocols and SOPs are incomplete. They can help to guide a decision or practice, but users need to remain mindful of the specific context. The goal is to create a guideline that is agile where it needs to be.[16] It is important that people understand the principles behind the guideline and can go off-script if the situation warrants. Application always depends on the right balance between standardization and informed judgement.

Non-routine decisions

This kind of decision involves making changes to the way in which an organization operates. It is the sort of decision that managers are typically trained to make at business schools and universities. The scale of this type of decision can vary from the introduction of autonomous teams within a particular department to major strategic decisions such as whether to take over another company or launch a new product. The key point about decisions that fall within this category is that they concern something that is 'new' to the organization – though not necessarily to the industry or other firms – and are thus subject to varying degrees of uncertainty regarding the outcome. Non-routine also means that there may be relevant research evidence available, but it may take effort to retrieve it. In this type of decision, the evidence needed must first be identified. This means that the first action often concerns understanding the problem (or opportunity) and defining the desired outcome.

In contrast to routine decisions, evidence for non-routine decisions is typically applied using a 'pull' approach: based on the problem to solve, the outcome to achieve and the organizational context involved, you can actively obtain evidence from multiple sources and succinctly summarize it to inform decision makers. Evidence summaries come in many forms. When it comes to summarizing scientific evidence, Critically Appraised Topics (CATs) and Rapid Evidence Assessments (REAs) are the form we most widely use. Both apply the same systematic approach to selecting the studies – the methodological quality and practical relevance of the studies are assessed based on explicit criteria; thus, the summaries are transparent,

Figure 13.2

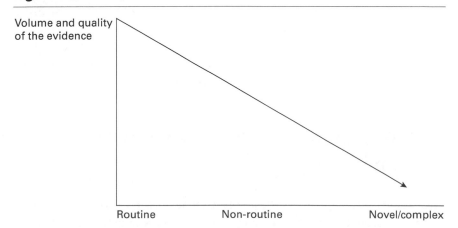

verifiable and reproducible. CATs are the quickest to produce and may take one skilled person a few days to produce. REAs might take two skilled persons several days or weeks to produce. A guideline on how to conduct a CAT is provided in Chapter 16. Although there is no harm in drawing up a separate summary for each evidence source (practitioners, organizational data, stakeholders and the scientific literature), we would recommend aggregating and synthesizing the evidence into one overall summary.

Novel/hyper-complex decisions

These decisions involve interventions that are not only new to the organization but also new to the industry at large (for example, introducing an innovative IT solution or starting a business unit in an emerging market). They often involve new or emergent conditions for which prior experience and historical knowledge provide little insight. Imagine a major technological breakthrough or a heretofore unheard-of environmental catastrophe. In such circumstances, evidence from the scientific literature is often not available, because the issues are too novel for scientific study. As a result, this type of intervention is typically subject to a high degree of uncertainty and involves many unknowns. Novel or hyper-complex situations involve considerable ambiguity – cues that signal the problem or possible solution can be so vague and confusing that they are hard to identify. This can be the case when technological changes bring unexpected consequences including new opportunities or unimaginable threats. In these situations, there is often very little or no quality evidence available (Figure 13.2), and as a result there is often insufficient evidence to inform decision makers. In these cases, there is no other option but to work with the limited evidence at hand and supplement it through a process of sense-making and learning by doing. This means pilot testing and systematically assessing outcomes of the decisions we take. In highly uncertain organizational environments, managers and leaders are likely to rely on constant experimentation and critical reflection in order to identify which things work and which things do not. We discuss how you can do this in the next chapter.

13.9 Dissemination, implementation and change

The methods of applying evidence mentioned in the previous section all represent different ways of providing decision makers with the best available evidence from multiple sources. In most evidence-based disciplines, however, dissemination of evidence is a major concern. For example, a survey of 950 US HR managers showed large discrepancies between what managers think is effective and what the current scientific research shows.[17] In medicine, it has been widely reported that evidence takes on average 10 to 15 years to be incorporated into routine general practice in healthcare.[18] The situation in other evidence-based disciplines such as education, policing and social welfare is not much better. As we will discuss in Chapter 15, whether the situation relates to a guideline, a checklist or a CAT, simply providing practitioners with the best available evidence unfortunately does not guarantee that they will use it. In fact, many reasons exist why practitioners – deliberately or unwittingly – disregard evidence. For this reason, a new field of science has emerged: implementation science, the study of methods to promote the uptake of evidence in routine practice. Whereas dissemination concerns the spread of evidence about a model, topic or intervention within an organization or a profession, implementation science concerns the uptake and usage of that evidence.[19] In this sense we need to make a distinction with the implementation of a management model, method or technique in the broader sense, such as the implementation of lean management or a new IT system. This type of implementation concerns methods or insights to facilitate organizational change and is thus related to the field of change management. Obviously, there is considerable overlap between the two fields, but whereas the implementation of evidence and evidence-based management is within the scope of this book (in particular Chapter 15), implementation as 'organizational change' is not. Nevertheless, we would like to dedicate a few words to the latter.[20]

Organizational change is risky. At least, that is what many change experts, consulting firms and management gurus claim. In fact, it is often (without the benefit of evidence) suggested that 70 per cent of all change initiatives fail.[21] For most experts, the reason is obvious: change initiatives fail because there is no sense of urgency, because there is no clear vision, because there is no commitment to the change goals, because the change leaders lack emotional intelligence, because... and so on. Just as in fields such as marketing, leadership or human resources, many (mostly self-proclaimed) change experts make strong claims about what does and doesn't work without providing any evidence. Here, too, there is a huge gap between what change experts think is effective and what the evidence shows. The only response to this dilemma is to take an evidence-based approach: conscientiously acquiring and appraising the best available evidence to determine whether claims regarding the best way to change or implement stand up to evidence-based scrutiny.[22]

Flowchart 13.1

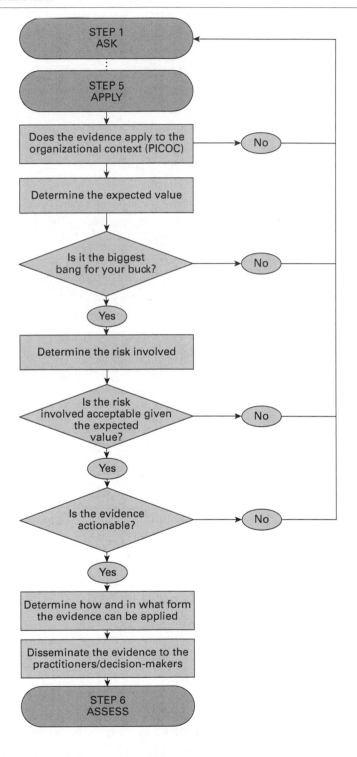

Notes and references

1 See, for example: CIPD Research Report (2017) 'Could do better? Assessing what works in performance management'

2 In science, generalizability is also referred to as external validity. Often two types of external validity are assessed: ecological validity (type of organization) and population validity (type of employees).

3 Drosdeck JM, Bansal, S and Peterson, A (2013) A personality trait analysis of surgeons and non-surgeons at different career points, in The International Conference on Residency Education, Royal College of Physicians and Surgeons of Canada

4 Closely related to the notion of expected value is the concept of expected utility. Whereas expected value simply calculates the monetary value, expected utility also takes into account the personal satisfaction and happiness that is derived from a certain outcome.

5 Harter, JK, Schmidt, FL and Hayes, TL (2002) Business-unit-level relationship between employee satisfaction, employee engagement and business outcomes: A meta-analysis, *Journal of Applied Psychology*, 87, pp 268–79

6 Barends, E, Plum, K and Mason, A (2017) Rapid evidence assessments in management: An example, in *Evidence-Based Management in Healthcare*, ed AR Kovner and TA D'Aunno, Health Administration Press, Chicago

7 Adapted from: Leonard, D (2017) What I was wrong about this year, *New York Times*, Opinion section, 24 December

8 Katz, J (2016) Hillary Clinton has an 85% chance to win, *New York Times*, 8 November

9 Butler, S and Topham, G (2017) Uber stripped of London licence due to lack of corporate responsibility, *The Guardian*, 22 September

10 McAllister, DJ (1995) Affect- and cognition-based trust as foundations for interpersonal cooperation in organizations, *Academy of Management Journal*, 38 (1), pp 24–59

11 Mesmer-Magnus, JR and DeChurch, LA (2009) Information sharing and team performance: A meta-analysis, *Journal of Applied Psychology*, 94 (2), pp 535–46

12 Idem

13 Scott, A *et al* (2010) The effect of financial incentives on the quality of health care provided by primary care physicians, *Cochrane Database of Systematic Reviews*, 2011 (9)

14 World Health Organization (2011) New scientific evidence supports WHO findings: A surgical safety checklist could save hundreds of thousands of lives [Online] http://www.who.int

15 This section is adapted from Rousseau, DM (2018) Making evidence-based decisions in an uncertain world, *Organizational Dynamics,* in press

16 The need for adaptive protocols: Rycroft-Malone, J *et al* (2009) Protocol-based care: the standardisation of decision-making?, *Journal of Clinical Nursing,* **18** (10), pp 1490–1500

17 Rynes, SL, Colbert, AE and Brown, KG (2002) HR Professionals' beliefs about effective human resource practices: Correspondence between research and practice, *Human Resource Management,* **41** (2), pp 149–74

18 See, for example, Morris, ZS, Wooding, S and Grant, J (2011) The answer is 17 years, what is the question: Understanding time lags in translational research, *Journal of the Royal Society of Medicine,* **104** (12), pp 510–20

19 Bauer, MS *et al* (2015) An introduction to implementation science for the non-specialist, *BMC Psychology,* **3** (1), p 32

20 The following section is adapted from the foreword the authors have written for: ten Have, S *et al* (2016) *Reconsidering change management: Applying Evidence-Based Insights in Change Management Practice* (Vol 16), Routledge, Abingdon

21 Beer, M and Nohria, N (2000) Cracking the code of change, *HBR's 10 Must Reads on Change,* **78** (3), pp 133–41

22 Stouten, J, Rousseau, DM and De Cremers, R (2018) Successful organizational change: Integrating management practice and research literatures, *Annals of the Academy of Management,* in press

ASSESS: Evaluate the outcome of the decision taken

14

You should measure things you care about.
If you're not measuring, you don't care and you don't know.

STEVE HOWARD

In the United States, the number of employees who work from home has tripled over the past 30 years. Many people still picture an employee working from home as a person in pyjamas watching videos on their laptop. Several empirical studies, however, suggest that this picture is not accurate and that remote working can have a positive effect on performance.[1] For this reason, James Liang, CEO of Ctrip, China's largest travel agency with more than 16,000 employees, considered implementing remote working for his call centre staff. To make sure his decision had the desired outcome (increased individual task performance), he first assessed the effect of remote working on a smaller scale. A sample of 250 employees was included in the assessment: employees with even-numbered birthdays were assigned to the group that works from home, while those with odd-numbered birthdays remained in the office as a control group. The trial lasted three months. Did the employees working from home resist staying in bed watching TV instead of doing their job? When Liang and his colleagues reviewed the outcome, they were stunned. 'It was unbelievable. The work-from-home employees were far from goofing off – they increased their performance by 13.5 per cent over those working in the office.' In addition, employees who worked from home also reported shorter breaks and fewer sick days and took less time off. Liang decided to introduce remote working for all call centre workers.[2]

Assessing the outcome of the decision taken is the sixth and final step of the evidence-based process. After we have Asked critical questions, Acquired, Appraised and Aggregated evidence from multiple sources and, finally, Applied the evidence to the decision-making process, we now need to Assess the outcome: Did the decision deliver the desired results? Unfortunately, many organizations fail to evaluate the outcome of their decisions – sacrificing one of the principal means to learn. Remember, the expertise you develop as a practitioner depends in large part on the accuracy of the feedback you get on your decisions – and how well you learn from it, as we discussed in Chapter 4. Systematically assessing the outcome of a decision taken is one of the key ways in which we can improve the quality of our decisions and it often leads us to challenge our assumptions, change our judgement and reconsider our conclusions. For this reason, assessing the outcome of our decisions is something we can and always should do, even – or particularly – in cases in which the preceding five steps of the evidence-based process yield little or no quality evidence. This may be the case, for example, with the implementation of new technologies or in an organizational context that changes rapidly. In those cases, we have no other option but to systematically evaluate the results of our decisions through a process of constant experimentation, punctuated by critical assessment of what worked and what didn't.

14.1 Types of decisions

In this chapter, we will present several methods for assessing the outcome of a decision taken. Before such an assessment can take place, however, it is important to remind ourselves of the types of decisions managers make, because to a large extent this determines how we can assess the outcome in an effective and reliable way. We provided an overview of common decision types in Chapter 13. A succinct summary is provided below.

Routine decisions

Routine decisions, which are often operational, are those that are made within an organization's existing set of rules and procedures. How much of a given product to stock in a shop? Who to hire to fill an existing role? How to deal with a customer complaint? Typically, we can assess the outcome of routine decisions using organizational data generated by systems available within the organization.

Non-routine decisions

Non-routine decisions involve making changes to the way in which an organization operates. The scale of this type of decision can vary from the introduction of autonomous teams within a particular department to major strategic decisions such as whether to take over another company or launch a new product. The key point about decisions that fall within this category is that they concern something that is 'new' to the organization – but not to the industry – and are thus subject to varying degrees of uncertainty regarding the outcome. Non-routine also means that we may not have standard ways to assess the outcome because existing organizational data are insufficient.

Novel/hyper-complex decisions

Novel or hyper-complex decisions involve interventions that are not only new to the organization but also new to the industry at large (for example, introducing an innovative IT solution or starting a business unit in an emerging market). This type of intervention is typically subject to a high degree of uncertainty and risk regarding the outcome and usually involves many unknowns. As a result, we often do not have standard ways to assess the outcome.

14.2 Assessing the outcome: Two preliminary questions

In this chapter, we present several methods for assessing the outcome of a decision. Before we can assess the outcome, however, there are two questions we need to answer first: 1) Was the decision executed? and 2) Was the decision executed as planned?

Question 1: Was the decision executed?

Decisions may be made but simply not executed. In an organization that produces physical products or where the decision makers are in the same building as those executing the decision, it may be possible to simply check whether a decision has been implemented through 'management by walking around'. In many organizations, those who execute the decision are located in different departments, buildings or even countries. In that case, it is worth checking whether the decision indeed has been executed. Even where a decision is clearly represented in new rules, procedures or training, it does not automatically follow that the decision has been carried out.

 Example

The executive board of an international bank decided that any bank account that has two or more 'Suspicious Activity Reports' (reports of activities likely to indicate the account had been used for illegal activity) should be closed. The bank's top executives, however, repeatedly ignored internal warnings that the firm's monitoring systems were inadequate, and that it was thus unclear whether the decision was fully implemented. During an audit of the US Justice Department several months later it indeed turned out that the decision was not implemented by one of their Latin American subsidiaries. This became a major factor in the bank being fined over 1 billion US dollars in a money-laundering case.

Question 2: Was the decision executed as planned?

This question pertains to what is referred to as 'implementation fidelity', which describes the degree to which a decision was executed as intended by the decision makers. It acts as a potential moderator of the effect of the decision and its intended outcomes. Put differently, the degree to which a decision or intervention is executed determines whether the decision produces the desired outcome. Interventions in areas such as medicine or engineering often have dramatic consequences if they are not carried out as specified (people die, bridges collapse). This is one of the reasons why we always need to assess implementation fidelity. Unless we make such an assessment, we cannot determine whether a lack of impact is due to poor implementation or the decision itself, and thus may lead us to draw false conclusions about the decision's effectiveness.

 Example

Tuberculosis is one of the top 10 causes of death worldwide: in 2016, more than 10 million people fell ill with tuberculosis and 1.7 million died from the disease. For patients with a specific type of tuberculosis, antiretroviral therapy was shown to have good results. Because the impact of implementation fidelity on the therapy's outcome was unknown, a controlled longitudinal study was conducted.[3] The outcome demonstrated that the overall mortality risk was 12.0 per cent. However, under complete implementation fidelity, the mortality risk was 7.8 per cent, suggesting that one-third of the mortality is preventable by implementation fidelity.

Implementation fidelity is commonly described in terms of three elements that we need to assess.[4] These are:

1 Content

The content of the intervention concerns its 'active ingredients': the actions, knowledge or skills that the intervention seeks to deliver to its recipients. For example, a company can decide that the leadership training for its managers should include general management skills (for example, goal setting, performance appraisal, time management) as well as interpersonal skills (for example, listening, questioning, negotiating).

2 Dose: Duration, frequency and coverage

The dose of the intervention refers to its duration, frequency and coverage (that is, percentage of the population involved in the intervention). For instance, in the example above it could be decided that the training should take three days, be repeated every four years and be mandatory for all middle managers. If an implemented decision adheres completely to the content, frequency, duration and coverage as determined by the decision makers, then we can say that fidelity is high.

3 Moderators

A high level of implementation fidelity is not easily achieved. In fact, there are several factors that may influence or moderate the degree of fidelity to which a decision or intervention is implemented. For example, the intervention may be very complex and entail multiple elements, the people that are supposed to implement the intervention may lack the necessary skills to do so, or the departments involved may have insufficient financial or human resources to carry out implementation. In those cases, it is likely that implementation fidelity is low.

14.3 Assess: The gold standard

When we assess the outcome of a decision, we are asking whether the decision had an effect on a particular outcome. This type of question (does X have an effect on Y?) is about cause and effect. Questions of this sort are hard to answer. Controlling the independent variable (cause/intervention) and separating it in time from the dependent variable (effect/outcome) can be very difficult. In addition, there are many confounding factors that may influence the outcome. When it comes to assessing the effect of a decision in a valid and reliable way, we need both a control group (preferably randomized) and a baseline measurement (Figure 14.1). As you may recall from

Figure 14.1

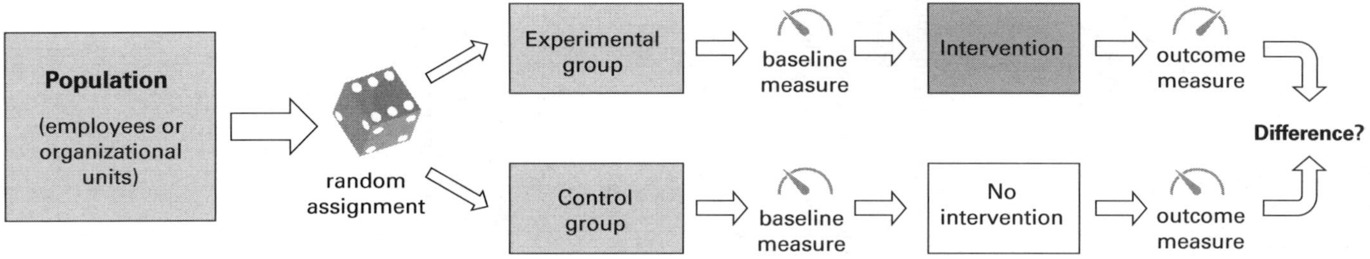
Population
(employees or organizational units)
random assignment
Experimental group
Control group
baseline measure
baseline measure
Intervention
No intervention
outcome measure
outcome measure
Difference?

Chapter 7, this type of design is known as a randomized controlled trial, considered the gold standard to answer cause-and-effect questions.

A randomized controlled trial (RCT) can be conducted quite easily. For example, in the case of a new service you can offer the service to a random group of customers, offer no (or a different) service to a control group, and then compare the results. Another example of an RCT is provided at the beginning of this chapter: employees of a call centre were randomly assigned to an intervention group (working from home) and a control group (working from the office). The outcomes of RCTs are simple to analyse, and the data easily interpreted. Another domain in which it is relatively easy to run an RCT is marketing, especially online marketing. For example, it is quite common to test the effectivity of online advertisements or web pages by randomizing potential customers to one of the two versions to determine which one performs better. This latter example is also referred to as A/B testing.

 Note

Not all experiments are created equal

In science, an RCT is sometimes referred to as a 'true experiment'. In daily life, an experiment means 'trying something out to see what happens', and is a synonym for 'pilot'. A true experiment (RCT) and a pilot, however, are two very different things. A true experiment is a research design with a high internal validity, whereas a pilot means 'trying out' something new (for example, a new product or service) to determine whether it can be introduced more widely. Most organizations run pilots (a well-known CEO of a large multinational once complained that his company had more pilots than British Airways), but not many organizations run true experiments. This means that when an organization says it has done an experiment, you should check whether it involved a pre-measure, a control group and random assignment. In some industries, running experiments (RCTs) is already standard operating procedure. If you order something at Amazon, you are almost certainly part of an experiment – testing products, prices and even book titles. Capital One, a US bank, conducts tens of thousands of experiments each year to improve the way in which the company acquires customers, maximizes their lifetime value and terminates unprofitable accounts.[5]

Baseline

As explained in Chapter 4, we tend to automatically infer causality because of our System 1 thinking (ie automatic, intuitive, heuristical). To determine whether a decision has an effect on a desired outcome, however, we first need to know what the situation was before the decision was executed. Thus, we need a baseline. In athletics, a baseline is essential. Without being sure that all athletes start at the same time (and thus have a similar baseline), we can't be certain that the winner was indeed the fastest. But a baseline is also essential in the realm of management and organizations. For example, in order to assess the effect of a new working procedure on employees' job satisfaction, we first need to know what their job satisfaction was before the new working procedure was implemented. Here too we need a 'baseline': a measurement of the metrics of interest before the decision was executed that we can use to compare to later measurements in order to assess the effect. A baseline is also often referred to as a 'before' measurement, whereas the one taken at the outcome is referred to as an 'after' measurement.

A baseline is not only essential in order to determine whether a decision has 'caused' an effect, but also to determine what causes what. For example, when the organizational data demonstrates a strong correlation between the level of supervisory support and subordinates' productivity, we are inclined to assume that supportive supervisors cause productive subordinates. However, without a baseline we cannot rule out what is known as 'reverse causality': subordinates may be productive because they have supportive supervisors, or supervisors may be supportive because they have productive subordinates.[6] When we don't have a baseline, we can't say with certainty whether it was the decision that caused a desired outcome.

Control

In a randomized controlled trial, we expose a group of employees or organizational units (sometimes referred to as an 'intervention' or 'experimental' group) to an intervention. This intervention or experimental group is compared with another group that is not exposed to the intervention (sometimes referred to as the 'control' or 'comparison' group). The control group serves as a benchmark for comparison against the intervention group. In the example above, we could obtain more confidence about the effect of supportive supervisors on subordinates' productivity by comparing the productivity of teams with a supportive supervisor with those with an unsupportive supervisor. To rule out alternative explanations for the increased productivity, however, we should assign subordinates or supervisors to the control and intervention groups 'at random'.

Randomization

Even when we use a control group, we still can't be 100 per cent certain that there were no (unknown) confounders affecting the outcome. The gold standard of outcome assessment therefore includes 'random assignment', a method to create control and intervention groups that include subjects (people or organizational units) with similar characteristics, so that both groups are similar at the start of the intervention. The method involves assigning subjects to one of the groups 'at random' (by chance, like the flip of a coin), so that each subject has an equal chance of being assigned to each group, and any possible distorting factor is equally spread over both groups. Thus, we can more confidently attribute any differences in the desired outcome to the decision.

 Example

A large Dutch food retailer is looking for ways to cut its operating costs. The Chief Operating Officer suggests opening up all stores one hour later on workdays. The company's executives are divided on the decision's potential impact: some argue that reducing the opening hours will result in a substantial decrease in sales, while others claim that the impact will be minimal. The company's board therefore decides to first assess the impact of the reduced opening hours by conducting an RCT. A sample of 100 stores is randomly assigned to the intervention (reduced opening hours) and the control condition (normal opening hours). After the trial has run for three months, the results demonstrate that the delayed opening hours do not result in any meaningful sales decline. The board therefore decides to implement later opening hours for all 1,200 stores.[7]

 Note

Random assignment is not the same as random sampling

Remember, as we explained in Chapter 7, random assignment is not the same as random sampling. Random sampling refers to selecting subjects (people, organizational units and so on) in such a way that they represent the whole population, whereas random assignment deals with assigning subjects to a control group and intervention group in such a way that they are similar at the start of the intervention. Put differently, random selection ensures high representativeness, whereas random assignment ensures high internal validity.

14.4 Assess: The silver standard

The gold standard – a randomized controlled trial – requires random assignment of individuals to units (teams, departments and so on) that serve as either an intervention or a control group. In most organizations, however, units were set up long before the intervention started, and the individuals within these units were often not assigned at random. An alternative option would be to randomize units rather than individuals, but that is feasible only for corporations with multiple, geographically dispersed sites, such as banks, chain stores, government agencies, or health-delivery organizations.[8] In addition, non-routine change interventions often concern new tasks and responsibilities, but people's tasks and responsibilities are never assigned 'at random'. In these cases, the gold standard is not feasible, so we have no other option than to go for silver instead.

Quasi-experiments

The biggest barrier to the gold standard is random assignment. For this reason, we must settle for a non-randomized controlled study, also referred to as a quasi-experiment. What makes quasi-experiments experimental is their use of both a control group and a before and after measurement. What makes them 'quasi' is the lack of random assignment of people or units to the control and intervention group. The lack of random assignment negatively affects the assessment's internal validity (trustworthiness). It is nevertheless worth doing them. In fact, in domains such as medicine many findings are based on non-randomized studies, especially when objections of an ethical nature come into play (for example, in research into the effects of smoking on the development of lung cancer it would not be ethical to induce one group of people to start smoking in order to see its health consequences). Non-randomized studies too can lead to robust empirical insight into a decision's effects, when repeated under varying conditions.[9]

Example

A financial services organization with 40 branches in the United Kingdom decides to set goals to enhance the performance of their mortgage sales agents. Because several scientific studies suggest that providing rewards can strengthen a person's goal commitment – which results in better performance – the company also decides to introduce performance-based rewards. To assess the effect of this decision the company measures the performance of 124 sales agents over a two-month period. Because it is not possible to randomly assign the agents to one of the two conditions (that is, since agents often work side by side and would learn, and possibly resent, differences in their reward allocations), 82 agents at 6 branches serve as the intervention group, and 42 agents at 4 branches serve as a control. The key performance indicator is the number of new mortgages sold. The average number of sales in the preceding year is set as a baseline level, and the agents receive a reward when attaining a particular level of performance: 105 per cent, 110 per cent and 125 per cent, with rewards of US $250, $700 and $1,500, respectively. At the beginning of the assessment, each agent chooses one of the performance goals and receives the corresponding award if the goal is achieved. Agents at three branches receive cash, while agents at three other branches receive 'points' that are redeemable for rewards listed in a catalogue. After two months, the outcome is assessed: the agents who set goals and received performance-based rewards sold on average 12.5 per cent more mortgages. However, it was also found that the agents who were offered cash rewards tended to set higher goals than those who were offered non-financial rewards, and as a result their performance was higher.[10]

Before–after assessment

When random assignment is not feasible, it is important that the subjects (people, organizational units) in the intervention group are similar to those in the control group. If the groups are not similar at baseline, the outcome of the assessment may be flawed. In large organizations with multiple branches, offices or departments it is often possible to find a control group that matches the subjects in the intervention group. In smaller organizations or those with a diverse population, however, a control group may be

Figure 14.2

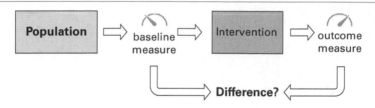

hard to achieve. The same counts for novel and hyper-complex decisions, and for large-scale change interventions. In those cases, it may be preferable to assess the outcome of the decision taken by only comparing the baseline with the outcome. This type of assessment is referred to as before–after measurement (Figure 14.2). A before–after measurement may also be more suitable for companies that prefer to implement the decision within the whole organization, rather than only in the units that were assigned to the intervention group.

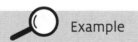 Example

A daycare centre has a clearly stated policy that children must be picked up by their parents by 5 pm. Nevertheless, some parents are often late and, as a result, at least one teacher must wait until the parents arrive. Because there is extensive research suggesting that people are sensitive to financial disincentives, the daycare centre manager decides to introduce a fine for tardy parents. To determine whether this decision has the desired effect, the centre keeps track of the number of parents who come late for four weeks both before and after the fine is introduced. In the first four weeks they register, on average, six late pickups per week. In the fifth week, the fine is introduced: parents who arrive more than 10 minutes late will receive a fine of US $3. This fine will be added to the parents' monthly bill (which is about US $380). To the manager's great surprise, in the four weeks after the fine is introduced the average number of late pickups goes up from 6 to 20. Apparently, the fine backfired. To find an explanation for this unexpected outcome, a focus group is held with some of the parents. From this focus group, the manager learns that putting such a small fine on a late pickup absolved the parents of the moral guilt they felt for being late.[11]

A before–after measurement is a simple and practical method of assessing the outcome of a decision. Because this type of assessment lacks both random assignment and a control group, however, the outcome is more prone to bias and confounders. For this reason, it is important that we use valid and reliable outcome measures to assess the effect (see below).

After-Action Review

When we do not (or cannot) obtain a baseline, it will be hard to assess the outcome of a decision taken. This is often the case in large-scale interventions, hyper-complex decisions, or change projects that have multiple objectives. But even in those cases, we should make an attempt to assess the outcome, for instance by means of an **After-Action Review** (AAR). First used by the US Army for combat training, an AAR is a structured, reflective evaluation of a recent set of decisions in order to evaluate their effectiveness. Meta-analyses have found that, when appropriately conducted, AARs can lead to a 20 to 25 per cent average improvement of the desired outcome (for example, performance, safety, attitudes).[12] Nowadays, AARs are used in many disciplines such as medicine, policing, education and aviation. The method is relatively straightforward: a facilitator leads individuals or teams through a series of questions that allow participants to reflect on a recent decision and uncover lessons learned in a non-punitive environment. The process may be formal or informal, and may last for minutes or hours, but the review always revolves around the same four questions:

1 What did we decide to do?

2 What actually happened?

3 How/why did it happen?

4 What should we do next time?

According to US Army guidelines, roughly 25 per cent of the time should be devoted to the first two questions, 25 per cent to the third, and 50 per cent to the fourth.[13] In addition, it was found that AARs are most effective when the following requirements are met:[14]

- **Developmental intent:** The focus of the review should be on learning and improvement, rather than evaluation or judgement. A developmental, non-punitive focus not only yields more honest and accurate feedback, but also enhances experiential learning.

- **Focus on specific events:** The review should focus on specific activities, episodes or events, rather than performance or results in general.

- **Multiple evidence sources:** The review should be informed by a variety of perspectives and evidence sources. For example, the review should include input from multiple participants and at least one additional source of evidence (such as organizational data).

14.5 Outcome measures

Reliability

When we assess the outcome of a decision taken, we want to make sure that our conclusions are valid and reliable. For this reason, we prefer to assess the outcome with before and after measurement and a (randomized) control group. The trustworthiness of an assessment, however, is first and foremost determined by the way in which the outcome was measured. The measurement of direct/objective outcomes (such as production error rate, staff turnover rate) is more likely to be valid and reliable than that of self-reported/subjective outcomes (for example, perceived error rate). In addition, when we assess the outcome of a decision by using organizational data generated by the company's systems, we need to check whether these data are accurate and reliable, and thus we must consider all aspects that were described in Chapter 9.

Performance measures

When assessing the outcome of a decision, we often have many types of measures available. One of the most widely used measures is performance. Organizations use various methods to measure performance. These methods vary in terms of complexity and are often expressed in a metric that contains both objective and subjective measures. Measuring performance, however, is difficult, since it depends on what is defined as 'performance' by the organization and how its customers perceive this performance. In addition, the correlation between subjective and objective performance measures tends to be rather low and therefore cannot be used interchangeably.[15] For this reason, we recommend you use primary outcome measures rather than indirect or aggregated performance metrics. In Table 14.1 we provide an overview of common primary outcome measures.

Table 14.1

Primary outcome measures		
Number of sales	Net profit margin	Job satisfaction
Number of units produced	Return on investment	Staff turnover rate
Number of production stops	Cost/benefit ratio	Absenteeism
Failure frequency rate	Overhead ratio	Retention
Production hours	Market share	Professional time utilization
Throughput time	Company value growth	R&D quota
Unused capacity	Customer profitability	Handling time
Occupancy rate	Customer satisfaction	Timeliness
Waiting times	Number of complaints	Revenue per employee
Number of innovations	Net promoter score	Profit per FTE
Number of patents	Brand awareness	Overtime per employee

Costs and benefits

Even the best decision may come with unexpected costs, so we should make a thorough cost-benefit analysis part of every assessment. On the internet, there are several analytics tools and templates (often freely) available. Many of these tools, however, do a poor job of identifying indirect and intangible costs (such as a decrease in customer satisfaction or drop in employee morale). Thus, when you conduct a cost-benefit analysis, you need to consult multiple sources of evidence (organizational data, professionals or stakeholders) to identify all the costs, financial and otherwise.

14.6 Assessing stakeholder effects

Decisions have both intended and unintended consequences. We are more likely to recognize the latter when we assess evidence from stakeholders regarding a decision's impact. In fact, stakeholders are an important source of information regarding issues we might need to manage in the aftermath of a decision. Unfortunately, some managers prefer to ignore the impact of their decisions on stakeholders, particularly those at lower levels or outside the firm.[16] This evaluation avoidance, however, undermines understanding of the full array of effects of organizational decisions. This is particularly a problem in non-profit organizations where positive results of interest to donors and funding agencies are emphasized while negative effects on clients and the community are downplayed.[17] In for-profit organizations, evidence from stakeholders can inform decision makers about the effects of their decisions on sustainability, community well-being and longer-term social consequences. Note that the values and concerns of stakeholders (in terms of decision outcomes they view as important) can be quite different from what managers believe them to be. For example, in global firms operating in developing countries, locals may be particularly interested in job security, and less accepting of cuts that are explained by market factors.[18] Thus effective (and ethical) decision-making includes systematic assessment of (potential) effects on stakeholders broadly.

14.7 Keep it simple!

The perfect is the enemy of the good. This old proverb also applies to assessing the outcome of a decision taken. We already pointed out that when the gold standard – a randomized control trial – is not feasible, we should go for silver instead: a non-randomized study, a before–after measurement or an After-Action Review. In general, it pays to conduct assessments that are easy to execute and that use minimal resources and staff. Running complex trials that take several months to execute is probably not the best strategy. Instead, we recommend focusing on small-scale assessments that can be automated through the company's existing information systems. Much of what you can learn from large-scale experiments you can also learn from a series of smaller tests. In addition, sometimes an honest and open After-Action Review of a failed decision generates more value than a rigorous RCT of a successful decision – provided that the organization is open to learning. The goal is not to conduct the perfect assessment – the goal is to learn and help the organization make better decisions. Because, as Eric Anderson, professor at Kellogg School of Management rightly states, 'What's surprising is not how bad decisions typically are, but how good managers feel about them. They shouldn't – there's usually a lot of room for improvement.'[19]

Flowchart 14.1

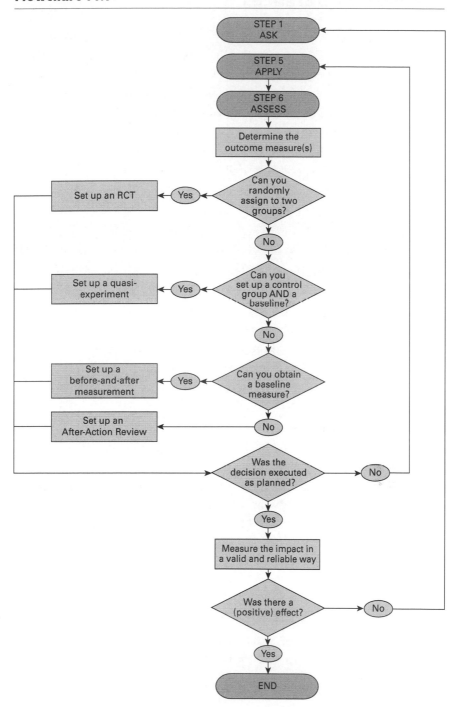

Notes and references

1 De Menezes, LM and Kelliher, C (2011) Flexible working and performance: A systematic review of the evidence for a business case, *International Journal of Management Reviews*, **13** (4), pp 452–74

2 This example is adapted from Ari Surdoval (2017) Why working from home should be standard practice, published on IDEAS.TED.COM on 20 September

3 Patel, MR *et al* (2015) The impact of implementation fidelity on mortality under a CD4-stratified timing strategy for antiretroviral therapy in patients with tuberculosis, *American Journal of Epidemiology*, **181** (9), pp 714–22

4 Carroll, C *et al* (2007) A conceptual framework for implementation fidelity, *Implementation Science*, **2** (1), p 40

5 Anderson, ET (2011) A step-by-step guide to smart business experiments, *Development and Learning in Organizations: An International Journal*, **25** (6)

6 Bass, BM and Bass, R (2008) *The Bass Handbook of Leadership: Theory, research, and managerial applications*, Free Press, New York

7 This example is adapted from Thomke, S and Manzi, J (2014) The discipline of business experimentation, *Harvard Business Review*, December

8 Eden, D (2017) Field experiments in organizations, *Annual Review of Organizational Psychology and Organizational Behavior*, **4**, pp 91–122

9 Petticrew, M and Roberts, H (2008) *Systematic Reviews in the Social Sciences: A practical guide*, John Wiley & Sons, London

10 This example is adapted from Presslee, A, Vance, TW and Webb, RA (2013) The effects of reward type on employee goal setting, goal commitment, and performance, *The Accounting Review*, **88** (5), pp 1805–31

11 This example is adapted from Dubner, SJ and Levitt, SD (2014) *Freakonomics*, INCA. The original study was published as Gneezy, U and Rustichini, A (2000) A fine is a price, *The Journal of Legal Studies*, **29** (1), pp 1–17

12 See, for example, Tannenbaum, SI and Cerasoli, CP (2013) Do team and individual debriefs enhance performance? A meta-analysis, *Human Factors*, **55** (1), pp 231–45

13 Garvin, DA (2003) *Learning in Action: A guide to putting the learning organization to work*, Harvard Business Review Press

14 Adapted from Tannenbaum, SI and Cerasoli, CP (2013) Do team and individual debriefs enhance performance? A meta-analysis, *Human Factors*, **55** (1), pp 231–45, as summarized by Wendy Hirsch in her blog on Team Improvement (11 December 2016, retrieved from wendyhirsch.com/blog/how-to-improve-teamwork)

15 See, for example, Forth, J, and McNabb, R (2008) Workplace performance: A comparison of subjective and objective measures in the 2004 Workplace Employment Relations Survey, *Industrial Relations Journal*, **39** (2), pp 104–23

16 Keltner, D, Gruenfeld, DH and Anderson, C (2003) Power, approach, and inhibition, *Psychological Review*, **110** (2), p 265

17 Julian, R (2016) Is it for donors or locals? The relationship between stakeholder interests and demonstrating results in international development, *International Journal of Managing Projects in Business*, **9** (3), pp 505–27

18 Lähteenmäki, S and Laiho, M (2011) Global HRM and the dilemma of competing stakeholder interests, *Social Responsibility Journal*, **7** (2), pp 166–80

19 Anderson, ET (2011) A step-by-step guide to smart business experiments, *Development and Learning in Organizations: An International Journal*, **25** (6)

Building the capacity for evidence-based management

15

Be the change that you wish to see in the world.

MAHATMA GANDHI

In 1954, Leon Festinger, a US social psychologist, read about a cult that believed the end of the world was nigh. The cult was led by 'Mrs Keech', a housewife from Chicago who claimed to have received a message from extra-terrestrials that on 21 December a great flood would extinguish all life on earth, although all 'true believers' would be rescued the night before by a flying saucer. Mrs Keech attracted a large group of followers who gave up their jobs, sold their homes and gave away all their possessions. Given the followers' strong beliefs, Festinger wondered how they would react when Mrs Keech's claim turned out to be false. To find out, he posed as a believer and infiltrated the cult. At midnight on 20 December the evidence was clear: no spaceship had turned up. The followers, however, concluded that this time the world had been spared because of the faith of their group. The next day they actively started to recruit new members.[1, 2]

We like to think that we base our judgements on evidence. After all, isn't this the hallmark of rationality? Of course, as explained in Chapter 4, our judgement is prone to cognitive biases that negatively affect the decisions we make. But when confronted with hard, undisputable evidence that reveals we should change our judgement, we do just that. Or do we? Unfortunately, as the example above demonstrates, simply showing the evidence is often not enough to change a person's beliefs.[3] We could argue that the cult members did not change their minds because they were stupid or foolish, and that this example doesn't represent the average manager. That argument, unfortunately, doesn't ring true. People's beliefs and judgements – including those of managers and business leaders – are part of a complex system that is resilient or stubborn (take your pick) in the face of contradictory evidence. As a result, simply showing your boss, colleagues or employees strong evidence may not be enough to change what they believe. In fact, as illustrated by the following experience of Jeffrey Pfeffer, renowned management professor at Stanford University, managers at times even choose to ignore the best available evidence:[4]

> A few years ago, while serving on the compensation committee for a publicly traded company, we were considering what to do about the CEO's stock options and our stock option programme in general. Just that day articles in the mainstream business press were published on research showing that stock options led to risky behaviour.[5] That research added to the growing body of evidence demonstrating that many executive pay practices not only did not enhance company performance, but led instead to misreporting of financial results.[6, 7] At the meeting, a vice president from Aon Consulting who was advising the compensation committee replied 'No' without any hesitation or embarrassment when I asked him first, if he knew about this research and second, if he was interested in me sending him the original articles or other information about the extensive research on stock options and their effects. What is particularly telling is that many people from other compensation consulting firms to whom I have related this story said it could have been their firm, too – that the perspective reflected is typical.

To give evidence-based management a shot at success, we need to increase the capacity of managers and organizations to prioritize quality evidence over personal opinion – and incorporate what the body of evidence indicates into their professional judgement. That, however, is easier said than done. In this chapter, we will discuss how you can build the capacity for evidence-based management – not only in yourself, but also among your peers, bosses and the organization at large.

15.1 Becoming an evidence-based manager

This chapter's opening quote from Gandhi has energized generations of people to act as change agents for a better world, by first starting with themselves. Evidence-based management also starts with ourselves. By becoming an evidence-based practitioner, you can inspire other practitioners and form the basis of an organizational culture that is itself evidence-based.

An approach of this kind is not only about mastering the six skills – Ask, Acquire, Appraise, Aggregate, Apply and Assess – but also the lifelong pursuit of personal and professional development as an evidence-based practitioner. This development typically involves three phases:

1 Developing a questioning mindset.

2 Making decisions more explicit.

3 Practising and learning every day.

Developing a questioning mindset

The absence of evidence-based decision-making is not so much due to a lack of knowledge about the evidence supporting or contradicting a decision (though that is a serious issue), but rather the absence of managers with a questioning mindset.[8] Wondering what works, what doesn't and why is the first step towards improving management practice. As discussed in Chapter 2, asking questions kicks off a deliberate search for evidence and leads to the active exploration of alternatives. This questioning also increases understanding by testing assumptions about problems, solutions and the outcomes of decisions. Developing a questioning mindset that appreciates the difference between trustworthy and less trustworthy evidence is a first step to becoming an evidence-based manager. Developing this mindset, however, is a career- (and maybe even life-) changing proposition.

An evidence-based practitioner thinks differently from other people. Evidence-based management is not just about applying skills and knowledge: it's about taking a different perspective on the organization and its day-to-day concerns. This shift starts with developing the habit of frequently asking yourself and others, 'What's the evidence for that?' Of course, raising questions can be scary, especially for those of us who fear making waves. But, once practised at it, we become comfortable asking, 'Is this your personal opinion based on your own professional experience? Is there any other evidence to support it?' This habit of asking questions has turned many evidence-based practitioners into the 'evidence squad', as they learn to apply their questioning mind in a manner that promotes raising critical questions without necessarily criticizing. A must here is to learn ways of raising critical questions in socially effective ways (read: civil and persuasive). To be effective, we need to avoid being dismissed as a mere naysayer. In addition, we need to learn when to ask these questions. For example, we should question the evidence regarding an important strategic decision at the beginning of the decision-making process (preferably when the problem to be solved is first defined). It's less effective to wait until it's at the CEO's desk for final approval. At the same time, don't be afraid to speak up when the available evidence contradicts established practice or political interests. A questioning mindset is the lifeblood of evidence-based management.

Making more mindful and explicit decisions

As a manager or leader, you make decisions all the time. But as an evidence-based practitioner, you should avoid making decisions on autopilot. Instead we need to foster mindful, explicit decision-making. The process of making decisions of this kind has two parts. The first concerns decision awareness, recognizing the numerous daily choices we and our organizations make. Try making a list of the events of a morning or afternoon at work. What situations did you encounter, and what did you do or say? We bet you make far more decisions or choices in a day then you realize. For this reason, evidence-based managers tend to make many decisions with the evidence they already have in hand. Thus, it is valuable to 'prime the pump'. This means acquiring and learning in advance the evidence useful for decisions you most probably will make. Priming the pump is especially useful for repeat decisions like hiring, running meetings, making purchasing decisions and the like. This can mean reading up on subjects related to important everyday decisions. But what about those decisions you cannot foresee? Of course, evidence-based management is not about taking an evidence-based approach to all decisions. Instead, it means paying attention to the number and type of decisions you make, and being able to recognize when evidence is important to pursue.

The second part of making more mindful and explicit decisions is paying attention to how decisions are actually made. Analyse an important management decision you have been involved in. Ask what was the problem to be solved? From whom or where was the available evidence in this decision obtained? What kind of evidence was available and from which sources? What evidence was used and what not? Did some types of evidence influence the decision more than others? Was evidence missing? What are the indicators that the decision was a success (or a failure)? How long did the whole decision-making process take? Making decisions more mindful and explicit prompts critical thinking and evidence-seeking behaviour. It means paying attention to how our decisions might be made differently. Doing so provides you with an opportunity to apply the six steps and skills described in this book – and to make decisions using the best available evidence.

Everyday practice and learning

Basing your management decisions on the best available evidence can be a turning point in your career as a manager or business leader. It is a big step, and not always easy. But the more you practise, the better and easier it will be.

As you become more experienced, you will develop more advanced evidence-based skills, such as searching in online research databases, critical appraisal of scientific evidence, or using Bayes' Rule to aggregate evidence from multiple sources. Effective practice and learning requires lots of repetition and exposure to a variety of different conditions (organizational settings, types of decisions and so on). But, as explained in Chapter 4, repetition and exposure alone do not necessarily result in greater expertise – a person still needs direct, objective feedback. This means that systematically assessing the outcome of decisions is a key way to improve your skills and knowledge as an evidence-based manager. In Chapter 14 we described several methods of assessing a decision. As you may recall, the best way to assess a decision's outcome tends to be a systematic before/after comparison and use of a control group, but sometimes a frank and thoughtful After-Action Review generates considerable value – provided we are open to learning from mistakes.

Effective practice, however, not only requires lots of repetition and objective feedback, but also the opportunity to practise using an evidence-based approach. The opportunity to practise means having a work environment that allows use of evidence-based skills. As a rule, it is determined by the amount of discretion and control you exert over how you do your work (ie professional autonomy). In a highly structured work setting (that is, with lots of rules about how a task is done), your opportunity to practise may be somewhat limited. Nonetheless, you still may be able to negotiate with your supervisor for the flexibility to apply an evidence-based approach – perhaps on a project or a change programme. A work setting that supports introducing evidence into conversations – at meetings, with staff, managers and clients – is a strong indicator of organizational readiness for evidence-based management.

15.2 Building evidence-based capacity among bosses and peers

We described above activities you can perform by yourself. However, unless you are running a one-person business on a desert island, evidence-based management involves other people, such as colleagues, bosses or clients. Therefore, the next step in building evidence-based capacity is introducing the approach to the people in your organization. In general, bosses and peers appreciate the professionalism and conscientiousness that evidence-based practitioners display. Yet, there still may be pushback, for example when decisions need to be quick or if there is lots of politicking and backbiting in your organization. In such cases, executives may choose to ignore the evidence and make decisions based on personal judgement ('I don't think we need more evidence – we all know what we need to do, so let's just get it done'). Even in work environments where evidence use is highly valued, if evidence challenges a boss or peer's closely held beliefs, it can activate defences and muddle their judgement.

Evidence alone doesn't change people's minds

Evidence alone does not change minds – political scientists have demonstrated this in many empirical studies. For example, in 2010 a landmark study showed that confronting people with hard evidence can backfire, making them more entrenched in their biases and misperceptions.[9] The reason for this counterproductive effect is simple: when someone presents us with evidence contrary to our beliefs, we can feel threatened and dig in our heels. Particularly when the evidence makes people feel stupid (that is, threatens self-perceptions regarding their intelligence and competence), they may put their porcupine needles up and dispute (or ignore) the facts. When this person is your boss or someone higher up in the organization, the evidence may even be perceived as undermining their formal authority. In addition, the human brain seems intrinsically reluctant to go back on a decision taken, even when the facts underlying the decision have changed. Put differently, we seem to be wired to stick to our judgements and deal with the consequences later.[10] As a result, when presented with contradictory evidence, individuals tend to dig in their heels and increase their commitment to an initial belief. This shouldn't surprise us. After all, many psychological mechanisms in the human mind induce self-justification, confirmation bias and a host of other self-protective mindsets. So, what can we do instead?

Giving the mind a way out

As a rule, when people feel threatened, their minds dig in rather than give in. The key is to trick the mind by giving it a way out.[11] For example, explain to a person that his or her judgement is right, given what he or she knows. But now new information has emerged – showing that the underlying facts have changed. Thus, it now makes sense that the person's judgement changes too. Keep in mind that the moment you (implicitly) belittle, ridicule or embarrass the other person with contradictory evidence, you've lost the battle.[12] Instead, as Robert Cialdini, Professor of Marketing and Psychology at Arizona State University and recognized 'persuasion' expert, explains, you must offer the other person a way in order to save face while getting out of his or her prior commitment: 'Well, of course that was your judgement a week ago, because this new evidence was not yet available.'[13]

Helping people to develop a new operating logic

A meta-analysis based on a large number of randomized controlled studies found that a well-argued and detailed debunking message was better at persuading people to change their mind than simply labelling their judgement as plain wrong.[14] Stripping out incorrect or unreliable information leaves a painful gap in a person's operating logic regarding how the world works. As a result, contradictory evidence is more effective when it provides information that enables people to develop a new logic or narrative that in turn legitimizes their change in judgement.

Enhancing people's understanding of science

An additional finding of the meta-analysis mentioned above was that enhancing people's understanding of science can increase acceptance of contradictory evidence. Rebutting bad science may not be effective, but asserting the methodological quality of trustworthy scientific evidence seems to be effective.[15] In Chapter 7, we provided several examples that can be used to educate your bosses and peers on what constitutes trustworthy evidence based on science. Including practical examples of reliable research findings enhances people's understanding even more, especially when doing so invokes an emotional reaction, ranging from fear (wow, cultural diversity can lead to task conflicts and poor communication) to relief (ok, increased absenteeism is not uncommon after a period of restructuring). Lastly, you should word evidence from scientific research in a way that passes the mother-in-law test. That is, you should be able to explain the findings to your mother-in-law.[16]

Increasing people's accountability

A trend promoting evidence-based management is public demand for accountability. Evidence-based medicine is not only about making better clinical decisions – it is also about the need to justify clinical decisions to others.[17] Accountability is a serious issue in management too. Managers, leaders and administrators often endure a great deal of criticism from various directions. Mismanagement, incompetence and misuse of power are the charges most commonly heard. As a result of this increasing social pressure, there is a strong drive for increased accountability. Accountability refers to the (implicit or explicit) expectation that one may be called upon to justify one's beliefs, actions or decisions. It implies that people who do not provide a satisfactory justification for their decisions will suffer negative consequences – ranging from disdainful looks and public outcry to discharge and prosecution.[18] Not surprisingly, a large number of studies indicate that increasing a decision maker's felt sense of accountability leads to more information-seeking behaviour, less implicit bias and greater openness to external evidence. In addition, managers and leaders who experience increased accountability regarding how they make decisions (process accountability) will be more open to evidence that challenges their beliefs than those who are held accountable only for the outcome of their decisions (outcome accountability).[19, 20] Increasing accountability in order to enhance more systematic evidence use is helped when the parties involved have influence over the decision process, for example as a supervisor, CEO, board member or stakeholders in a position to publicly review decisions (for example, shareholders or review committees).

Take small steps and pick your battles

It is tempting to try to apply all at once the skills and knowledge this book presents, but instead we advise caution and mindfulness. Evidence-based management challenges existing beliefs and conventional management practice. Your bosses, peers and clients may need time to get used to this new approach. Instead of flooding them with organizational data, stakeholder input and scientific evidence, take small steps and focus on one or two aspects of evidence-based management at a time. You might make a habit of providing bosses and peers with succinct plain language summaries of relevant studies on important issues. You might collect and share relevant organizational data as they become available. In doing so, pick your battles. An evidence-based manager need not take an evidence-based approach to all decisions since some battles are not worth fighting – some arguments are lost before they even begin. For example, some people are so certain of their beliefs that no amount of evidence can change their minds. Those persons are, by definition, fundamentalists, to which an evidence-based argument is doomed to fail. On the other hand, over time an accumulation of wins through big and small uses of evidence to improve decision quality can really pay off.

15.3　Building evidence-based capacity in your organization

The final step of building evidence-based capacity concerns the organization at large. The cultural meaning and value of evidence varies across firms, with technical and clinical organizations potentially being more receptive. For example, Google Inc structures its employee-selection procedures around both research findings and organizational data in order to avoid unconscious bias in its promotion and hiring decisions.[21] However, making evidence-based management organizational and not just personal, involves raising collective awareness about the added value of evidence for management-related decisions. Broadcasting the idea of evidence-based management to the larger organization can involve a variety of interventions – from conversations and lunchtime meetings in which new research findings are discussed to citations of research in internal memos, reports or policy papers. At the same time, an organization's capacity for evidence-based management is largely determined by its leadership and culture.

Organizational culture and leadership

An essential prerequisite of organization-wide evidence-based management is senior leadership that promotes an EBMgt 'culture'.[22] A global survey suggests that managers tend to have positive attitudes towards evidence-based management, and a large majority believe use of scientific evidence improves the quality of managerial work – while lack of time is commonly seen as a major barrier. You can overcome such barriers by having a senior management that promotes an organizational culture where it is psychologically safe for members to raise concerns about evidence quality and where supports are in place to acquire the best available evidence before making important decisions. This prerequisite is underscored by a recent systematic review finding that supportive leadership and organizational culture are key factors in the implementation of evidence-based practice.[23]

Building an evidence-based culture can take a lot of forms. It can be bottom-up, as the distinctive style in which individual managers practise, make decisions and lead their teams. Or it can be top-down, led by the board or senior leadership in order to create a basis of common understandings and shared values ('this is the way in which our company makes decisions'). Finally, it can also be intervention-driven, introducing evidence-based initiatives in a drive for culture change. For example, process changes such as the sustained implementation of After-Action Reviews can alter several cultural features including values, norms and patterns of behaviour. When you promote an evidence-based culture, opportunities for intervention include:

- **Focus of attention:** What does the organization pay attention to, what is measured and what is controlled? Does the organization focus on sustaining decision quality or on short-term outcomes? Do managers pay attention to developing employees' capacity to think critically and encourage them to use multiple sources of evidence when making decisions?

- **Reactions to crises and critical incidents:** What messages does the organization send when problems arise? In a crisis, employees look to their leaders for signals reflecting the organization's key values. When all eyes are on you, the evidence-based leader has a valuable opportunity to convey the organization's priorities. For example, if a failure occurs, is learning appreciated more than avoiding being caught making mistakes? Do employees see a commitment to evidence-based processes for improving the organization's practices, or do they suspect a cover up or a blame game?

- **Reward systems:** Who is selected? Who gets promoted? Who leaves? How important rewards are allocated can signal the value leaders place on members who follow an evidence-based approach. On the other hand, efforts to promote an evidence-based management culture are undermined if good evidence-based practitioners leave while less conscientious managers are promoted.

- **Modelling:** How might evidence-based management actually look in this organization? Members need to see how people in jobs like their own might take an evidence-based approach. It helps to make visible how managers diagnose problems in an evidence-based fashion, search for evidence, assess outcomes and so on. Importantly, calling attention to the processes through which people make decisions and making them transparent can both educate organization members regarding evidence-based decision-making and enhance their trust in the organization.

Organizational resources

Finally, organizations need resources in order to successfully build the capacity to practise evidence-based management. You can think of organizational resources in terms of three categories: ability, motivation and opportunity to practise.[24]

Ability

Building collective evidence-based skills and knowledge among organization members requires training people in the six skills we have detailed in this book. This training is particularly effective if it starts with senior leadership and then cascades throughout the organization. By training senior leaders first, we take a step towards changing the work environment in the direction of a more evidence-based organizational culture.

Motivation

Creating a critical mass of people who support evidence-based management helps to create new organizational norms regarding evidence use in decision-making. Training is a start for developing such norms. The interventions we have described above for culture change are themselves motivation-altering mechanisms. Managers who act as a role-model and reward their employees for using evidence in making decisions are creating new incentives and supports that motivate the organization's uptake of evidence-based management. Importantly, norms that support evidence-based management are enhanced by making it psychologically safe for members to ask critical questions regarding the organization's decisions and practices.[25]

Opportunity to practise

Opportunity to practise refers to the support that the organization provides to engage in evidence-based management. Examples of such support include staff who can easily search for relevant studies in research databases; information systems that can capture and process organizational data enabled by an IT department that supports basic statistical analyses; HR-systems routinely gathering professional and stakeholder evidence, and HR professionals able to design in-house questionnaires, conduct surveys and run focus groups; staff who can develop reliable outcome measures and conduct RCTs, quasi-experiments or After-Action Reviews. Some organizations have installed so-called Evidence Assessment Teams, whose members are tasked with obtaining evidence on a practice question or pending decision. Other organizations have appointed a Chief Evidence Officer, responsible for ensuring that the company uses the best available evidence to inform its decision makers. All these types of support make a huge difference in the amount of time involved in making evidence-based decisions, and thus substantially increase employees' opportunity to practise evidence-based management.

 Note

No one-size fits all

Like other kinds of organizational change, building a culture supporting evidence-based management involves a bundle of mutually reinforcing practices – not a simple fix or silver bullet. A key lever in promoting an evidence-based management culture is supportive leadership that promotes collective ability, motivation and opportunity to practise evidence-based management. The support leaders provide can take many forms and we advise learning by doing. Start first with building critical abilities and an understanding (motivation) of why taking an evidence-based approach is important for your organization and then work towards creating opportunities to practise that help evidence-based management go native in your workplace.

15.4 Some final words

With this chapter on building evidence-based capacity we have reached the end of this book. We hope the insights, tools and checklists provided will help you in taking an evidence-based approach to the problems, opportunities and solutions you encounter in your daily practice and help your organizations make better decisions. This chapter started with how to become an evidence-based practitioner and ended with how to build the organization's evidence-based capacity. Still, we believe, this book should end with building evidence-based capacity within the society at large.[26] To this end, we would like to draw attention to the words of one of our proof readers: 'What I take from this book is the career- and life-changing value of taking an evidence-based approach, which is fostering an inquisitive mind that appreciates the difference between trustworthy and less trustworthy evidence. It is not only committed to helping managers and organizations make better decisions, but also is about making this world a better place.' Decisions made by managers have a profound impact on the lives and well-being of people the world over. As Henry Mintzberg, famous management thinker, once said, 'No job is more vital to our society than that of a manager. It is the manager who determines whether our social institutions serve us well or whether they squander our talents and resources.'[27] By ignoring evidence, billions of dollars are spent on ineffective management practices, to the detriment of employees and their families, communities and the society at large. As evidence-based practitioners, we have a moral obligation to change this situation. We can do this by helping organizations to find the best available evidence, to critically appraise its trustworthiness, and to encourage critical thinking and dialogue about assumed problems and preferred solutions. Let's not forget that evidence-based practice started as a movement with ambitions that surpass the realm of individual practitioners and organizations.

As we close, we are reminded of what Amanda Burls and Gordon Guyatt, two of the movement's pioneers, have said, 'evidence-based practice is not just about changing a person's skills and knowledge, it's giving them a totally different perspective on the world... It's an activist thing. We want them to get out... and change the world'.[28] Let's get out and do it.

Notes and references

1   Adapted from Suls, J (2017) [accessed 8 December 2017] Leon Festinger, *Encyclopaedia Britannica* [Online] www.britannica.com/biography/ Leon-Festinger

2   This story is described in detail in Festinger's book *When Prophecy Fails* (1956, University of Minnesota Press, Minneapolis) and helped him develop Cognitive Dissonance Theory, a widely studied psychological phenomenon in which people attempt to minimize the discrepancy between their beliefs and the actual evidence.

3   Syed, M (2016) [accessed 8 December 2017] Chilcot: Why we cover our ears to the facts, *BBC News Magazine* [Online] www.bbc.com/news/ magazine-36744911

4 Pfeffer, J (2012) Foreword, in *The Oxford Handbook of Evidence-Based Management*, ed DM Rousseau, Oxford University Press

5 Sanders, WM and Hambrick, DC (2007) Swinging for the fences: The effects of CEO stock options on company risk-taking and performance, *Academy of Management Journal*, 50, pp 1055–78

6 Dalton, DR, Certo, ST and Roengpitya, R (2003) Meta-analyses of financial performance: Fusion or confusion? *Academy of Management Journal*, 46, pp 13–28

7 Burns, N and Kedia, S (2006) The impact of performance-based compensation on misreporting, *Journal of Financial Economics*, 79, pp 35–67

8 Kovner, AR and Rundall, TG (2006) Evidence-based management reconsidered, *Frontiers of Health Services Management*, 22 (3), p 3

9 Nyhan, B and Reifler, J (2010) When corrections fail: The persistence of political misperceptions, *Political Behavior*, 32 (2), pp 303–30

10 Burnett, D (2017) The neuroscience of no regrets: Why people still support Brexit and Trump, *The Guardian, Science*, 9 November

11 Varol, O (2017) Facts Don't Change People's Minds. Here's What Does, *Heleo*, 8 September [Online] https://heleo.com/facts-dont-change-peoples-minds-heres/16242/

12 Ibidem

13 Adapted from Garcia, C (2017) Alphachat, Robert Cialdini on persuasion, *Financial Times*, 3 April

14 Chan, MPS *et al* (2017) Debunking: A meta-analysis of the psychological efficacy of messages countering misinformation, *Psychological Science*, 28 (11), pp 1531–46

15 Gawande, A (2016) The mistrust of science, *New Yorker*, 2 (3), p 4

16 Eden, D (2017) Field experiments in organizations, *Annual Review of Organizational Psychology and Organizational Behavior*, 4, pp 91–122

17 Daly, J (2005) *Evidence-Based Medicine and the Search for a Science of Clinical Care* (Vol 12), University of California Press

18 Lerner, JS and Tetlock, PE (1999) Accounting for the effects of accountability, *Psychological Bulletin*, 125 (2), p 255

19 See, for example, Scholten, L *et al* (2007) Motivated information processing and group decision-making: Effects of process accountability on information processing and decision quality, *Journal of Experimental Social Psychology*, 43 (4), pp 539–52

20 It should be noted that this outcome is moderated by individual differences in analytical intelligence and rational thinking style. See De Langhe, B, van

Osselaer, SM and Wierenga, B (2011) The effects of process and outcome accountability on judgment process and performance, *Organizational Behavior and Human Decision Processes*, 115 (2), pp 238–52.

21 Bock, L (2015) *Work rules!: Insights from inside Google that will transform how you live and lead*, Hachette, London

22 There has been an ongoing debate within the scientific literature regarding the use of the terms 'culture' and 'climate', and whether they represent the same thing. The general consensus is that culture represents the more stable and enduring traits of the organization: it reflects fundamental values, norms, assumptions and expectations, which, to some extent, reside in societal culture. Climate, on the other hand, is thought to represent a more visible manifestation of culture, which can be seen as its 'mood state', at a particular moment in time. An excellent overview of the differences and overlap of these two terms is provided in: Denison, DR (1996) What is the difference between organizational culture and organizational climate? A native's point of view on a decade of paradigm wars, *Academy of Management Review*, 21 (3), pp 619–54.

23 Flödgren G, Parmelli, E and Doumit, G (2011) Local opinion leaders: Effects on professional practice and health care outcomes, *Cochrane Database of Systematic Reviews*, 8

24 Rousseau, DM and Gunia, B (2016) Evidence-based practice: The psychology of EBP, *Annual Review of Psychology*, 67, pp 667–92

25 Nembhard, IM and Edmondson, AC (2009) Making it safe: The effects of leader inclusiveness and professional status on psychological safety and improvement efforts in health care teams, in *Elaborating Professionalism: Studies in practice and theory*, ed Clive Kanes, pp 77–105, Springer, Netherlands

26 Part of this section is adapted from Rynes, SL, Rousseau, DM and Barends, E (2014) From the guest editors: change the world: Teach evidence-based practice!, *Academy of Management Learning & Education*, 13 (3), pp 305–21

27 Mintzberg, H (1990) The manager's job: Folklore and fact, *Harvard Business Review*, 53, pp 12–20

28 Barends, EG and Briner, RB (2014) Teaching evidence-based practice: Lessons from the pioneers an interview with Amanda Burls and Gordon Guyatt, *Academy of Management Learning & Education*, 13 (3), pp 476–83

Guidelines for critically appraised topics

16

As explained in Chapter 13, evidence is often summarized to inform decision makers. When it comes to summarizing scientific evidence, Critically Appraised Topics (CATs) are the most widely used. A CAT provides a quick and succinct assessment of what is known (and not known) in the scientific literature about an intervention or practical issue by applying a systematic approach to selecting the studies – the methodological quality and practical relevance of the studies are assessed based on explicit criteria; thus, the summaries are transparent, verifiable and reproducible. CATs are easy to conduct and may take a skilled person only a few hours to days to produce. In order to be quick, a CAT makes concessions in relation to the breadth, depth and comprehensiveness of the search. Aspects of the search may be limited to produce a quicker result:

- **Searching**: a limited number of databases may be consulted, and unpublished research is often excluded. Sometimes a CAT may be limited to only meta-analyses.

- **Data extraction**: only a limited amount of key data may be extracted, such as year, population, sector, sample size, main findings and effect size.

- **Critical appraisal**: quality appraisal may be limited to methodological appropriateness.

Due to these limitations, a CAT is more prone to selection bias than a systematic review or rapid evidence assessment. A practitioner's need for obtaining evidence rapidly should hence always be greater than the risk related to lacking a completely comprehensive review of the evidence on the topic.

Steps in the CAT process

A CAT involves the following steps:

1 Background

2 Question

3 PICOC

4 Inclusion criteria

5 Search strategy

6 Study selection

7 Data extraction

8 Critical appraisal

9 Results

   9.1 Definitions

   9.2 Main findings

10 Conclusion

11 Limitations

12 Implications and recommendations

16.1 Step 1: Background – What is the context of the CAT question?

The background should clearly state what was the rationale for the CAT and explain why the question being asked is important. You may also indicate how it might relate to a wider understanding of a general problem. Most CATs occur in the context of a specific organization. You should address this context (for example, sector, history, characteristics), help specify the rationale for the CAT and explain why the question is important for the organization, its members or its clients. In formulating the CAT question, it is important to reflect on the potential stakeholders relevant to the general problem being addressed in order to tap deeper insight into the issues involved (for example, internal stakeholders such as employees at different organizational levels or external stakeholders like clients or the community).

 Example

As a change consultant, I am expected to contribute to the realization of organizational change. The outcomes of change can be both positive and negative, depending on the type of change and the specific individual or group affected. Particularly when the change has predominantly negative outcomes (eg lay-offs), I think it is of utmost importance that the change process is fair and just. I am curious about the impact procedural justice has on the way people perceive the outcomes of organizational change.

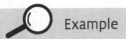 Example

Interviewing and who got what job how are the most talked about subject on campus. Most students are getting ready to find either internships or full-time jobs this summer. It is widely believed that smiling during a job interview may increase your chances of getting hired. This CAT was conducted to understand whether this claim is supported by scientific evidence.

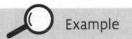 Example

Hoping to imitate the innovative and flexible work environments found at start-ups and companies like Google, my organization's Executive Director is considering implementing a bullpen style, open-plan layout. Currently, our office is divided into individual workspaces with half walls. The Executive Director and Controller both have private offices. With 15 employees working in a relatively small space, I worry that the distractions created by a new, open layout may undermine our ability to focus and to be productive at work. To draw a more informed conclusion on the effect that such a layout might have at our office, I have gathered and assessed the quality of available scientific evidence, outlined key findings and summarized their practical implications.

16.2 Step 2: Formulating the CAT question – What does the CAT answer?

You can use a CAT to answer many different types of questions. For the purposes of this guideline, we split these into 'impact' and 'non-impact' questions. This distinction is not ideal but reflects the fact that the most common CAT questions are about:

- the effect of an intervention, factor or independent variable;
- the drivers (antecedents) of a certain outcome.

Impact questions

Example

What is known in the scientific literature about the impact of goal setting on the task performance of sales agents?

Example

What is known in scientific literature about the impact of smiling during job interviews: Do people who smile more have better chances of getting hired?

Example

What is known in the scientific literature about the impact of flexible work schedules on task performance?

Example

What is known in the scientific literature about the effect of open-office layouts on workers' task performance?

Non-impact questions

You can, however, use CATs to answer a range of other questions, which can be grouped as:

- Needs: What do people want or need?
- Attitude: What do people think or feel?
- Experience: What are people's experiences?
- Prevalence: How many/often do people/organizations... ?
- Procedure: How can we implement... ?
- Process: How does it work?
- Exploration: Why does it work?

Example

Main question:
- What is known in the scientific literature about the prevalence of burnout among nurses in the United States?

Supplementary questions:
- What is burnout?
- What are the symptoms of burnout more widely and for nurses more specifically?
- Are there reliable and valid instruments available to measure burnout?

16.3 Step 3: PICOC

A PICOC is a mnemonic used to assist reviewers to search for studies that are relevant to your organizational context (see Chapter 2). Your PICOC will help you to determine whether the findings of a study will be generalizable and applicable to your organizational context. More specifically, your PICOC helps to answer the question whether your population, outcome of interest and organizational characteristics are so different from those in the study that its results may be difficult to apply.

16.4 Step 4: Inclusion criteria – Which studies will be considered?

One of the features that distinguishes a CAT from a traditional review is the pre-specification of criteria for including and excluding studies. The inclusion criteria (also referred to as eligibility criteria) help the reviewer(s) to determine whether a study will be included in the CAT when reviewing its abstract and/or full text. The inclusion criteria should be guided by your CAT question and objectives, and by the outcome measures that you will be considering to answer your question. They define the studies that the search strategy is attempting to locate.

 Example

Inclusion criteria:

- Date: published in the period 1990 to 2018.
- Language: articles in English.
- Type of studies: quantitative, empirical studies.
- Study design: only meta-analyses or controlled studies.
- Measurement: a) studies in which the effect of goal setting on organizational outcomes was measured, or b) studies in which the effect of moderators and/or mediators on the outcome of goal setting was measured.
- Outcome: task performance.
- Context: studies related to workplace settings.

Exclusion criteria:
Studies including goal setting as part of health-, lifestyle- or treatment-related interventions.

16.5 Step 5: Search strategy – How should the studies be sought?

Based on the question, you next have to conduct a structured search for all relevant studies in the international research literature. In the first instance, you should concentrate your search on relevant bibliographical databases using clearly defined search terms. At the very least, conduct your search using ABI/INFORM from ProQuest and Business Source Premier from EBSCO. Depending on the CAT question, you may also need to search in databases that are aimed at neighbouring disciplines such as psychology (PsycINFO), education (ERIC) or healthcare (PubMed).

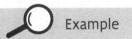 Example

The following three databases were used to identify studies: ABI/INFORM Global and PsycINFO. The following generic search filters were applied to all databases during the search:

1 Scholarly journals, peer-reviewed.

2 Published in the period 1980 to 2018 for meta-analyses and the period 2000 to 2018 for primary studies.

3 Articles in English.

A search was conducted using combinations of different search terms, such as 'job interview', 'employment interview', 'selection interview' and 'smiling'.

Documentation of the search

It is important that the search conducted is transparent, verifiable and reproducible. For this reason, the search process should be clearly documented,

Table 16.1

ABI/INFORM Global, PsycINFO peer-reviewed, scholarly journals, July 2016		
Search terms	ABI	PSY
S1: ti("job interview") OR ab("job interview")	76	231
S2: ti("employment interview") OR ab("employment interview")	122	368
S3: ti("selection interview") OR ab("selection interview")	70	130
S4: S1 OR S2 OR S3	259	583
S5: ti(smil*) OR ab(smil*)	736	2,673
S6: S4 AND S5	7	5

preferably in the form of a table that shows which search terms were used, how search terms were combined and how many studies were found at every step. Table 16.1 is an example.

In Chapter 6 you can learn the skills necessary to successfully conduct a systematic, transparent and verifiable search in online research databases such as ABI/INFORM Global, Business Source Premier and PsycINFO.

16.6 Step 6: Study selection – How should you select the studies?

In general, a search will yield a large number of studies – sometimes more than one hundred. Some studies will not be directly relevant to the research question and PICOC. Hence, the next step is to screen them to check that they meet the inclusion criteria. Screening is usually a two-stage process: the first involves reviewing the abstracts and the second, reviewing the full studies.

Review abstracts

This involves reading the abstracts that have been found through searching. Each abstract should be compared against the inclusion criteria and if the abstract meets the criteria then the full study should be read. Not all abstracts will contain information on all the inclusion criteria (this is particularly a problem with electronic searching). In these cases, decisions need to be made on whether or not to include the study on the information available. When in doubt, the study should be included.

Review full studies

You should read the full article and compare it against the inclusion criteria.

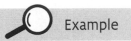 Example

Selection took place in two phases. First, the titles and abstracts of 83 studies identified were screened for their relevance to this CAT. In case of doubt, the study was included. Duplicate publications were removed. This first phase yielded 2 meta-analyses and 12 controlled and/or longitudinal studies.

16.7 Step 7: Data extraction – What information should you extract?

Data extraction involves the collation of the results and other information of the studies included. From each study, information relevant to the CAT question, such as year of publication, research design, sample size, population (eg industry, type of employees), outcome measures, main findings, effect sizes, weaknesses and the final level of trustworthiness (see Chapter 7) should be reported, preferably in the form of a clearly structured table. Table 16.2 is an example.

16.8 Step 8: Critical appraisal – How should the quality of the studies be judged?

Methodological appropriateness

You can usually find a study to support or refute almost any theory or claim. It is thus important that you determine which studies are trustworthy

Table 16.2 Methodological appropriateness: which design for which question?

Author and year	Sector/ Population	Design and sample size	Main findings	Effect size	Limitations	Level
Abraham and Graham-Rowe (2009)	General population, multiple organizations	Systematic review; 2/3 RCT; 1/3 quasi-experimental, 8 studies; N = 624	Worksite physical activity interventions, which include specific goal setting, goal reviews (ie follow-up) and graded tasks, have a small, positive impact on fitness-related outcomes	Small	Limited relevance to the review question	AA
Bandura and Locke (2003)	General population, multiple organizations	Traditional literature review, N = unclear	Discusses the importance of self-efficacy for understanding, predicting and changing people's performance or goal attainment. Self-efficacy is stated to be related (based on meta-analytical findings from previous studies), among others, to more proactive (self-set) goal setting, challenging goals and faster goal attainment, as well as effort and performance.	No effect sizes provided	No systematic search, no information regarding design of included studies	D
Brown (2005)	Canadian government, employees in a training programme	Randomized controlled trial, N = 74	Both participants who were urged to do their best and those who set proximal (shorter-term) as well as distal (= longer-term) goals had increased transfer of training (= maintenance of learned material over time and generalization of learned material from the classroom to the workplace context) relative to those who set only distal outcome goals. There was no significant difference in the transfer level of participants urged to do their best and those who set proximal plus distal goals. In addition, there was no difference between the experimental conditions regarding the effect on self-efficacy. This supports the conclusion that distal outcome goals are not effective in bringing about an increase in transfer when participants are learning new skills.	Small	Short time frame between training and measurement (six weeks)	A

Fu (2009)	Industrial sales agents, multiple organizations	Before after, with double post-test (3 months and 6 months) N = 143	The study indicates further that self-set goals fully mediate the relationship between assigned goals and selling effort (ass goals impact ssg and then selling effort). In addition, the longitudinal data indicate that company-assigned goals, self-set goals, and selling effort all positively influence future new product sales, but not self-efficacy (not significant). Interestingly, the results of the study fail to confirm an inverted, U-shaped relationship between assigned goals and effort.	Moderate	No serious limitations	C
Schweitzer et al (2004)	Undergraduate studies, US, lab setting	RCT, n = 159	Results of a laboratory experiment utilizing high, low, increasing, decreasing and 'do your best' goal structures across multiple rounds provide evidence that depletion mediates the relationship between goal structures and unethical behaviour, and that this effect is moderated by the number of consecutive goals assigned.	Very small	Students, artificial setting	A

(ie valid and reliable) and which are not. You should first determine and grade the trustworthiness of a study by its methodological appropriateness as explained in Chapter 7.

 Example

The overall quality of the studies included was high. Of the four meta-analyses, three included randomized and/or non-randomized controlled studies and were therefore qualified as level A or AA. The remaining meta-analysis was graded as level C, because it was insufficiently clear what type of studies were included. The actual level of evidence of this meta-analysis (and as a result the overall quality of the studies included in this CAT) may therefore be higher. All three primary studies used a cross-sectional design and were therefore graded level D.

 Example

After critical appraisal of the 24 studies, only four studies were included. Most studies were excluded because they had serious methodological shortcomings. One of the studies included concerned a systematic review, representing the results of 18 studies. The overall quality of the included studies, however, was low. For instance, all but two of the studies included in the systematic review were self-report surveys, and due to heterogeneity between studies it was not possible to calculate a pooled estimate of effect. The three single primary studies used a cross-sectional design. As a result, the trustworthiness of the scientific evidence supporting the following main findings is very limited.

Effect sizes

An outcome can be statistically significant, but it may not necessarily be practically relevant: even a trivial effect can be statistically significant if the sample size is large. For this reason, you should pay little attention to the *p*-value but instead assess the 'effect size' as described in Chapter 7.

16.9 Step 9: Results – What did you find?

Step 9.1: Definition: What is meant by X?

Most CAT questions include one or more key elements/constructs, for which several definitions are available. In this step, you should provide an overview of the most common definition(s).

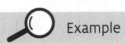

Example

An incentive is commonly defined as 'something that arouses action or activity'.[1] In the domain of management, incentives can be defined as 'plans that have predetermined criteria and standards, as well as understood policies for determining and allocating rewards'.[2] Incentives include all forms of rewards (and punishments) that are based on an employee's performance or behaviour. Promotions, grades, awards, praise and recognition are therefore all incentives. However, financial incentives such as money, bonus plans or stock options are the most commonly used. Formally, incentives differ from rewards. Incentives refer to all stimuli that are provided in advance, whereas rewards are offered after a given performance. In the scientific literature and management practice, however, these terms are used interchangeably.

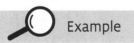

Example

A smile is defined as a pleased, kind or amused expression, typically with the corners of the mouth turned up and the front teeth exposed. A neutral expression is a blank facial expression characterized by neutral positioning of the facial features, implying a lack of strong emotion.

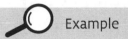

Example

The concept of self-managing teams is referred to in various ways, using terms such as 'autonomous groups', 'shared' or 'self-directed teams'; all of these terms refer to teams that are hallmarked by autonomy. We use the term 'self-managing teams' to cover all of the different descriptions of this concept. Cummings and Worley (2005) refer to the standard definition of autonomous groups as 'groups responsible for a complete product or service, or a major part of a production process. They control members' task behaviour and make decisions about task assignment and work methods'.[3]

Step 9.2: Main findings

In this section, you should provide an overview of the main findings relevant to the CAT question. For each finding, you should present the main evidence from the CAT, including its level of trustworthiness and (if available) effect size. Often three to six findings are presented.

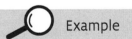

Example

1   **Smiling is weakly correlated with job interview success (level D)**
    Putting on a smile may be advantageous by comparison with remaining neutral, which may be seen as reflecting a lack of interest or involvement. But there are other factors at play too during the interview and just smiling is weakly correlated to success.

2   **Quality and timing of the smile also has an influence on the overall impression and subsequent decisions (level D)**
    Dynamic authentic smiles generally lead to more favourable job, person and expression ratings than dynamic fake smiles or neutral expressions. Furthermore, authentically smiling interviewees were judged to be more suitable and were more likely to be short-listed and selected for the job. Hiring was maximized when applicants smiled

less in the middle of the interview relative to the start and end. This research suggests that job type is an important moderator of the impact of smiling on hiring.

3 **An anxious facial expression is negatively correlated with job interview success (level B)**
Candidates who are anxious in the job interview receive significantly lower ratings of interview performance and are less likely to be hired for the job.

 Example

1 **Difficult and challenging goals have a moderately positive effect on performance (level A)**
Numerous meta-analyses have demonstrated that difficult, challenging goals have a moderately positive effect on performance, compared with easy goals. Goals must therefore be made as difficult but realistic as the individuals can cope with. In addition, goals must be challenging and stimulate the individual motivation.

2 **However, when employees must first acquire requisite knowledge or skills to perform the task, specific and challenging goals can have a large negative effect on performance (level A)**
Several randomized controlled studies have demonstrated that when a task requires the acquisition of knowledge before it can be performed effectively, a general goal (eg 'do your best') leads to higher performance than a specific high goal. In fact, when knowledge acquisition is necessary for effectively performing a task, setting a specific but extremely high performance goal can lead people to ruminate on the potential negative consequences of failure rather than focus on task-relevant ways to attain the goal.

3 **In addition, when employees need to acquire knowledge or skills in order to perform a set task, or when the task involved is complex, then behavioural goals and learning goals tend to have a more positive effect on performance than outcome goals (level A)**
In addition to the findings reported above, several randomized controlled studies have demonstrated that when a simple task

is involved, an outcome goal (focused on results) leads to higher performance than urging people to do their best, whereas when a complex task is involved, a learning goal (eg adopting a specific number of strategies or procedures to perform the task correctly) leads to higher performance than either an outcome goal or urging people to do their best.

4 **The effect of goal setting varies across workers' ability levels (level C)**
   A recent controlled study found that low-ability workers for whom goals were likely to be challenging increased their performance by 40 per cent in the goal-setting treatment with respect to the baseline while high-ability workers achieved the same level of performance across treatments. This finding confirms the outcome of previous studies that 'ability-based' goals are more effective at improving performance than a 'one-size-fits-all' approach, where everyone is assigned the same performance target.

16.10 Step 10: Conclusion

You should make the conclusion of your CAT a concise statement (of two or three sentences) on the main findings on the CAT question.

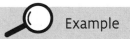 Example

Scientific research literature supports my assumption that a fair change process is important to realizing successful change, given the moderate positive effect of procedural justice on organizational outcomes. Although the effects are mostly small to medium, the indications are that there is indeed a positive relationship between procedural justice and acceptance, commitment and behaviour during organizational change.

Example

We can conclude that financial incentives can have a positive impact on performance, also known as the 'price effect'. However, financial incentives also have a negative impact on the intrinsic motivation of employees, which is known as the 'crowding-out' effect. The net result of these two opposing effects determines a possible gain or loss in performance. In addition, the net effect is influenced by several mediating and moderating variables.

 Example

Goal setting is one of the most powerful and evidence-based interventions for enhancing performance, provided that moderating factors such as goal attribute, type of task, organizational context and employee characteristics are carefully taken into account.

 Example

The scientific literature does not support the claim that ethnic or cultural diversity leads to higher team performance.

16.11 Step 11: Limitations

In a CAT you are aiming to provide a balanced assessment of what is known (and not known) in the scientific literature about an intervention or practical issue by using a systematic methodology to search and critically appraise empirical studies. Nevertheless, all CATs have limitations. In your CAT you should explicitly describe any limitations and discuss how they possibly impacted the findings of the assessment. Below is an example of a description of limitations that are inherent to CATs.

Example

Concessions were made in relation to the breadth and depth of the search process. As a consequence, some relevant studies may have been missed. A second limitation concerns the critical appraisal of the studies included. This CAT did not conduct a comprehensive review of the psychometric properties of the tests, scales and questionnaires used. A third limitation concerns the fact that the evidence on several moderators is often based on a limited number (sometimes only one) of studies. Although most of these studies were well controlled or even randomized, no single study can be considered to be strong evidence – it is merely indicative. Finally, this CAT focused only on meta-analyses. As a consequence, relevant findings may have been missed. Given these limitations, care must be taken not to present the findings of a CAT as conclusive.

16.12 Step 12: Implications and recommendations

Once you have used the evidence found to answer the CAT's main question, you should use the final part of the assessment to relate the findings to the background of the CAT and the PICOC described in steps 1 and 2. For example: Is the evidence supportive of current practice? What are the estimated benefits and harms? What, based on the evidence found, are your specific recommendations for action? Importantly, how might you consider the concerns and interests of different organizational stakeholders in your recommendations?

Example

The fair process effect in organizations is observed when change leaders increase aspects of their decision-making process, specifically consistency, accuracy, lack of bias and openness to employee input. When procedural justice is not taken into account, employees may feel treated unfairly and resistance to change may increase. To actively design a fair change process, the six classic criteria for procedural justice specified by Leventhal (1980) may serve as a useful checklist.[4] These criteria can be turned into practical guidelines for the purpose of organizational change as follows: a) the change approach needs to be consistently applied to all employees at all times; b) it needs to be impartial, ie prejudice or stereotyping are eliminated; c) the information on which decisions are based needs to be accurate; d) opportunities should be provided to correct or change plans or processes; e) those responsible for the organizational change (the change managers or leaders) need to represent the interests of all stakeholders affected by the change; and f) the ethical standards and values of those involved should never be disregarded.

Example

Financial incentives can be used to increase the employee motivation and performance needed to support change. However, upper management should have a clear vision about the change in performance or behaviour that it desires, as it requires different approaches to incentivizing. Intrinsically motivated employees executing interesting tasks and quality outcomes should be encouraged by indirect incentives (eg opportunities to do valued activities) in order to avoid eroding that motivation. Direct financial incentives are effective when extrinsic motivation and quantitative performance need to be stimulated. Upper management should therefore frequently 'calculate' the proposed net effect (positive price effect versus negative crowding-out effect) when defining a pay plan. Lastly, if the plan is designed to increase team performance, all incentives should not be distributed equally, as this may harm individual motivation.

Example

This CAT indicates that Emotional Intelligence (EI) is not a radical new construct in leadership. Even though EI has (some) positive effects, these effects can also be explained by the overlap with other psychological constructs. In addition, the claims made by well-known consultancy firms such as Hay Group that 'EI can make the difference between a highly effective and an average professional contributor' is not supported by the outcome of this CAT. For this reason, I advise against investing in training courses that claim to develop our executives' EI.

16.13 Checklist

Table 16.3

1 Have you clearly described the background and context of the CAT question?
2 Does the CAT address a clearly focused question? Is it clear what the CAT will answer?
3 Have you used the PICOC framework to focus the CAT question?
4 Have you clearly defined the inclusion criteria (eg population, outcomes of interest, study design)?
5 Have you conducted a comprehensive literature search using relevant research databases (ie ABI/INFORM, Business Source Premier, PsycINFO, Web of Science, etc)?
6 Is the search systematic and reproducible (eg were searched information sources listed, were search terms provided, were search results reported)?
7 Have you selected the studies using explicit inclusion and exclusion criteria?
8 Have you clearly described the key features (year of publication, population, sample size, study design, outcome measures, effect sizes, limitations, level of trustworthiness) of all studies included?
9 Have you assessed the methodological appropriateness of each study using predetermined quality criteria?
10 Have you provided definitions of the key elements/constructs in the CAT question?
11 Have you clearly described the assumed causal mechanism?
12 Have you provided an overview with the main findings, including their level of trustworthiness and effect size?
13 Have you provided a clear, succinct conclusion on the main findings on the CAT question?
14 Have you clearly described all limitations and discussed how they may impact on the findings of the CAT?
15 Have you clearly described what the implications for practice are?

Notes and references

1 Incentive (nd) [accessed 14 October 2017] *Merriam-Webster* [Online] https://www.merriam-webster.com/dictionary/incentive.

2 Greene, RJ (2010) *Rewarding Performance: Guiding principles; custom strategies*, Routledge, Abingdon

3 Cummings, T and Worley, C (2005) *Organizational Development and Change*, South-Western, Ohio

4 Leventhal, GS (1980) What should be done with equity theory? in *Social Exchange*, ed KJ Gergen, MS Greenberg and RH Willis, pp 27–55, Springer, Boston, MA

GLOSSARY

After-Action Review: Structured, reflective evaluation of a recent set of decisions in order to evaluate their effectiveness.

Assumption: A belief, claim or hypothesis that is accepted as true (or as certain to happen), without evidence.

Baseline: A measurement of the metrics of interest before a decision was executed that we can use to compare to later measurements in order to assess the effect. A baseline is also often referred to as a 'before' or 'pre' measurement.

Bayes' Rule: Method to estimate the probability of a claim, assumption or hypothesis being true given the available evidence.

Benchmark: Metrics that are tied to standards or best practices within the industry.

Big data: A massive volume of both structured and unstructured data that is so large it is difficult to process using traditional data analytics techniques.

Blinding: Concealing the group membership (experimental group vs control group) of individuals in a study where research participants do not know which group they are in. Double blinding occurs when neither the research participant nor the researcher knows which group an individual is in.

Boolean operators: Logical operators used to join search terms. Standard Boolean operators are "AND", "OR", and "NOT". Named after mathematician George Boole.

Business intelligence systems: System that analyses business data and presents actionable information to help managers and other users make informed business decisions.

Cognitive bias: Systematic pattern of deviation from rational or logical judgement based on inherent and unconscious psychological processes. Well-known examples are confirmation bias, availability bias, group conformity and authority bias.

Cohen's rules of thumb: Heuristic to determine the magnitude of an effect found in a study.

Confounder: A third variable that distorts (confounds) the relationship between two other variables.

Confidence interval: Provides the upper and lower boundaries between which we expect – usually with a 95 per cent certainty – the true value of a point estimate (mean, percentage or effect size) to fall. Used to determine the precision of an effect size.

Construct: An idea or theory that exists as an abstraction. When a construct is measured or operationalized the result of that actual measurement is referred to as a variable (ie, a variable is empirically observed and may take different values). For example, organizational commitment is a psychological construct describing an individual employee's attachment to the organization. It can be measured using a variety of questionnaire-based scales.

Control group: A group (sometimes referred to as an 'intervention', 'treatment' or 'experimental' group) that is exposed to a condition or situation expected to have an effect (the assumed cause), which is then compared with another group (known as the 'control' or 'comparison' group) that is not.

Correlation: The degree or strength of a (linear) relationship between two variables. The relationship may be positive (an increase in one variable is associated with an increase in the other) or negative (an increase in one variable is associated with a decrease in the other). The square of correlation indicates how much variation in one variable is explained by the other.

Covariation: The phenomenon that when the value of one variable changes, the value of the other one alters as well. See also correlation.

Critical appraisal: Process of systematically judging the quality or trustworthiness of a unit of evidence.

Cross-sectional study: A study in which a large number of data or variables is gathered only at one point in time. It provides a 'snapshot' of the current situation. Often referred to as 'survey'.

Data: Numbers, words, figures, symbols, sounds, dates, images, etc without context.

Data dredging: An unsystematic effort to find patterns in a data set without first formulating a hypothesis. Highly prone to finding false and nonreplicable patterns, it is sometimes referred to 'fishing' or 'p-hacking'.

Data warehouse: A large, integrated database that contains the data of multiple separate information systems.

Delphi Method: A qualitative, interactive method, involving a group of experts or professionals who anonymously reply to a questionnaire or a set of statements and subsequently receive feedback in the form of a 'group response', after which the process repeats itself.

Devil's advocate: A person who expresses an opinion that disagrees with the prevailing point of view, for the sake of debate or to explore the thought further.

Double-barrelled questions: Questions that ask respondents to evaluate more than one concept. An example is 'How organized and interesting was the meeting?'

Effect size: A quantitative measure of the strength of a relationship, or the degree of difference between two groups, controlling for the bias that sample size introduces.

Evidence: Information supporting (or contradicting) a claim, assumption or hypothesis.

Expected value: The (often monetary) outcome expected from the decision.

External validity: The extent to which results or findings can be generalized to other contexts or to people not included in the original study(s).

Focus group: A set of six to ten people who are asked about their perceptions, feelings, opinions, or attitudes towards a product, service, idea, or – in case of an evidence-based approach – asked about an assumed problem or proposed solution.

Generalizability: Extent to which the evidence also applies to other populations or organizations.

Goodness of fit: Metric that indicates if (and how) the observed (true) values in a dataset differ from the values as predicted by a regression.

Google Scholar: A search engine developed by Google that provides a simple way to broadly search for scholarly literature, including research articles.

Heuristic: A mental shortcut that helps us make judgements quickly without having to spend a lot of time researching and analysing information.

Information: Data relating to something or someone and considered meaningful or useful.

Internal validity: The quality or trustworthiness of a given study, reflects the extent to which the research design controls for or rules out methodological bias.

Key Performance Indicator (KPI): Key Performance Indicators are measurable values that provide information regarding the extent to which an organization is achieving its goals. Typically, these are composite indicators such as the ratio of revenues generated relative to the number of customers or customer-related activities; these indicators provide information on the pay-off associated with specific kinds of organizational activities.

Law of the Large Numbers: Law that states that the larger the sample size, the more accurate its predictions regarding characteristics of the whole population. Thus, when we use a small sample of organizational data, the metrics and KPIs based on that sample are most likely to deviate from the 'true' value.

Leading question: A question that guides a person toward a desired answer by suggesting what the answer should be.

Likelihood (vs probability): Indicator of the probability that an event will occur.

Logic model: A framework used for both decision making and evaluation that represents the logical connections expected between resources, activities, outputs, and outcomes, allowing assumptions to be surfaced and evaluation of the actual effects that resources and activities have on an organization's outcomes.

Longitudinal research: Study that involves repeated observations (measurements) of the same variable(s) over a certain period of time (sometimes even years).

Measurement error: The difference between a measured value and its true value.

Mediator: A variable that causes the relationship between two other variables, for example between an antecedent and a consequence a mediator might be a psychological process that intervenes between them. For example, having a supportive boss might lead to increased employee commitment to the organization through the mediating effect of trust in management.

Meta-analysis: A statistical approach combining the results from multiple studies in order to obtain a trustworthy estimate of effect sizes and to resolve uncertainty when studies find different results.

Methodological appropriateness: Indicates if the way a study is designed is the best way to answer the study's research question.

Methodological bias: Systematic pattern of errors or deviations from population values or true scores; these errors are introduced by some feature(s) in the research design. Methodological bias can occur when a certain kind of answer is encouraged and another kind of answer discouraged, for example, social desirability bias can lead individuals to agree with positively worded questions and disagree with negatively worded questions regardless of the actual content of the questions.

Methodological quality: Indicates the strengths and weaknesses of the way a study is conducted.

Moderator: A variable that affects the relationships between two other variables, for example, when the relationship between performance and job satisfaction is affected by whether rewards are contingent on performance.

Null hypothesis: The hypothesis or belief that there is no difference between two treatment groups or no relationship between two variables, aside from bias or measurement errors.

Pearl growing: Browsing through the references of a relevant article (the 'pearl') to identify other relevant articles. Also referred to as 'snowballing'.

Peer-reviewed journal: Articles submitted to these journals are first evaluated and critiqued by independent, anonymous scientists in the same field (peers) to determine whether they merit publication in a scientific journal.

PICOC: A conceptual tool to help you find evidence that takes into account your professional context. The PICOC acronym stands for Population, Intervention, Comparison, Outcome and Context.

Placebo: A substance or treatment with no therapeutic or systematic effect. Placebo effects reflect non-specific factors that can influence a research subject's response to experimental conditions. Placebo effects should be ruled out when looking at effects of treatments or interventions since participating in a study can itself alter the behaviour or attitudes of participants.

Predictive model: A statistical model to make a prediction. May refer to any statistical model that is used to make predictions (such correlations and regressions), but in the realm of 'big data' it often refers to a model that uses complex algorithms derived from advanced data-analytic techniques based on artificial intelligence or machine learning.

Prior (probability): The initial estimate of how probable it is that a hypothesis (claim, assumption) is true to start with, that is, without the benefit of the available evidence.

Probability: the extent to which an event is likely to occur, measured by the ratio of the favourable cases to the whole number of cases possible.

Professional expertise: The experience and judgement of managers, consultants, business leaders and other practitioners – differs from intuition and personal opinion because it reflects the specialized knowledge acquired by the repeated experience and practice of specialized activities.

Pseudo-science: A collection of beliefs or practices erroneously believed to be based on the scientific method (eg astrology).

Qualitative research: Research that uses data that are not expressed in numbers. These data are usually obtained from interviews, focus groups, documentary analysis, narrative analysis or participant observation.

Quantitative research: Research that uses data that are quantified in various ways, that is, measured and expressed using numbers. These data are usually obtained from surveys, tests, financial reports, performance metrics or statistics.

r-squared: Indicates the extent variation or differences in one metric can be explained by a variation or differences in a second metric.

Random assignment: Assigning subjects to different groups 'at random' (by chance, like the flip of a coin), so that each subject has equal chance of being assigned to each group, and any possible distorting factor is equally spread over both groups.

Random selection/random sampling: A sampling method in which all subjects of a group or population have an equal and independent chance of being selected. Random selection reduces the chances of selection bias.

Range restriction: Occurs when a metric in a dataset has a more limited range (minimum and/or maximum value) than it has in the whole population. As a result, the correlation between that metric and another metric can be constrained.

Red team: Team used by a company to challenge assumptions, unearth preconceived notions, and identify symptoms of bias (especially confirmation bias and groupthink) that could affect professional judgement.

Reliability: The degree to which the results of a measurement can be depended upon to be accurate. Related to the consistency or repeatability of measurement results.

Regression: The prediction of an outcome metric from one predictor metric (simple regression) or several predictor metrics (multiple regression).

Regression coefficient: Tells you how much the outcome metric is expected to increase (if the coefficient is positive) or decrease (if the coefficient is negative) when the predictor metric increases by one unit.

Replication: The process of repeating or reproducing an experiment or intervention to see if its outcomes are trustworthy.

Representativeness: Indication of how well the data obtained from a sample accurately represents the entire population. The more representative the sample, the more confident we can be that we can generalize the evidence to the whole population. See also generalizability.

Research design: The 'blueprint' of a study that describes its steps, methods and techniques used to collect, measure and analyse data.

Residual plot: A graph that shows if (and how) the observed (true) values in a dataset differ from the values as predicted by a regression.

Risk acceptance: The level of risk a manger or organization is willing to accept – also referred to as risk appetite.

Science: A systematic enterprise that builds knowledge by accumulating results based on testable hypotheses.

Scientific literature: Scientific studies published in peer-reviewed academic (scholarly) journals.

Scientific method: Systematic observation, measurement, and experimentation in order to formulate, test, and modify hypotheses.

Selection bias: Also referred to as sampling bias, occurs when your selection of practitioners leads to an outcome that is different from what you would have gotif you had enrolled the entire target audience

Semi-structured interview: Interview that consists of a limited number of key questions that define the topic or issue to be explored while allowing the interviewer to explore relevant information not thought of beforehand.

Significance (statistical): Statistical metric that is often – but incorrectly! – presented as the probability that a scientific hypothesis is true, or the probability that the findings were produced by random chance alone.

Small numbers problem: See Law of the large numbers.

Snowballing: See pearl growing.

Social desirability bias: Respondents' natural tendency to want to be accepted and liked, which may lead them to provide 'socially desirable' answers, especially to questions that deal with sensitive subjects.

Structured Query Language (SQL): A standardized programming language used to 'query' a database by extracting the data in a readable format according to the user's request.

Stakeholder map: Map that illustrates the potential array of stakeholders related to a specific decision.

Stakeholders: People (individuals or groups) whose interests affect or are affected by an organization's decision and its outcomes.

Standard deviation: A measure that tells us how much the data deviates from the average, often abbreviated as SD.

Structured interviews: Interviews that uses a fixed format in which all questions are prepared beforehand and are asked in the same order. To ensure that answers can be reliably aggregated and comparisons made, all persons are asked the same questions.

System 1: The fast, effortless thinking system that operates automatically with little voluntary control and that uses intuition or heuristics to make decisions fast.

System 2: The slow, effortful reasoning system that draws heavily on our cognitive resources and requires attention and concentration.

Systematic review: A structured literature review that reviews the complete published and unpublished scientific literature relevant to a specific question. It follows a pre-set procedure for identifying, searching, coding and synthesizing findings from the entire body of relevant research. Compares to a meta-analysis, which is a quantitative analysis of an entire body of studies, summarizing its findings in terms of effect sizes. Some systematic reviews also include meta-analysis.

Thesaurus: The controlled vocabulary of an online research databases that lists words grouped together according to similarity of meaning, including synonyms, antonyms and related words.

Truncation: A searching technique used in databases in which a word ending is replaced by a symbol: often an asterisk (*) – in order to find singular and plural forms of words and variant endings

Trustworthy: Deserving of trust or confidence, used in EBMgt to refer to the extent to which evidence is reliable and valid.

Unstructured interview: Interview that lacks predetermined questions (see also structured- and semi-structured interview).

Validity: The extent to which a concept, measurement or result is consistent with the real world.

Variable: An empirical observation liable to vary or change, typically measuring a more abstract concept or construct (above).

Weaknesses: Limitations to the trustworthiness of evidence based on presence of bias, cognitive or methodological and/or low reliability or validity.

Workflow systems: Systems that manage the execution of a business process.

INDEX

NB: page numbers in *italic* indicate figures or tables